Cher Krause Knight

POWER AND PARADISE

in Walt Disney's World

VIVA FLORIDA 500.
1513-2013

A Florida Quincentennial Book

This book is neither authorized nor sponsored nor endorsed by the Disney Company or any of its subsidiaries. It is an unofficial and unauthorized book and not a Disney product. The mention of names and places associated with the Disney Company and its businesses are not intended in any way to infringe on any existing copyrights or registered trademarks of the Disney Company but are used in context for educational purposes. The opinions and statements expressed in the quotations and text are solely the opinions of those people who are quoted and do not necessarily reflect the opinions and policies of the Disney Company and its businesses or the University Press of Florida.

Library of Congress Cataloging-in-Publication Data
Knight, Cher Krause.
Power and paradise in Walt Disney's world / Cher Krause Knight.
pages cm
Includes bibliographical references and index.
ISBN 978-0-8130-4912-0 (alk. paper)
1. Walt Disney World (Fla.)—History. 2. Disney, Walt, 1901–1966.
3. Amusement parks—Florida. I. Title.
GV1853.3.F62W3453 2014
791.068759'24—dc23
2013044106

University Press of Florida
15 Northwest 15th Street
Gainesville, FL 32611-2079
http://www.upf.com

For Beatrix Marcel—

I love you the whole world.

contents

figures

acknowledgments

Many people helped me as I researched, wrote, and edited this book. At the University Press of Florida, I thank John Byram for his initial interest in the text, and Sonia Dickey, Amy Gorelick, Sian Hunter, Dennis Lloyd, Shannon McCarthy, Meredith Morris-Babb, and Marthe Walters for their assistance through all of its editorial and production phases. The faculty and administration at Emerson College, particularly my colleagues in the Department of Visual and Media Arts, have been very encouraging throughout the project. The department's staff and graduate assistants have been wonderfully helpful, too. I am especially appreciative of the sabbatical the college granted me, which afforded dedicated time to work on the project, as well as of a Faculty Advancement Fund Grant I was awarded to support the book's production. My collaborators and friends at Public Art Dialogue have also been unwavering in their kindness. And my students at Emerson College remain a constant source of fun and inspiration. Mentors and good friends Therese Dolan, Harriet F. Senie, and Gerald Silk all read the work in various stages—many thanks for your suggestions and insights, as well as those of the blind reviewers, which I am sure have made this a better book. My friends, whether they be those I see regularly or only catch up with periodically, have sustained me with their thoughtfulness and humor.

Several family members have accompanied me on research trips to Disney World, and so I must thank these loyal traveling companions: Earl and Janice Knight; Denise, Jack, and Jessica Petonak; Elaine and Harold Krause; and Brooke and Beatrix Knight. Were it not for Elaine and Harold Krause, my terrific parents, I doubt I would have even written this book. They took me on my first pilgrimage to Disney World, in 1976, and on many more visits thereafter. It was never just another family vacation when we went to Disney World, but a journey to be savored and one we continue to share. There are simply not enough words to thank my husband, Brooke Knight, who is patient, perceptive, and caring beyond measure. In particular, I want to thank him and our daughter, Beatrix Marcel, for their many daddy-daughter outings that gave me the time and space I needed to really think through Disney. Without both of you I could not have told this story. Beatrix, thanks for being proud of and loving me, and for your seemingly endless supply of enthusiastic wonder—the world is an adventure, and I am the luckiest person as I get to share it with you.

Power and Paradise in Walt Disney's World

The Good, the Bad, and the Ugly

Disney World and Academia

Fantasy and reality often overlap.
—Walt Disney, *Wisdom* magazine, December 1959

I fell in love with Disney World at eight years of age. Like most first loves, this was a crush: a heady mix of infatuation with blind devotion. As I grew up, the love remained but was increasingly transformed and more complex. No longer was this devotion unexamined, a development due not only to my gradual progression into academia. As a curious and excited visitor to Disney World, one begins to simply notice things over time, some of them reassuring and others prompting pesky questions. Can a formula for happiness really be devised, and this happiness subsequently manufactured? If so, is a theme park a sustaining vehicle for the delivery of such happiness? What forms of control are exerted over visitors while at Disney World? How are connections to things Disney maintained once we leave the parks and return home? Questions like these, which never go away no matter how deeply I am immersed in Disney's World, led me to write this book.

The new Walt Disney Family Museum opened its doors on 1 October 2009, in three historic buildings located in San Francisco's Presidio. Its stated mission is to "present the life and achievements of the man who raised animation to an art, transformed the film industry, tirelessly pursued innovation, and created a global and distinctively American legacy," emphasizing "the real story of Walt Disney, the man, told by him and others who knew him well."[1] The museum was spearheaded by Walt's daughter, Diane Disney Miller, and is supported by the Walt Disney Family Foundation (a separate entity from the Disney Company, though the company lent much of the displayed material). Richard and Katherine Greene, "Disney historians" with a track record of unqualified enthusiasm for their subject, are its founding curators.[2] Even with their best intentions to share "the real story," one anticipates points of omission obscuring a full picture of Walt and his creations. And yet Randy Malamud, writing for the *Chronicle of Higher Education*, is optimistic about this place. Of course, the museum emphasizes the creativity and "organizational and technological complexities" of Disney's work. But there is a desire to impart information about the person as well as his artistic and business endeavors, "a valuable corrective" returning us "to the actual flesh-and-blood man behind the curtain" instead of the "hugely overdetermined figure" Walt became. In addition to the revolutionizing innovations (the multiplane camera) and aspiring plans (for Epcot) on display, one also finds boxes of Jell-O and cans of Hormel chili (Walt's favorite foods). Malamud praises the "curatorial evenhandedness" of the accounts presented here, including episodes we might expect to be pruned out: Disney's "unfortunate testimony" before the House Un-American Activities Committee, for example, and an acrimonious animator's strike (1941) during which Walt attempted to thwart union efforts while workers fought for rights such as being included in screen credits.[3] Jason Sperb once remarked that given Disney's "immeasurable impact" on the United States and around the world, "academic criticism has scarcely scratched the theoretical surface."[4] Thus, perhaps the most encouraging aspect of the Walt Disney Family Museum is its professed attitude toward scholars. For decades the Disney Company has effectively shut out most academics from its archives. All archival research requests are "subject to approval from the legal department": Malamud could not find any scholar granted access in recent years. But Richard Benefield, the museum's founding executive director, insists that academics are encouraged to use the museum and can apply for access simply with a description of research plans. It remains to be seen if the museum will actually maintain such an open-door policy, but at the moment this is a welcome change from the restrictive and sometimes hostile treatment scholars received from the Disney Company. Though Malamud worried the museum would be "a hagiography, or a glorified gift shop, or a propagandistic reification of the Disney empire," he found that it "isn't any of those things." Instead, the museum "historicizes Disney's work and compels us to think twice about how we appraise it."[5] This book is also about thinking twice.

I began really thinking about Disney World, and researching it, more than twenty years ago. I wanted to better understand why I was drawn to the place, how it works in the ways it does, and why so many other people also have deeply emotional responses to it. Back then, Disney studies was not an established field, and the explosion of texts examining Disney from a multitude of perspectives had not yet arrived. There were also far fewer unofficial texts and insider tell-alls. I remember going to conferences, frustrated at being called the "Disney Girl" and defending the inclusion of my work in sessions instead of talking about its merits or lack thereof. I met many Disney detractors, who annoyed me as they proudly boasted of having never gone to the theme parks. Things have changed. Today there is more scholarship on Disney, much of it excellent. Perhaps it is not so bad being the "Disney Girl" after all.

My purpose here is to provide both analysis of and anecdotes describing the experience of being at Disney World in all of its complexities. I draw equally upon my background as an academic and as a visitor. These first-hand experiences are essential, legitimizing components of my research, and are emphasized throughout the text: I would not write this book if I hadn't been to Disney World many times over. When your field research requires you to stand in winding queues for Space Mountain, you appreciate the value of lived experience—and overheard conversations—as much as critical theory. As an art historian, I initially conceived this text through the perspective of art and architectural history. But Disney World engages many discourses, and so by necessity I have taken an interdisciplinary approach addressing many fields: American and cultural studies; sociology; visual, material, and popular culture; urban planning and environmental design; cultural anthropology; critical studies; and theology. Here I explore traditional art historical concerns such as aesthetics and artistic intent, but audience response issues common to cultural studies practices are foregrounded, too. My aim is to shift the language conventionally used to describe relationships between mass audiences and media products (including artworks and theme parks). I often use the term "shared culture" rather than "popular culture," as the latter implies a segregated system composed of those who study that culture on the one hand, and those who participate in it on the other. To my mind, the term "shared culture" is a better one; it suggests that those of us who study such cultures also help make them and regularly take part in them. Disney World offers an especially fertile environment in which to interrogate the muddled boundaries between supposedly "high" and "low" cultures, while advocating for the increased agency of all kinds of audiences. Theme parks are well suited to the concept of shared culture, which pushes matters of audience engagement to its center. In particular, shared culture counters theming's critics, such as Ada Louise Huxtable, who asserted "there is something fundamentally disquieting when the knowledgeable join the naïve in trashing the richer reality," a claim she rightly thought might draw charges of elitism.[6] Huxtable retains her "right to remain unenchanted" by Disney, but she cannot decide which experiences are imbued with the greatest richness for others, "knowledgeable" and allegedly otherwise. That said, I want to mindfully question "widespread assumptions" about Disney—the company and the man— rather than taking either at face value.[7]

My hope is that this book is inclusive of multiple audiences. I realize some readers may not receive it with open arms. Journalist Hank Stuever suggests academics are "smitten" with Disney, as it engages so many critical issues (urban planning, mass media, feminism, racism, government, the environment, commerce, art).[8] But I would add that this scholarly fascination often retains doses of repulsion, as if one is dating a person she is embarrassed to introduce to her friends. Furthermore, Kevin Shortsleeve detects a "collective anxiety" inhibiting the dialogue on Disney. Critics' "widespread mistrust of the company" is fueled by its touting of collaborative efforts and democratic processes, while simultaneously exerting centralized forms of control to vigilantly snub out negative publicity.[9] Although there exist serious and fair studies of Disney (Stephen Fjellman's *Vinyl Leaves* comes immediately to mind), Disney bashing is still a regular academic practice, and the literature on the subject can be quite fractured. I believe that criticism of Disney World, in particular, has too often eluded the place's intricacies. Two predisposed camps that have advanced polarized views should be mentioned here: academics who do little to hide their disdain for Disney's parks and the mass adoration they inspire;[10] and authors whose wholesale celebrations of the parks are written under the Disney Company's auspices.[11] I will consciously avoid aligning myself with either camp, and instead provide critical analysis without necessarily dampening my enthusiasm. Clearly, I am not a "neutral" party: I have a sustained affection for Disney World, and it would serve no one well to pretend otherwise. That said, my affinity derives in part from its unexpected nuances and even contradictions. I like it that Disney World heightens the frictions of social life: between public and private spheres, consumptive impulse and contemplative thought, enthusiastic celebrations and nagging doubts.

My relationship with Disney World is complicated. I love visiting it, and have been there so many times that I have honestly lost count. Each time I find something new to consider, but this excitement is not unchecked. My fondness for Disney is coupled with hesitations about the larger picture it projects onto our collective cultural screen. This book, however, is not a comprehensive study of all things Disney. Others (notably Steven Watts and Michael Barrier) have already meticulously mapped Walt's biography and impressive contributions to animation and film, and it is not my objective to trek this terrain again. Instead, I concentrate squarely on the Florida resort, Walt Disney World, which actually contains four separate theme parks. Disney's other endeavors (including the earlier Disneyland and the later foreign theme parks) are pursued here in service to my primary subject. Walt Disney was not interested in building amusement parks: he wanted to create parks using a *theme* as "a frame that orders narrative and shapes experience."[12] His first park, Disneyland in Anaheim, California, was Disney World's precursor and also the major catalyst for building the second, larger resort. Walt's dissatisfaction with the encroaching sprawl of tourist traps, quickly developed to siphon off of Disneyland, spurred him to "correct" what he thought had gone wrong in California. When Art Linkletter asked Walt why he wanted to build another park, Disney responded to "do it better."[13] (Consequently, Disneyland remains a more localized park, while Disney World is a destination resort attracting international audiences.) This book resists the tendency of much Disney literature to speak about the theme parks—and Disney products in general—as if they were interchangeable. Instead, I focus on Disney World as the project in which Walt became most invested, personally and financially, before his death. Walt took decisive measures to insulate his Floridian resort. Though hotels, gas stations, and souvenir shops would come in the wake of Disney World, as they had at Disneyland, now they were held at bay by a vast, impenetrable buffer zone. After the close of the 1964–65 World's Fair, organizer Robert Moses had urged Walt to take over the fairgrounds, but Disney knew these were not big enough for his dreams, and New York's climate was far too seasonal. With a generous budget for land, lacking when he built Disneyland, Walt turned his attention to Florida.[14] The importance of Florida as a site that represented opportunity, renewal, and visionary fantasy to Disney cannot be underestimated. Walt's obsessive focus on Disney World offers insight into one man's ambitions. But beyond Walt, Disney World has a massive community of devotees, as well as a considerable amount of detractors, for whom it has profound cultural relevance. Admittedly, Walt's vision is not universally shared.

My methodology throughout the book is correlative: I offer several readings of Disney World, interrelated in their examinations of its reach of power and function as a sort of paradise. By turns Disney World is considered as a pilgrimage center, a utopia, a fantasy city, and a technological and global microcosm. For each of these four contexts I provide precedents, though their use here is not strictly historical: in some cases we have known sources for Disney's resort, and in others there are looser associations. One might ask: "Why bother with sources for which definitive roots cannot always be proven?" My answer is that such comparisons help banish long-standing cultural assumptions, especially those that likely sell short Disney World's meaning and impact. There is a great advantage in knowing that Walt Disney actually did work for World's Fairs when studying Disney World, but there is also much value in understanding how this place relates to well-established archetypes, such as a medieval pilgrimage center, even if Walt did not cite the source directly. This correlative approach, however, is not accidental. I took pains to make sure the comparative examples were not cherry-picked but rather allow us to see how primary themes in the history of the built environment and human creativity persist at Disney World. The need for community, desire to intensify experience, and impulse to enhance existence beyond the everyday extend through the most traditional historical forms to perhaps the least expected, a theme park.

It occurred to me during the writing of this book that its structure literally adopted that of the Disney World parks, most especially the Magic Kingdom. The chapters examining Disney World as a pilgrimage site, a Garden of Eden, a fantasy city, and a contemporary World's Fair are individual thematic sections (though with connections to the others), much like Disney's "lands." In this respect, the introduction is an entry gate, and the first chapter is Main Street, U.S.A., setting the stage for what comes in the following pages. As noted several times throughout the text, Main Street is the only conduit in and out of the Magic Kingdom, and so the concluding chapter provides an opportunity to reconsider some of the terrain covered, as well as new thoughts on the future of the Disney Company. Chapter 1 reflects on the impetus for Walt to build Disney World, and his carefully crafted dual persona as a savvy businessman and dedicated visionary. A discussion of the Disney Company's synergistic business model is provided so that its successes and failures are better comprehended. Chapter 1 also offers a brief examination of the postmodern ideas that remain key to Disney World's physical and conceptual operations, particularly its use of simulations (*simulacra* in postmodern jargon). This first chapter is intended as a foundational one, offering information on the history and evolution of the Disney Company and its parks. The following chapters combine contextual research and critical analysis with a more internal dialectic, as I share experiential accounts of my time spent in Disney's parks to inform my scholarly observations. Chapter 2 examines Disney World as a pilgrimage site predicated on its rites of passage, temporary communities transcending normal social constraints, spatial planning, and corporeal and symbolic transitions, or *liminality*. Although comparisons to traditional pilgrimage centers point up distinctions between touristic and spiritual practices, I contend that many Disney World visitors engage in, at least, quasi-religious pilgrimage. Today, pilgrimage may be less a matter of a journey's risk than a destination's ability to generate memorable experiences.

Chapter 3 addresses Disney's desire to create his own Garden of Eden, aligning this urge with examples of landscape tourism: places where natural elements were "corrected," mapped, and marketed as playful respites from daily existence. Rising from the swamps of Florida, Disney World enjoys a nearly seasonless climate, and an ample buffer zone sets it apart from the everyday world's imperfections. Walt also intended his theme parks to prescribe and reinforce "proper" behavior, imbuing Disney World with utopian—if often unattainable—ambitions. Chapter 4 looks at other tourist destinations, particularly Las Vegas, that employ theming techniques and loose historical references to create immersive experiences for wide audiences. While inducing consumptive impulses is clearly a primary goal, the resulting fantasy spaces are not easily dismissed as solely commercial. Increasingly popular, planned communities (often developed near such tourist destinations, including Disney's own Celebration) attempt to perpetually extend the "holiday" state of mind.

Chapter 5 brings us to the profound influence that World's Fairs, especially those in the United States, had upon Walt Disney. The fairs offer keen insight into the conception and planning of Disney World, particularly Epcot (an acronym for the Experimental Prototype Community of Tomorrow). Disney's work developing attractions for the 1964–65 World's Fair (New York City) provides evidence of his fondness for these grand events and illuminates his desire to build an ideal city. Divided into two sectors (one devoted to technology and the other to world cultures), Epcot prompts us to reconsider which products, technological revolutions, and social movements point the way toward "progress" and what kinds of relationships Americans want to foster with their global neighbors. Finally, the conclusion addresses charges against Disney as a monopolizing transnational corporation that exports mediocre tastes. It also provides observations about Disney World's state of health as an entertainment destination and questions its sustainability for the future. While impressive—and even troubling—Disney's efforts to establish the Florida resort as a self-governing entity did not make it impervious to "moral" threats, economic decline, and enterprising competitors. Despite Walt's controlling vision, it is Disney World's employees and visitors who continually reinvent the place, ever more on their own terms.

Before going forward, I wish to clarify several things about the images in and field research for this book. Many Disney studies contain few if any illustrations, as the company is notoriously protective of its trademarks, properties, and products. The omission of such images in these studies underscores the level of control Disney exercises over its corporate identity. (Michael Sorkin illustrated his essay on Disneyland with a single view of the sky above the park, describing it as "the first copyrighted urban environment in history.")[15] The Disney Company does not officially permit reproduction of its images without having editorial approval of accompanying text: of course, I could not surrender such. Fortunately, Disney World is well known through widely available visual sources, so in this book you will find other compelling images—some rarely if ever linked with Disney—intended to invite novel comparisons. Finally, a note about how I conducted my field research. I have always paid my own way into Disney World, and was a tourist among other tourists whenever there. Other than a backstage tour I took in 2011 (see especially the conclusion), I have generally avoided asking employees or visitors questions. My role has been to observe and listen (and overhear) rather than to lead discussion. In full disclosure, I am a member of the Disney Vacation Club (a vacation home time-share), which has affected my research, especially as I have often stayed on property while working and sometimes took advantage of "Extra Magic Hours" (a perk for resort guests granting access before and after official opening and closing times to select park attractions).

There is something I have noticed over the years about academics: despite our good intentions, we do not always do the best job of communicating passion for our given fields, or we forget why we had fallen in love with these in the first place. In fact, sometimes we actually quash such passions, burying them in heaps of theory. Disney World is a very real place, offering individual lived experiences to those who choose to interact with it. Critics who pride themselves on never having visited the Disney parks opt out of the chance to have their own experiences, whatever these may be. This book is, for me, an opportunity to see Disney World in its unvarnished totality and find out if, as a participant in our shared culture who also happens to be an academic, I still experience a sort of impassioned discovery there as the place first imparted to me when I was eight. I do not expect the same spellbound wonder to exist—I am a lot older now—but I want to see if the joy remains.

one

Smart Business and Simulations

Walt Disney and His World

To all who come to this happy place: Welcome. Disneyland is your land. Here, age relives fond memories of the past, and here youth may savor the challenge and promise of the future. Disneyland is dedicated to the hard facts that have created America—with the hope that it will be a source of joy and inspiration to all the world.

—Disneyland dedication plaque inscription, 17 July 1955

To me, [Disneyland's] a piece of clay. I can knock it down and reshape it to keep it fresh and attractive. That place is my baby, and I would prostitute myself for it.

—Walt Disney, *Look* magazine, 11 February 1964

Walt Disney (5 December 1901–15 December 1966) had fantasized about building a theme park of his own since the 1930s. Having taken his two daughters to many amusements parks on "daddy's days" over the years, he appreciated their spectacles and technology. Yet he was dismayed at the filthy and congested facilities, haphazard organization, dishonest showmen, and salacious, unimaginative entertainment he encountered all too often.[1] Walt's wife, Lillian, a former "ink and paint girl" at the Disney Studio, asked him, "Why do you want to build an amusement park? They're so dirty." He later recalled his answer: "I told her that was just the point—mine wouldn't be."[2]

By 1948 Walt considered opening a park for his employees and friends on a vacant lot in Burbank, near the studio. His memo envisioning this unrealized "Mickey Mouse Park" described what would become primary features at Disneyland, including a railroad, "Western Village," and a "village green," noting that the park would be very "inviting."[3] On 17 July 1955, Walt finally opened his first park—like none that had existed before—Disneyland, in Anaheim, California. Here his enchanting stories and their beloved characters were freed from the boundaries of movie screens and comic books and translated into a three-dimensional immersive fantasy environment. Walt conceived Disneyland as a theatrical experience, merging the space of the park with the sensation of watching movies to forge a new kind of entertainment. A filmic sensibility pervades both Disneyland's structure and content as visitors traverse through massive stage sets, taking in highly composed scenes leading from one to the next. Walt's "Imagineers," who designed the park, focused on the "art of the show," ensuring all elements big and small enhanced the visual storytelling. Each attraction and themed "land" was mapped out as an edited progression of long shots and close-ups leading to "peak moments," as if glimpsed through a lens. The effect was intended to transform visitors into "actors in a dramatic experience . . . being affected by and simultaneously affecting the plot and the sequence of the narrative."[4] Disney landscape artist Bill Evans remembered, "Walt kept emphasizing . . . that he wanted the public to participate. He wanted them onstage."[5] As biographer Neal Gabler describes it, "Disney reconceptualized the amusement park as a full imaginative experience, a *theme* park, rather than a series of diversions."[6] Indeed, Disneyland was the first park to be fully themed; all of the characters, costumes, food, architecture, landscaping, transit, music, and merchandise were interrelated to create a fantastic atmosphere where everything was cleaner and friendlier than in daily life. And not only would this new place entertain visitors—it was intended to educate and enlighten them as well.

Today, many cultural analysts suggest that our society functions as an "experience economy" in which events and encounters, not just goods and services, are profitable products. Consumers willingly pay to have memorable, fulfilling experiences staged for them. Joseph Pine and James Gilmore trace the roots of this economy to Walt Disney, citing how the experiential effects of his movies evolved into the immersive worlds of his theme parks. They argue that Disney experiences are among the most effective and richest because these encompass all four aspects of experience: entertaining, educational, escapist, and aesthetic.[7] Stellar customer service and pristine environs would not be enough to keep crowds coming: Disney must provide experiences that foster a sense of community, intensify lived existence, and enrich daily life. In an experience economy, an individual's consumption practices can help define one's identity, making the physically and emotionally immersive experiences Disney offers particularly desirable.[8] Not surprisingly, Disneyland was the first theme park to be marketed nationally.

Most amusement parks were seasonal places for local residents that grew by accretion without comprehensive planning. Walt believed he could do better and briefly enlisted the help of Pereira and Luckman Architects. But Walt's friend and neighbor Welton Becket, an architect, advised Walt to design Disneyland for himself, and so Disney Studio staffers took up the job. Consultants thought Walt's venture was unwise—amusement parks throughout the United States were closing at the time—but he persisted.[9] Even his brother and business partner, Roy, was skeptical and only allowed $10,000 of studio money to be invested in the $17 million Disneyland scheme. To raise the rest, Walt borrowed on his life insurance policy, sold his vacation home, and struck an agreement with the American Broadcasting Company to create a weekly television series, *Disneyland* (1954–58), in exchange for help financing the park.[10] Subsequently, Walt and his inner circle designed Disneyland in secrecy in an abandoned Glendale warehouse. In its first seven weeks of operation the park received more than a million visitors; within a year it grossed $10 million; a decade later, nearly a quarter of all Americans had visited it. After six years Walt bought out ABC (and another partner, the Western Printing and Lithograph Company) and owned the park outright. Despite Disneyland's commercial success, Walt had grown dissatisfied with it shortly after its opening. Encroaching urban sprawl threatened his pristine park, and Walt had secured just enough land for his theme park and parking lots. As Disneyland's popularity swelled, so did the number of motels, restaurants, and souvenir stands, all eager to cater to its visitors. Anaheim was becoming a tourist jungle, and Walt could do little to stave off its impending overdevelopment. So he resolved to build another park, one that would be bigger—and better, he asserted—than his first attempt in California.

In many ways, Walt's life story was built on visionary capitalism. He overcame setbacks such as the 1923 bankruptcy of his first company, Laugh-O-Gram. In the early years, neither he nor his brother Roy took a salary, plowing all profits back into their business. Roy claimed he often wanted to give up, but Walt patiently nurtured quality in their products rather than seeking quick financial returns.[11] Although Walt never graduated from high school, his hometown of Marceline, Missouri, gave him a diploma, and he had numerous honorary degrees from the likes of Harvard and Yale Universities. Disney received more than seven hundred awards in his lifetime, including thirty-two Oscars, four Emmys, and the Presidential Medal of

Freedom in 1964 (the highest civilian award given by the American government). And then at 9:35 a.m. on 15 December 1966, Walt, a chain-smoker for most of his life, succumbed to cancer after having his left lung removed the month before. As he lay dying in St. Joseph's Hospital, across the street from his Burbank studio, Walt remained consumed with Disney World. Though he did not live to see it completed, his Florida resort has welcomed nearly a billion people from around the globe since its 1971 opening.

The Disney Formula

To outsiders, the cheerful demeanor of [Disney's] employees, the seemingly inexhaustible repeat business it generates from its customers, the immaculate conditions of park grounds, and more generally, the intricate physical and social order of the business itself appear wondrous.

—John Van Maanen, "The Smile Factory"

Reflecting on the scope and grandeur of his company, Walt remarked, "I hope we never lose sight of one thing—that it was all started by a mouse."[12] That mouse, which Walt wanted to name Mortimer until his wife suggested the friendlier-sounding Mickey, has become the company's most recognizable icon. For many people Mickey instantly conjures up potent memories: childhood days spent watching *The Mickey Mouse Club* and Disney cartoons; trips to the theme parks; one's first watch emblazoned with the Mouse. Mickey also symbolizes the Disney Company: embodying American notions of the self, bound by self-enforced moral codes, and oozing with plucky optimism. At first a spindly, angular rodent, Mickey gradually became a more rounded, anthropomorphic figure, decked out in shoes and gloves. He quickly enjoyed widespread appeal in his role as the good-natured everyman, particularly in the United States, where his humor was a welcome antidote to the Great Depression's bleakness.[13] Although the Disney Studio made respected nature documentaries and live-action features, its animated works have remained the most admired and influential. It is also in the animations that the roots of the theme parks are most clearly discerned, particularly in their aesthetic exaggerations and quick transitions from one moment to the next. Likewise, the early Mickey Mouse shorts (1928's *Steamboat Willie* being the first) and the *Silly Symphony* series (started 1929) conjured magical worlds beyond the constraints of time and reason, though never so disordered as to undermine conventional rules and widely shared values.[14]

Ever since his early days as a filmmaker, Walt maintained tight control over his company. After completing his first series of *Oswald the Lucky Rabbit* cartoons in 1928, Walt tried to negotiate a better deal with distributor Charles Mintz. Instead he learned that their mutual contract had stripped Walt of copyright control, leaving Mintz free to hire Disney artists to produce Oswald himself. Determined this would never happen again, Walt proclaimed: "We're going to start a new series . . . about a mouse. And this time *we'll* own the mouse."[15] From that point on Walt acted as his own distributor, retained ownership of his films and the independence of his studio, held strict copyrights on his company's creations (including patenting his characters), and had the last word on all projects. His democracy of "commercialized togetherness" had a clear chain of command: "Everybody gets his say. Then I decide which ideas we'll use."[16] After a fight with Roy, Walt formed Retlaw (Walter spelled backwards) Enterprises in January 1953, a private company that held the sole lucrative rights to the "Walt Disney" name, which it then licensed to Walt Disney Productions (later to become the Walt Disney Company under Michael Eisner) for merchandising.[17] Walt also formed WED (Walter Elias Disney) Enterprises (now Walt Disney Imagineering, again changed under Eisner) and called the people who worked there "Imagineers."[18] The term, coined in 1952, combined "imagination" and "engineer" to designate members of Walt's creative think tank, as well as those possessed of the technical know-how to pull off Disney's fantastical schemes. Today the Imagineers design and develop Disney's parks, resorts, and attractions. Although these require vast collaborative efforts, the Imagineers' work is still largely subsumed under the moniker of Walt Disney. Walt's oft-told "bee story" reconciled any disparities between such collective endeavors and notions of fairness and credit:

> You know, I was stumped one day when a little boy asked, "Do you draw Mickey Mouse?" I had to admit I do not draw anymore. "Then you think up all the jokes and ideas?" "No," I said, "I don't do that." Finally he looked at me and said, "Mr. Disney, just what do you do?" "Well," I said, "sometimes I think of myself as a little bee. I go from one area of the studio to another and gather pollen and sort of stimulate everybody." I guess that's the job I do.[19]

But Walt's contributions should not be minimalized or overlooked. Writing a year before Disney's death, journalist Stephen Birmingham described Walt as a "catalyst," noting that "everything his organization does is filtered through his eyes, his ears, his taste, his personality, he *is* the one who does create."[20]

Although Walt died more than forty years ago, the Disney Company continues his legacy of exercising seemingly unparalleled control over its interests. This has already been noted of the films, and it is also true of the company's publishing ventures. Disney publishes a massive amount of literature (magazines, brochures, and training handbooks) for use by employees, stockholders, and a select public. It also publishes encyclopedias codifying Disney lore, books about its business practices, collections of Walt quotations, and travel guidebooks under its own imprints (Hyperion and Disney Editions). Unapologetically laudatory texts, written for and copyrighted by Disney, are frequently sold as souvenirs at the parks: although their authors enjoy access to vast archives, they must comply with the company's terms of use, including approval of completed manuscripts.[21] Of course, many sources are written without the assistance or endorsement of Disney, such as behind-the-scenes accounts of its business operations after Michael Eisner became chief executive officer in 1984.[22] (Not coincidentally, Disney's legal department simultaneously became "zealously litigious.") There is also abundant information available on the Disney parks—guidebooks, trivia, detailed accounts of the attractions, employee memoirs—some published under Disney's auspices and some not. These vary in credibility, quality, depth of knowledge, and sympathy for Disney. Kevin Yee's fond memoir of working at the parks recounts employee pranks, romances, and mishaps to underscore how Disney's magic prevails, even on 9/11. Meanwhile, Chris Mitchell's tell-all offers tales of employee partying and drug use and the SOP (Sex On Property) Club.[23] More decidedly critical analyses of Disney also range considerably. The exhibition catalog for *Designing Disney's Theme Parks: The Architecture of Reassurance* (curated by art historian Karal Ann Marling) helpfully contextualizes the first major showing of Disney concept drawings, photographs, models, and videos. But given the unprecedented access to the Imagineering collections, its essayists were inclined to cast favorable eyes on Disney.[24] On the other hand, a predisposition to dislike the company clearly permeates *Inside the Mouse*, by The Project on Disney (a team of three academics and a photo-essayist).

In addition to films and books, Disney markets many other goods and experiences. The popularity and dissemination of any Disney product relies, of course, upon the indoctrination of willing consumers. *The Mickey Mouse Club* series (1955–59) nicely accomplished such by targeting postwar American youth, the first generation to grow up with television. The club's audience was groomed for brand loyalty, trained to recognize its advertisers' logos, and encouraged to perceive technology as fun. And it was easy to become a club "member": all one needed was a TV set, then becoming a common fixture in homes across the country. *The Mickey Mouse Club* cleverly intertwined adolescent desires to belong to a larger culture with messages promoting consumerism as a form of good citizenship.[25] The club attracted a fairly homogeneous group: young, white, affluent suburbanites, an audience Walt also wanted to cultivate for his parks. But Disney had recognized the power of television even earlier, embracing it while most film producers still fearfully viewed it as unwelcome competition.[26] The weekly *Disneyland* series, which premiered on 27 October 1954, featured his park as a "living set for the t.v."[27] The following year, Disneyland's opening was telecast live coast-to-coast in a ninety-minute special hosted by Art Linkletter, Ronald Reagan, and Bob Cummings. Ironically, Disney employees called this "Black Sunday" due to several misfortunes, including a gas leak that temporarily shut down Fantasyland, and Walt cursing when he thought his microphone was off.[28] But the *Disneyland* series left a lasting imprint on viewers. Its format "recapitulated the thematic structure of the park," with sections devoted to cartoons, nature, science, and frontier tales.[29] As Marling observes, "Disneyland was the first made-for-TV place, in which the fictive content of the programming dictated the honest-to-gosh activity of Americans in physical space." Witnessing the construction of Disneyland as it progressed, viewers became acquainted with the park and had an "emotional stake in its success" even before it opened. Disney's TV shows appealed to suburbanites aspiring to family unity and upward mobility. The theme parks made their American Dreams seem accessible, exemplifying the social harmony and visual tidiness they had sought in bridge clubs and manicured lawns.[30]

Walt reputedly disliked advertising, yet he was one of the first to fully apprehend the possibilities of "meshing . . . mass media content, merchandising, and promotion in his 1950s theme park."[31] About 25 million viewers saw *The Mickey Mouse Club* each week, while 50 million tuned in to *Disneyland*. Though critics labeled Disney a "sell-out," Walt ignored them, relishing the opportunity to pitch his products "directly to the audience without any middleman."[32] By establishing an interconnected web of Disney goods and experiences (films, TV shows, music, memorabilia, toys, theme parks, etc.) the company encourages circuits of cooperative and diversified consumption. Such efforts have been intensified to the current day. For example, the Disney Channel and Radio Disney target a specific "tween" demographic, while Disney Cruises (launched in 1998) are aimed at the whole family. Disney even offers its own credit card via Chase. And though it had sold the underperforming Disney Stores in 2003, it has since bought back the chain from Children's Place. In 2009 Disney started D23 (the company was founded in 1923), an official fan community with an extensive website and members-only perks. The biennial D23 Expo, a multi-day convention with exhibits, screenings, celebrities, and field trips, was also inaugurated in 2009.

Disney's theme parks are vital links in its chain of self-promotion. Most of their attractions, stage shows, parades, and souvenir merchandise cull imagery directly from Disney films and television. Thus the company cultivates an eager, ready-made audience that arrives at the parks with prior knowledge of Disney characters and tales. Eisner described this as the "inside/outside" strategy: private usage of Disney products at home is complemented by their consumption in public forums like movie theaters and theme parks. Personal experiences are subsequently channeled into collective social memories, uniting people via "core cultural ideas and stories."[33] Disney devotees often become lifelong customers not only because the company has a reputation for quality entertainment, wholesome values, and family fun but because it offers a nearly endless supply of experiences and goods to fuel its "magic." The Disney Company has "given new meaning to the term *synergy*" in its "process of orchestrating entertainment production, distribution, and marketing into a lucrative whole."[34] Disney's synergy relies heavily upon customers' abiding emotional ties to its characters, as the company continually modifies, updates, and promotes them across media platforms.[35] It also requires a compelling message to communicate: the invitation to join like-minded folks and immerse yourself in experiences that make you feel special.

Understanding the persuasive power of immersion, Walt decided to secure a captive audience at Disney World. In California, the inconsistencies of daily life kept trespassing on his park; in Florida he made certain to block out any external distractions. In a way, Disney World is placeless: despite its national and regional associations, its buffered insulation distinctly separates it from the outside world. In a related way, it is also timeless: there, present-day moments are layered with references to both the past and the future. Walt had lamented that completed films were unable to be reworked, and instead conceived his parks as in continuous states of change, available to tinker with and become ever more "perfect."[36] Unruly elements and routine worries were edited out of the parks, distilling Walt's idealism to its most positive, purified essence (what John Findlay calls "Disney Realism").[37] The resulting sense of order can be constricting or anxiety-ridden for some people, but many visitors draw comfort from it.

Shortly after Disneyland opened, Walt determined that outsiders who did not follow his way of doing things could ruin the theme park experience, so he developed his own employee-training program and accompanying terminology. To this day, Disney University (founded in 1955) indoctrinates workers with the company philosophy and values. The "Traditions" class provides orientation, and training on how to "create happiness" via "emotion management." Trainees also learn Disney Speak: park employees are "Cast Members," Disney customers are "Guests," and an accident is an "incident." Disney Speak also emphasizes the theatrical nature of the themed experience: a uniform is a "costume," working is to be "on stage," and a ride is an "Adventure." Cast Members, handpicked and groomed for the "Disney look," are predictably alike: clean-cut and pleasant.[38] (As one Disney park official simply stated, "We require conformity.")[39] Applicants with less experience are actually preferred, as they can be trained from the start in the Disney way. For example, Cast Members are never to sit on the job, point with a single finger (they must use two or the entire hand), break character, or in any way compromise the Disney magic.[40] The goal is to provide service-oriented entertainment via teamwork in an environment where the Guests are always right and their expectations are continually exceeded. By spoiling its customers, the company primes them "to reflexively buy Disney products."[41] Despite its restrictive requirements, the company remains a sought-after employer. Tammy Gutierrez, who has played Snow White and trains others to perform as Disney characters, attests that her work is fulfilling and feels special: "You have to bring energy and spirit to the role—make it real. We're not people dressed up in costumes. Anyone can do that."[42]

Lee Cockerell, former executive vice president of operations at Disney World for more than ten years, insists that the company's success rests upon respectful treatment of its Cast Members (employee turnover is a third of the industry average), who are then motivated to care for Guests in kind. He maintains this is not feel-good propaganda but rather "a rational, muscular, no-nonsense business strategy" that yields customer and employee satisfaction via its "people-centered culture."[43] Business analyst Douglas Shuit concurs, describing the Disney formula as "a mix of common sense, strictly defined corporate values and nonstop attention to detail." Disney's blend of business strategies—particularly its "people-management ideas" and emphasis on customer satisfaction—have been so successful that other organizations, ranging from BMW to Arkansas Childrens Hospital, send their employees to study them. Off-site and on-property workshops and seminars are offered through Disney Institute, "a citadel of knowledge about professional development," where the company's practices are yet another product for sale.[44] (The original Disney Institute, 1996–2003, featured educational programs such as animation and cooking. Today it no longer has a main public campus.) Disney has built and sustained remarkable brand loyalty, both among its customers and employees, an achievement that other companies desperately hope to replicate. Yet while they can mimic management practices, it will be difficult for such enterprises to imitate Disney's uncanny ability to be ahead of the curve in its business decisions, an admirable though elusive trait.

Disney's purchase of the land in Florida is a prime example of its adeptness at recognizing opportunities others may overlook, and taking advantage of them. In the mid-twentieth century most developers considered central Florida nothing but a swampy real estate wasteland; instead, Disney envisioned unfettered possibilities. After studying various locations, Walt chose an area outside of Orlando, purchasing 27,443 acres (twice the size of Manhattan, or equivalent to the whole of San Francisco) in Orange and Osceola Counties for the bargain price of about $5.5 million (less than $200 an acre; he had paid $4,500 an acre in Anaheim).[45] He intended to use most of the land as a buffer for his resort so that all of the chaos, visual disharmonies, and pressures of the outside world would not trespass upon his orderly microcosm. His company also established the Reedy Creek Improvement District (see chapter 5 and the conclusion) to insulate Disney World from the jurisdiction of Florida's state government. The initial cost of Disney World was $400 million ($275 million over the estimated cost), which was largely financed by the Disney Company itself. Though it did not open until five years after his passing, Walt had already conceived a master plan that he described in detail to Roy, pointing with his fingers at the hospital room's ceiling to sketch the layout on the night before he died.[46] Construction on the massive project began in May 1969, but after the first contractor claimed that a 1971 deadline for opening day simply could not be met, Disney formed its own construction company with crews working seven days a week. On 1 October 1971 the Magic Kingdom theme park debuted with much fanfare and immediately distinguished itself from its precursor. Disneyland was not even finished when it opened; Disney World was a more polished package from the start. And to maintain its veneer of well-organized composure, the televised dedication ceremony was filmed when the Magic Kingdom was closed.[47]

As previously noted, Walt viewed his parks as perpetually in progress, despite the high degree of detail he demanded for them. Disney World initially offered only the Magic Kingdom theme park (1971; a variation on Disneyland) and several resort hotels (the Polynesian and the Contemporary).[48] Today Disney World is the largest single-site employer in the United States (with sixty thousand Cast Members), and it operates every day of the year.[49] In addition to the Magic Kingdom, there are now three other theme parks: Epcot (an acronym for the Experimental Prototype Community of Tomorrow, 1982), largely inspired by the World's Fairs; Hollywood Studios (1989; formerly Disney-MGM Studios, renamed in 2008), based on the film and television industries;[50] and Animal Kingdom (1998), a hybrid of zoo and theme park attractions. There are also two water parks: Typhoon Lagoon (1989) and Blizzard Beach (1995). (River Country, themed as an "old-fashioned swimmin' hole," was the first water park but has since been closed.)[51] Over time Disney World has evolved to include golf courses, spas, convention facilities, campsites, numerous luxury to budget-priced resorts, Disney Vacation Club time-share properties (with more than one hundred thousand member families who are greeted "Welcome Home" each visit), ESPN's Wide World of Sports complex (1997, formerly Disney's Wide World of Sports), and a Wedding Pavilion (1995). Disney's Boardwalk (1996) offers nightclubs, restaurants, and shopping. In Downtown Disney (1996) there is Marketplace, an extensive shopping village with eateries; and West Side, featuring themed restaurants and more shopping. Downtown's Pleasure Island (1989) was once populated by nightclubs and then slated for renovation as Hyperion Wharf, an upscale dining and shopping enclave aimed at adults. The company recently announced a more ambitious plan, however, which includes the renovation and expansion of Downtown Disney into Disney Springs: a mixed-use shopping, dining, and entertainment sector with theming inspired by Floridian waterfront towns. Here Marketplace and West Side will be refurbished and joined by the new Town Center, while Pleasure Island becomes The Landing (phased construction is planned, commencing in 2013 and to be completed in 2016).[52] These seemingly inexhaustible offerings and the availability of multi-day admission passes ensure that many visitors,[53] having so much to see and do, never leave Disney property during their entire vacations and even stay for longer visits. The Walt Disney World resort is "an enveloping experience of destination tourism that the small California site could never be."[54] It is also the most popular site to visit in the world, welcoming approximately 46 million people annually.[55] According to Stacy Ritz, "That Disney is a world unto itself is undisputed: At any waking moment, its 43 square miles contain more people, traffic, hotels and restaurants than most cities. But more than this,

Disney World is also a state of mind. In a single generation, Disney World placed its stamp on the American psyche, sharing the dreams of one man with an entire nation. For here, in 1971, Walt Disney offered the world its biggest playground. And the world accepted."[56]

Before Disney World, Florida had "many more-or-less equal tourist attractions" throughout the state, but a lot of these quickly became outmoded and unpopular. As Bob Sehlinger queries in his "unofficial guide" to Disney World: "When was the last time you planned your vacation around a trip to Jungle Larry's Safari Park?"[57] The answer is probably "Never!" and due, at least in part, to Disney's efforts to distinguish its parks from other attractions with brand-name cachet and a reputation for high quality. Disney Guests know what to expect: "a well-defined, prepackaged, indefinitely repeatable experience."[58] This formula has been emulated worldwide at other entertainment venues, which attempt to imitate Disney's design principles, attention to detail, integrated merchandising, and coherent theming. Yet Disney World remains the gold standard: superior in its clarity of vision, obsessive cleanliness and maintenance, consistency and excellence of experiences provided, and commitment to employee training and customer service. Novel but never too avant-garde, Disney World is a conceptually lucid and ultimately reassuring place, one where fantasies are realized.[59]

Simulations, Anyone?

We live everywhere already in an "esthetic" hallucination of reality.

—Jean Baudrillard, "The Orders of Simulacra"

Disney World is about appearances. How things look matters a lot there—helping move stories along, defining spaces, immersing the senses. Disney utilizes simulations (*simulacra; simulacrum* is the singular) of famous venues and nostalgic settings to conjure up somewhat familiar but not always specific places. It is easy to dismiss this tactic as the amassing of a shallow collection of facades, but I believe this is not really the case. Visitors to Disney World are not duped by its simulations but are savvy consumers of these, as we will see in the coming chapters. Simulation remains a key concept in postmodern theory. Although there is continued debate about the meaning of "postmodernism," we can broadly describe it as the synthesizing of eclectic and varied sources—past and present, indigenous and multicultural, "high" and "low." Perhaps the most useful way to conceive postmodernism is not as a summation of history but as a stopping point for reconsideration as we make our way through history's unrelenting cycles. Disney World's early years coincided directly with the postmodern aesthetics and theory that flourished in the United States during the 1970s and 1980s (especially after key French texts became available in English translations). The beliefs espoused and practices enacted at Disney World are in sympathy with postmodernism, particularly in the use of immersive simulations to transform and enhance daily existence. It should also be noted that the Disney Company is a conspicuous patron of decidedly postmodern places and spaces, having repeatedly commissioned venerated postmodern architects to design high-profile projects.

Numerous critics have analyzed the Disney parks' innate postmodern qualities, citing the prevalence of "pastiche" and "controlled" planning of space and architecture.[60] Unfortunately, it became common to write off the parks as neatly aggregated, sanitized simulations that offer sad replacements for true adventure. Fredric Jameson crankily complained that postmodernists randomly cannibalize "dead styles," producing a culture of "depthlessness."[61] Meanwhile, Michael Sorkin singled out the Disney parks specifically, worried that visitors would be so seduced by simulation as to forfeit their interpretative faculties.[62] Supposedly Jean Baudrillard is more forgiving of postmodernism than Jameson or Sorkin, repeatedly warning his readers not to dismiss simulations as "artificial" or "inauthentic." But he also believes that simulations create hyperreality ("the meticulous reduplication of the real"), overriding history while simultaneously inducing nostalgia for such. Thus the simulacrum, "an identical copy for which no original ever existed," allows us to "be there" without "being there" at all. Baudrillard sarcastically praises Americans as being liberated from Europe's rigid intellectualism and oppressive ideals, claiming Disneyland is "real" for a country that lacks a long historical past.[63] Roland Barthes, however, challenges the notion that a "copy" or simulation impairs judgment, limits meaning, or is inherently inferior. He acknowledges that a "text" (a book, film, theme park, etc.) may direct its "reader" (including a viewer or visitor) toward a specific meaning chosen in advance by its "author" (creator). But Barthes also asserts that even tightly controlled texts cannot suppress an individual's prior knowledge and personal preferences.[64] Thus despite Walt's efforts to manage Guests' interpretations (carried on in perpetuity by his company), our reactions to Disney World can be guided but never completely prescribed; ultimately, we discern and assign meaning to our own experiences.

Umberto Eco is critical of Disney's parks, but he tries to embrace their escapism. In his legendary essay "Travels in Hyperreality" (1975), Eco describes time and space as compressed by simulations and designates the Disney parks as pinnacles of hyperreality. But his concept of the "absolute fake" (purported to be more "real" than the original) does not bear out at Disney World. The simulations found there clearly announce their function as such rather than being exact replicas; no one mistakes these for the Eiffel Tower in Paris or a castle in the German woods. Eco, too, knows this, acknowledging that Disney "not only produces illusion" but also confesses it.[65] In fact, much of the pleasure to be had at Disney World comes from recognizing and negotiating its simulations. Architects and urban planners were among the first to celebrate Disney's simulations for their substance instead of surface value. Early on, *New York Times* architecture critic Paul Goldberger acknowledged Disney World's profound potential to shape the built world, suggesting that its cleanliness, advanced technologies, effective crowd control, and efficient public transportation might establish it as "the most important city planning laboratory in the United States." Visitors are not tricked by Disney simulations, he concluded, but knowingly play along with the "elaborate, intricately conceived hoax . . . and share in its irony."[66] I agree that Disney World can be quite ironic, but it is neither a "hoax" nor a stand-in for someplace else. It is a special place where wide-ranging references and rich associations are accumulated in thoughtfully designed spaces. Often its attractions do not have a single or specific antecedent, but engage more generalized sensibilities and sources (think of Space Mountain's merging of science-fiction lore with aspects of actual space exploration). Disney's simulations do not debase or replace history—they recontextualize it.

We now live in a post-postmodern age, in which "fakery, in large part, is a matter of context," and "fakes, in the right context, can become real." In this "re-mix" culture we are used to navigating the spatial and temporal junctures between the physical and virtual worlds, and readily acknowledge the importance of replication in our learning processes. Today's "bricolagic orientation" is an active one in which we sample simulations "to create new art forms authentic to the ways" we now live.[67] This orientation is well suited to Disney World, encouraging us to experience the place unencumbered by dismissive prejudgments. Disney World is a collage: it synthesizes passing references into novel juxtapositions, without the expectation of fixing meaning.[68] It does not bastardize or compete with the sources from which it gleans inspiration; rather, it absorbs these into a genuinely unique composite. Anthropologist Stephen Fjellman is wary of Disney World's corporatism and potential for "cognitive overload," but he still admits: "I love it! I could live there. . . . It gets me to think, to remember, and to make up new fantasies. I appreciate its civility and safety. I crave its contradictions. I like walking in its streets."[69] I do not want to live in Disney World, but like Fjellman, I appreciate how it gets me to think, most especially about its contradictions. It is, as Nicholas Sammond reminds us, a place "both symbolic and actual."[70]

two ▶ Keeping the Faith

Disney World as a
Pilgrimage Center

I ask of myself, "Live a Good Christian life." Towards that objective I bend every effort in shaping my personal, domestic, and professional activities and growth.

You don't build it for yourself. You know what the people want and you build it for them.

I don't want the public to see the world they live in while they're in the park. I want them to feel they're in another world.

—Walt Disney, *Walt Disney: Famous Quotes*

Walt Disney was a complex man, motivated by an odd mix of faith, commerce, and altruism. The quotations above support this contention, as Walt voiced his desires to lead an honorable life and serve others, though we can infer that success in business also mattered. In the third quotation Walt is his most visionary self, talking of how his park offers concrete transcendence from the everyday world. But with such ambitious goals, Walt became an easy mark for skeptics, who oversimplify his ideas or discredit his sincerity. Yet in this chapter I argue that Walt did achieve some of his loftiest aspirations, including his explicit aim to provide transcendent experiences. In particular, I believe that at Walt's parks, most forcefully and specifically at Disney World, he created ceremonial spaces and established ritual practices that are akin to those of pilgrimages throughout the centuries. By no means are the similarities between Disney World and traditional pilgrimage centers merely coincidental. Rather, it is clear that Walt and his company purposely fostered intense—even unquestioning—devotion to their creations and actively encouraged travel to sites where firsthand experiences with these creations could be had. I know this argument may offend at least some people, especially as I explore the anthropological and theological dimensions of pilgrimage as related to Disney World. The social functions of conventional pilgrimage are clearly met there, but I suggest that the place can also satisfy spiritual needs for some of its visitors. Broad-based appetites for direct contact with Disney's creations have transformed the trek to Disney World into a genuine form of pilgrimage.

Theologian Émile Durkheim insisted that "there are no religions which are false. All are true in their own fashion; all answer, though in different ways, to the given conditions of human existence."[1] To view Disney World as imbued with spiritual potential, we must resist the urge "to rigidly separate the secular and the religious," acknowledging that such division "is not ultimately a viable frame of reference" here.[2] Instead, my claim depends upon an understanding of religion that emphasizes its ability to fulfill widely shared human needs for community, comfort, and celebration. David Chidester offers an excellent description of religion along these lines: it helps us navigate what it means to be human, orient ourselves in time and space, and sort out our beliefs about supposedly supernatural beings. This conception of religion views pilgrimage as a quest for sacred time and space, a longing to exceed routine moments lived in ordinary places. Chidester concludes that Disney does a sort of religious work at its parks, "through the symbolic, material negotiations over the ownership of the sacred terms and conditions of being human in a human place."[3] Eric Michael Mazur and Tara Koda extend the case for Disney spirituality even further, proposing that Disney represents a contemporary mode of religious expression in the United States, which generates images of adoration, concepts of morality, and strong emotions. Since Disney's products are well marketed, its symbols are widely dispersed and circulated, implying that its model of faith is descended from capitalism.[4] (Interestingly, some churches are now emulating Disney's principles to attract and retain worshippers.)[5] There is no doubt that commerce plays an important role at Disney World, as it did at many traditional pilgrimage centers, but I believe there is more to Disney World's spiritual force than its ability to satisfy consumptive impulses.

Walt's legacy has an omnipotent presence in our culture; Disney media and merchandise seem to be everywhere, and its theme parks have achieved cult status. I assert, however, that Disneyland and the foreign parks are satellite shrines: Disney World is the seat of power. No Disney park fully replicates another, and none of the others can rival Disney World in its wide-ranging themes and vast physical terrain. Disney World is where the company's clout is most visible, accumulated in its most-concentrated form, and implicitly consecrated by millions of loyal devotees. Walt spent the last years of his life planning for and fixated on Disney World: it represents not only his vision but also his heart. This chapter explicates how Disney World is less like a conventional tourist site and more like a traditional pilgrimage center in space, rituals, and functions. Many of Disney World's visitors go there for more than a diversionary vacation: they seek to relieve anxieties and forget worries, to feel restored and uplifted. John Hench, former vice president in charge of design for Imagineering, said that Walt dreamed his parks would make people feel "more self-assured, stronger, alert, and much more alive."[6] Evidence suggests that he succeeded: more than 70 percent of Disney World Guests are repeat visitors, a staggering statistic attesting to the meaning and significance of this place.[7] That I count myself among those who return again and again made me realize I must be some sort of pilgrim, too.

From Tourist to Pilgrim

Now when one risks so little and experiences so little on the voyage, the experience of being there somehow becomes emptier and more trivial. When getting there was more troublesome, being there was more vivid. When getting there is "fun," arriving there somehow seems not to be arriving any place.

—Daniel Boorstin, *The Image: A Guide to Pseudo-Events in American Society*

Unfortunately, the contemporary traveler is often disparagingly dismissed as a lazy or unimaginative tourist. With convenient transportation, comparative affordability, and increased leisure time at our disposal, we can sacrifice less and yet travel more easily than ever before. Given these circumstances, it might be assumed that very few pilgrims exist anymore. But when we reframe the concept of pilgrimage for the contemporary age, the personal meaning and social relevance of a journey can overtake the notion that it must require logistical or physical difficulties. Pilgrimage is not an anachronistic practice—it morphs over time and varies by culture. While it originates from spiritual traditions, it was never a strictly religious practice. Even medieval pilgrims journeyed to fulfill worldly functions. They made pilgrimages not only for spiritual reasons but also as penance or punishment, seeking redemption; or to be healed; and even to find adventure and satisfy curiosity.[8]

A useful typology differentiating between "explorer," "traveler," and "tourist" was constructed by Paul Fussell. The explorer "seeks the undiscovered" and "risks of the formless and unknown," while the tourist gravitates toward the security of commercialized sites "prepared for him by the arts of publicity." The traveler mediates between exploration and tourism, fusing "the excitement of the unpredictable" with "the pleasure of 'knowing where one is.'" The tourist has a bad reputation as an uncritical simpleton, made worse by touring in groups. Those who think of themselves as intellectuals tend to frown on mass tourists, though they often engage in similar travel activities.[9] In an increasingly globalized world, genuine exploration is difficult to have, especially when the tourism industry so carefully manages even remote travel. But while critics grumble that traditional pilgrimage is in danger of becoming "'mere' tourism," we must consider the possibility that tourism "becomes for some the new pilgrimage."[10]

To build the case for Disney World as a pilgrimage center, consider that all pilgrims—religious and secular, past and present—engage in the same three-stage process: they journey away from their homes and daily routines, experience transition at a pilgrimage site, and later reincorporate into society.[11] Each pilgrim travels "through a terrain of culturally constructed symbols" in which historical narratives and visual imagery, usually circulated beforehand, condition expectations and experiences. Once home, any souvenirs acquired become especially potent: they are proof of the trip taken and a means of disseminating the pilgrimage center's power.[12] A Muslim is expected (if one can afford it and is able-bodied) to make at least one hajj to Mecca; in American society at least one visit to Disney World is nearly obligatory for middle-class families. Upon return the Muslim person enjoys a newly elevated status; a child back from Disney World is the envy of her peers.[13] Growing up I relished each family vacation we had at Disney World, particularly because I knew that when we got home every kid on our block would be eager for me to share tales of what we saw and did. Trips to Disney World have come to mark plateaus of achievement in American culture as well. In the past, prominent political and religious figures undertook pilgrimages;[14] now, Super Bowl champs and medal-winning Olympians proclaim "I'm going to Disney World!" when asked what they will do next.

Throughout the history of the built environment is an abiding desire to find and be with others, to feel that one belongs. This longing coincides with the social functions of pilgrimage. Although the decision to undertake a pilgrimage may be individual, a pilgrim often seeks a sense of community (*communitas*): perhaps traveling in a group, congregating to dine and lodge, or trading stories. The members of such a community may have different cultural backgrounds, but they share some common codes of conduct and goals. Even if their community is temporary, it brings with it momentary liberation from daily obligations and roles, though the pilgrimage is still bound by rituals and structure. Pilgrims are rarely drifters: they come together in organized manners at supervised sites. In this way, pilgrimage "reinforces the existing social order," as it hinges on some collective ideals.[15] But simultaneously it can subvert the established social fabric. Free from the constraints of home, pilgrims can experience enlightenment and transcendence, but also transgression as inhibitions are loosened. When one nears a pilgrimage center the aura of sacredness supposedly increases, but secularization increases too, as markets, fairs, and festivals offer further opportunities to find community.[16] As a combination of "devotion with pastime and mirth," pilgrimage satiates both our divine and worldly selves.[17] Yet claims for the legitimacy and confluence of all kinds of pilgrimages are undermined by charges that "pseudo-places" have supplanted "actual" ones, implying that some experiences—particularly of reputedly "untouched" historic sites—are more authentic than others. But such an argument does not account for personal variations of experience: we may share ideas about a place and engage in communities particular to it, but our own intentions, emotions, and memories ultimately shape our encounters.[18]

Marita Sturken has studied the phenomenon of cultural memory (as apart from historical accounts or strictly personal memories), describing how it is produced and widely dispersed through media, images, and cultural products. She contends such memory is "crucial to the understanding of a culture precisely because it indicates collective desires, needs and self-definitions" and helps people "imbue the past with value in the present." Within this context of cultural memory she notes the rise of nostalgic forms of tourism (especially in the United States), which focus on public performances of national citizenship and family bonding.[19] At Disney World, memorable experiences are purposefully generated within its coherently themed framework, often pitched toward the small communities we call families.[20] As a child I felt especially close to my parents on our trips there, believing that Disney experiences were unique and even more special because we shared them. Disney smartly cultivates such emotional attachments by encouraging visitors to share their memories. For example, at DisneyParks.com/memories visitors post still images, videos, and stories that emphasize the happiness and fulfillment the parks have brought them. The company also fosters a sense of urgency around the act of memory-making, imploring the would-be pilgrim not to "wait a moment longer. There's a Disney memory waiting for you right now!": "Everyone knows the treasure that memories can be. They connect us with the people we love and bring us a smile whenever we need one. And Disney memories? They're magical things that dance in our dreams and live happily ever after in our hearts."[21] Memories are a meaningful commodity at Disney World, and there is no fear of running out of the magic to fuel them. Company spokesman Terry Brinkoetter admits that emotionalism is the "heart and soul of our business. Disney is not shy. We go for the heartstrings."[22]

Sacred and Sainted?

I believe firmly in the efficacy of religion, in its powerful influence on a person's whole life. It helps . . . keep you attuned to the Divine inspiration. Without inspiration, we would perish.

—Walt Disney, *Walt Disney: Famous Quotes*

Throughout history many places have become pilgrimage sites, among the best known being Mecca, Canterbury, Lourdes, and Rome. Such traditional pilgrimage centers share several distinguishing qualities, including an arrangement of space that promotes ritual movement and circulation through the site; the use of shrines and symbols that draw upon knowledge gathered prior to visiting the center; and the ability to inspire intense devotion among visitors. Disney World, too, has all of these qualities, and compelling comparisons could likely be built between it and the places mentioned above. But when examining Disney World's physical layout, devotional figures, and symbolic rites in closer detail, the undeniable similarities it bears to pilgrimage practices from the Middle Ages make the most convincing case for it as a genuine pilgrimage center. My aim here is to look at the most direct parallels that can be drawn between Disney World and traditional pilgrimage centers; I decided it would be helpful if I could identify a particular medieval pilgrimage site that functioned much like Disney World, and determined that Santiago de Compostela was a persuasive match. Compostela was one of the most popular pilgrimage centers during the Middle Ages, and pilgrims still journey there today. Thus there is the distinct advantage of having accounts of its pilgrimage, both then and now. But what makes Compostela an especially apt choice for comparison to Disney World are the consistent similarities between the two, too frequent and overt to be merely coincidental. That said, I am not arguing that Walt or the Imagineers patterned Disney World specifically upon Compostela; I have found no evidence to support such a claim. But I do believe that the likenesses underscore persistent, recurring themes in the history of our built environment: a desire to foster community, intensify human experience, and provide a break from daily life. Furthermore, it is clear that Walt and his designers purposefully conceived Disney World as a ritualized space for devout followers, who were conditioned beforehand to participate in the rites and recognize the symbols enshrined there. Historically, pilgrimage rituals have ranged from formal ones, performed in a fixed order and having very specific symbolism, to those that are flexible in sequence and meaning. Disney World deftly coalesces formal and informal rituals, inducing processional movement through its symbolic spaces while allowing for choice in direction and even interpretation.[23]

One logical way to begin a comparison between Santiago de Compostela and Disney World is with brief introductions to their respective devotional figures. Both places rely on broadly disseminated stories, ensuring that visitors are familiar with these tales and their heroes prior to making a pilgrimage. Compostela's development as a pilgrimage site hinges on two specific legends concerning Saint James the Great (also called the Elder), one of the twelve apostles and allegedly a blood relative of Jesus.[24] The first story focuses upon his preaching of Christianity on the Iberian Peninsula and his subsequent beheading under Herod Agrippa (around 44 AD) after returning to Jerusalem. Purportedly, James's followers took his body back to Spain on a miraculous weeklong journey in a stone boat, and it was buried and forgotten about for hundreds of years as Roman persecution brought war and depopulation. In the ninth century a hermit named Pelagius supposedly found the enshrined relics, making James the only apostle to be buried west of Rome. As news of this discovery spread, Archbishop Gelmirez and Compostela Cathedral authorities endorsed and promoted their city as a pilgrimage center, and King Alfonso II declared James the patron saint of Spain. The second legend is much simpler, casting James as the "Moorslayer," said to have appeared on a white horse in 844 to guide the Christians to victory over the Moors at Clavijo.[25] As the Crusades proceeded, James was celebrated as Christian Spain's savior and the patron saint of the Reconquest.

Instead of making an analogy to a saint, David Chidester views Walt Disney as a sort of divine designer, framing the "invention of the Magic Kingdom" as a creationist myth in which Disney fashioned "alternative worlds" offering "new ideals of . . . solidarity" as well as models for "human possibility and experimentation."[26] It is true that Disney's creations provide comfort and joy to many people; they can even have healing effects as a respite from cynicism and worry. After his brother died, Roy claimed that Walt's influence lingered "like a living presence" over the Disney Studio and remained a "driving force" behind everything it did.[27] This impact is still felt today as Walt's "good works" are carried on through his disciples, the Imagineers. His spirit also continues to live through the ageless Mickey, Disney's eternal ambassador of goodwill, authenticated and copyrighted by the company as its exclusive property.[28] Although Mickey is not a saint in terms of canonization or other religious conventions, it is fair to claim that he functions as a patron saint at Disney World. Mickey is a universally recognized and loved symbol, embraced by people from all walks of life. The early animations in which he debuted (see chapter 1) emphasized his role as the everyman, making him a sympathetic character to the masses. But Mickey is also a "Renaissance Man" capable of extraordinary cunning and nimble feats.[29]

Compostela is nationalistically significant for Spaniards, although there are persistent doubts that Saint James was ever in Spain. Many historians believe that church officials fabricated the transportation and "discovery" of his relics there, perhaps to help subdue Moorish domination and occupation. But beyond such political motivations were commercial ones, too, as the minor town of Compostela quickly became one of the most powerful pilgrimage centers of the Middle Ages. Today Compostela remains a thriving pilgrimage site, suggesting that its spiritual magnetism or drawing power is derived from its mystical meaning, cultural associations, and civic identity,[30] rather than the historical veracity of its legends. Saint James—whether his relics are really there or not—endures at Compostela as a symbol of spirituality and patriotism. Likewise, both Mickey Mouse and Disney World have strong nationalistic associations. Karal Ann Marling comments: "In a pluralistic society, where experiences of church, school, ethnicity, and the like were not apt to be universally shared, Disney motifs constituted a common culture, a kind of civil religion."[31] In a similar vein, John Updike described Mickey as a patriotic and positivist figure: "He is America as it feels to itself—plucky, put-on, inventive, resilient, good-natured, game."[32] As the seat of Mickey's power, Disney World was designed to articulate "strong American cultural themes like individualism, freedom, and self-actualization."[33] It should be noted, however, that many of Disney World's pilgrims come from outside the United States. The Global Disney Audiences Project analyzed the reception of Disney products in foreign countries, emphasizing variations in the company's marketing practices abroad. Not surprisingly, the project found that Disney World attracts many international Guests, who often view a trip there as a status symbol or a rite of passage.[34]

Travel literature played an essential role in cultivating Compostela's famed status as an international pilgrimage site. Practical data initially passed by word of mouth were eventually collected in and circulated through pilgrims' guidebooks. The first of these offered basic information on lodging and way stations along pilgrimage routes as well as the measurement of distances. Gradually the format evolved to include rates of exchange, maps, and phrase books. The most renowned guide to Compostela (and the Western world's first tourist guidebook) is contained in the twelfth-century *Liber Sancti Jacobi*, more commonly known as the *Codex Calixtinus*.[35] The *Codex* comprises five books: its fifth, *The Pilgrims' Guide*, was by far the most popular. It provided a Basque vocabulary glossary, priced tolls, analyzed water quality, gave tips on avoiding extortionist custom officials, and assessed road and lodging conditions in Compostela and the towns along its pilgrimage routes. *The Pilgrims' Guide* also listed "must see" relics and shrines, outlined travel routes and sightseeing itineraries, and concluded with a detailed description of the city and cathedral that asserted Saint James's body was there "in its entirety."[36] Focusing on pragmatic matters more than spiritual ones, *The Pilgrim's Guide* was "a medieval do-it-yourself manual" that became a model for subsequent books and is used to this day.[37] The prevalence of such literature throughout history reminds us that many pilgrims were not seeking surprises but wished to be informed and reassured. Similarly, today's Disney World pilgrim has a vast and comprehensive body of travel literature from which to choose, both official and unsanctioned.[38] Bill Burke's "crowd-sourced compendium" is a contemporary pilgrim's guide aimed at "mousejunkies" who frequent Disney World and try to replicate the feeling of being there in their homes (including Burke, who plays the Magic Kingdom's entrance music on a loop in his house).[39] Social media have also expanded the ability to share travel tips and tales. During my last few pilgrimages to Disney World, Facebook was my pilgrim's diary: posts both verified the journeys and extended the *communitas* experience, at least to my Facebook "friends."

Compostela and Disney World also share considerable physical similarities in terms of geography and layout. Each is located on a peninsular outcropping of land and carefully planned to enhance its function as a pilgrimage center. During the Middle Ages, trade routes laid the economic and structural foundations for pilgrimage as a tourism industry, with Compostela being one of the first consciously developed tourist sites. At the height of its popularity, the city was made more accessible with new bridges and roads policed by the Order of the Knights of Santiago.[40] The Cluny monks, with monasteries on the southwestern pilgrimage route through France and Spain, were Compostela's most ardent promoters, disseminating travel literature, sponsoring pilgrims, and organizing trips to other pilgrimage centers.[41] A medieval pilgrim to Compostela had four major land routes to choose from, originating in northern France and moving toward the city through other pilgrimage sites and over the Pyrenees.[42] El Camino de Santiago (the Way of Saint James), reputedly walked by Saint Francis of Assisi in the twelfth century, remains popular even now (with a travel center on Facebook). Walking El Camino today, one is guided by yellow arrows on the road, trees, rocks, and buildings. Those who provide proof of completing a minimum of sixty-three miles by foot, bicycle, or on horseback receive a certificate conferred since the thirteenth century.[43] Once arriving in Compostela, many pilgrims linger to enjoy its hospitality and spectacles; a few press on to the extremely remote Finisterre (*Finis Terrae* or end of the world), which was the westernmost point known during the Roman Empire.[44]

Although pilgrims can enter Compostela from different points, those traveling its classical route, the French Road, make a highly directed progression through its ritual space. At the entrance one can purchase a scallop shell (the symbol of Saint James) before proceeding past the Bonaval Convent and the Cruceiro deo Homo Santo (Stone Cross of the Holy Man) to the Porta do Caminho, a way gate, marking the city's walled boundaries. The street of Casas Reales takes visitors past several churches until reaching the Cathedral of Compostela. The first church was built over Saint James's supposed tomb in the ninth century, but the city attracted so many pilgrims that around 1078 construction was begun on a grand Romanesque cathedral to accommodate the crowds (fig. 1).[45] Once inside the cathedral, pilgrims followed along the ambulatory, performing rituals and viewing relics before arriving at their primary destination, the reliquary arc of James. (The arrangement is like queuing up on lines at Disney World, where visitors wind around stanchions past themed elements and pre-shows on their way to the most popular rides.)[46] By the twelfth century Compostela had become the most visited site of Christian devotion; an estimated half million pilgrims from all over Europe made the trek there in the eleventh and twelfth centuries alone. The roads to and from the city became clogged with pilgrimage traffic. For safety's sake pilgrims often traveled in organized groups,[47] though Compostela's routes were well known and many people believed Saint James would protect them on the way to his city.[48] Compostela became the everyman's pilgrimage destination, popular not only for religious reasons but also for its desirable location and the relative ease of travel there. Thousands of people still make the Compostela pilgrimage every year.[49] Like Disney World, the city has peak seasons coinciding with good weather and holidays. In order to better accommodate these conditions, Saint James's feast day (a public holiday originally on 30 December) is now celebrated in late July. Clearly, the agendas of pilgrimage and tourism happily coexisted at Compostela, and continue to do so.

All pilgrims undergo a stage of transcendence, coinciding with the crossing of a physical or symbolic threshold (a *limen*).[50] Distinctions have been drawn between "liminal" pilgrimages, undertaken mostly for obligation, and more playful "liminoid" journeys. But as we have seen in the example of Compostela, the liminal and liminoid often overlap and coincide, which also happens during pilgrimage to Disney World. Although travel there is obviously leisurely, Disney's temporary break from daily life is definitively liminal and ultimately reinforces the existing social order to which its pilgrims eventually return. Here play is productive work, and structured activities help us organize our understandings of the world. Disney World's liminal boundaries are clearly marked by entry gates, enclosing walls, and vegetation separating its celebratory precincts from ordinary ones. We are consciously aware of being "in" or "out" of this space, and also "in on" or "left out" of the fun. In his groundbreaking study of Disney World, anthropologist Alexander Moore argues that this bounded ritual space directs people to make specifically liminal progressions akin to even the most conventional pilgrimage centers.[51] From Disney World's inception, its designers inscribed tightly regulated and synchronized patterns of movement to enhance visitors' experiential encounters there. On practical terms, it is essential to efficiently move crowds "who would easily overwhelm a less rationalized theme park," so Disney keeps us moving on foot, through rides, and, of course, into shops.[52] But motion signals spiritual as well as spatial transitions, as Disney's pilgrim constantly crosses through symbolic and commercial thresholds. The first of these is encountered as

Figure 1. West facade of the Cathedral of Santiago de Compostela, Galicia, Spain. Architects: Bernard the Elder, Master Mateo, and others; architect of the west facade: Fernando Casas y Nóvoa. Built ca. 1078–1122; restored 1738–1750. The Metropolitan Museum of Art, William Keighley Slide Collection. Photograph © William Keighley (1889–1984).

you enter the company's property (or at the airport, where resort Guests can board Disney's free Magical Express bus, thereby discouraging pilgrims from renting cars and going elsewhere). All visitors to Disney World approach the complex via Disney-owned and -operated highways, punctuated by brightly colored signage. Billboards advertise Disney alone. Driving on the company's smooth roads through its immaculate property, one senses a shift, noting there are none of the literal or figurative potholes of daily life. After four and a half miles of buffer zone, those riding in personal vehicles must surrender them to elaborate parking lots. Each lot is divided into named sections fortifying the corresponding park theme, which helps Guests remember where they parked and sets the mood for the day's adventure. Having exited these vehicles, we surrender some control over our mobility but can then become carefree passengers, joining fellow pilgrims on trams zooming us to entrance plazas.

As described in chapter 1, Disney World actually contains four different theme parks; at this point I wish to focus on the Magic Kingdom, the only one of the four planned in detail and on which construction began prior to Walt's death in 1966. Although he talked at great length about Epcot, that park did not open until 1982, and in its final form it varies greatly from what Walt envisioned (see chapters 4 and 5; Disney's Hollywood Studios and Animal Kingdom were not conceived during his lifetime). Our liminal progression through Disney's space is enhanced at the Magic Kingdom, where Guests make an additional journey to enter the park proper by boarding a monorail or voyaging across the man-made Seven Seas Lagoon on a ferryboat.[53] Next, everyone passes through admission gates and into one of two entrance tunnels under the railroad platform, where signs proclaim "Here you leave today and enter the world of yesterday, tomorrow and fantasy."[54]

Visitors then emerge onto Main Street, U.S.A., the only passageway to the rest of the park.[55] This extended transition into the Magic Kingdom is time-consuming, yet Walt insisted upon such a plan, believing this would help structure it as a total experience. Once inside, the park is laid out in the rough shape of an oval, mostly hemmed in by the Disney World Railroad. The plan recalls Baroque capital cities, evoking a sundial (a seventeenth-century icon for the solar system) as its avenues encircle the seat of sovereign power. As Moore observes: "This settlement pattern is the Magic Kingdom's most pervading symbolic statement . . . the expression of a world order thought to run mechanistically by divine clockwork."[56]

Main Street channels pilgrims into the circular plaza fronting Cinderella's Castle, where *Partners,* a bronze statue memorializing Walt and Mickey, resides.[57] Walt conceived his fiberglass castle as a "wienie"—a conspicuous landmark leading visitors like a trainer using frankfurters to coax animals into performing.[58] More elaborate and majestic than Sleeping Beauty's Castle in Disneyland, at 180 feet Cinderella's Castle is the Magic Kingdom's tallest structure, providing orientation from anywhere in the park. From the castle's plaza radiate wide pedestrian walkways leading to various themed "lands," each marked by a signature gateway charting our procession from one space into the next: variations in music, foliage, paving, lampposts, and even garbage cans offer noticeable but never jarring thematic transitions. The Magic Kingdom was originally divided into six distinct lands. In Fantasyland fairy tales come to life. Adventureland transforms visitors into explorers of the tropics. The pioneering spirit of the Old West is evoked at Frontierland. Liberty Square focuses on colonial American history. In Tomorrowland the future is—was?—today. Main Street celebrates small-town life. (A later addition to the lands designed for the youngest visitors, Mickey's Toontown Fair, was closed in 2011 to make way for the recent revamp and expansion of Fantasyland). Kevin Yee likens these themed lands to a prism, "refracting American public consciousness and character into its constituent parts": nostalgia for the past, optimism for the future, playful escapism, a desire to explore and conquer nature, and a taste for the "exotic."[59] Within each land are various attractions reinforcing the respective theme. Lined up in winding queues, Disney pilgrims experience a heightened sense of awareness as they draw nearer to the rides, somewhat like Buddhist or Hindu pilgrims circumambulating at shrines. Moore suggests that Disney's attractions engage us in "mini-phases of separation, transition, and reincorporation."[60] We are usually plunged into darkness, where we can confront fears and discover universal moral truths, and then returned to the light, frequently through a tunnel evoking accounts of near-death experiences. In this way Disney denies the grim realities of death, rendering them inert and unthreatening (Vincent Scully quipped that even the "skeletons in the haunted houses are jolly fellows after all").[61]

Today, as in the Middle Ages, trade in Compostela is concentrated around its cathedral. As Marilyn Stokstad describes it, "the city must have seemed more like a commercial than a religious center. The streets were lined with shops, taverns and hospices catering to the pilgrims' needs."[62] In the square adjacent to the church was the Paraiso, where medieval pilgrims found moneychangers and innkeepers and bought all types of goods, including medicine, wine, shoes, and souvenirs. Of particular interest are the souvenirs, which functioned as sacred traces providing proof of a completed pilgrimage and supposedly a deity's existence, as well as advertising the site.[63] Souvenirs make memory tangible, ensuring that distance from a place is less likely to diminish devotion to its ideals. The most popular souvenirs at Compostela were scallop shells from the beaches of Galicia, symbols of the saint and his good works (James is often pictured in pilgrim's garb with the requisite shell).[64] By the twelfth century, lead badges replicating these became Compostela's official emblems, and church authorities tried to control their sale much as the Disney Company authorizes and merchandises its products.[65] Today Compostela pilgrims can buy everything from bottle openers to T-shirts, along with their shells.

In the Middle Ages relics were exchanged, relocated, or traveled on fund-raising campaigns, making them accessible to broader publics. Likewise, Disney scatters its "relics" around the globe, giving would-be pilgrims multiple opportunities to consume its merchandise and media. At the theme parks souvenirs become even more exclusive, tagged to designate the specific park at which they were purchased. And at the parks Guests can also conduct financial transactions in Disney Dollars (legal tender at an even exchange rate with American currency). Similar to colorful chips in a casino, Dollars emblazoned with Disney's signature characters do not seem like "real" money, so Guests more willingly plunk them down, or hold onto them as souvenirs. Of course, the most widely known and loved character is Mickey, and the company invests considerable resources to bolster pilgrims' emotional connections to its Mouse. In an effort to make him easier for animators to draw, Disney transformed Mickey's original wiry frame into a series of curving forms, enhancing his benign image.[66] The company made the Mouse truly iconic through a clever (and trademarked!) visual shorthand—three conjoined circles representing Mickey's ears and head. This emblem is widely disseminated at the theme parks, being incorporated into nearly every attraction, restaurant, shop, and hotel. In addition to easily recognizable Mickeys (in the shape of waffles, e.g.), there are hidden ones everywhere, enticing visually adept Guests to discover Disney's entrenched symbolism. What started as an inside joke for Imagineers has grown into an obsession for pilgrims, who scour Disney parks for *authentic*—not decorative but purposefully concealed—"Hidden Mickeys" (most usually the classic three-circle silhouette). Steve Barrett, author of *Hidden Mickeys*, notes that this once "benign pastime" has become a "mission," fostering a sense of community among Mouse seekers.[67] The time and resources devoted to seeking Hidden Mickeys, the intimate knowledge required to locate them, the primacy placed upon verifying their "authenticity," and the repeat visits spurred by the rodent treasure hunt underscore pilgrims' intense dedication to Disney.

In addition to the Hidden Mickeys, Imagineers supply other insider references that only the most attentive and devout pilgrims apprehend. Often these refer to attractions, citing opening dates or the names of their Imagineers. In this way, the history of Disney World is both physically and conceptually embedded in the park itself: the individual features may change over time, but the pilgrimage site remains intact. As former Disney employee Kevin Yee explains, such "magical" details constitute the "Disney Difference," depositing "layers of meaning and history onto a form of entertainment often enjoyed on the strengths of its surface value alone. They impart ulterior significance to the attractions and the people who design them, and ultimately remind us why we found them so special in the first place." Impeccably researched and implemented, these details immerse pilgrims in a "rich sub-culture of homages, tributes . . . intricate trivia, and rich backstories . . . which do the heavy lifting of enchanting our imaginations."[68] Such remarkable attention to detail and the desire to codify the historic specialness of the place elevate Disney World beyond everyday theme park to a kind of spiritual center, both for its pilgrims and its designers.

Jon Pahl admits that a trip to Disney World can prompt "a desire for a more compassionate world," but he worries that its pilgrims worship spectacle and technology—that we bask in idealized notions of innocent progress and world peace while ignoring the violence, poverty, and suffering beyond Disney's compound.[69] Disney World is surely a "touristic space" designed for the performance of rituals to comfort and divert us.[70] But such spaces can be usefully beneficial, as long as the visitor is a "willing accomplice, rather than a stooge."[71] Corruption abounded at traditional pilgrimage centers, where relics were falsified and absolution was bought. But at Disney World the simulation of its relics is known to, anticipated by, and even applauded by its pilgrims. There we are invited to squelch fears and test ourselves in its safe environment. As Hench explains it: "Actually, what we're selling through the park is reassurance. We offer adventures in which you survive a kind of personal challenge. . . . But in every case, we let you win."[72] The Imagineers treat Disney World as a sacred place that "rejuvenates the body, stimulates the mind and inspires the spirit. It is a source of happiness and a fountain of learning." But they also maintain it can only be brought to life through the faith of Disney's pilgrims: "The magic is real, and its spark lives in you!"[73]

Main Street, Americana, and Induced Nostalgia

... all evidence suggests Disney meant well.

—Hank Stuever, "America Loves to Hate the Mouse"

As described above, the Magic Kingdom offers its pilgrims themed lands where time and space are collapsed in supposedly quintessential images, derived largely from American culture. We may venture into the future, cruise the jungle, or tame the Wild West, but the framework shaping these experiences is that of middle America, whose citizens were taught how to interact with the park through Disney film and television. I believe that among these themed lands, Main Street, U.S.A., was the nearest and dearest to Walt's heart: based upon his personal experiences and memories, it discloses the wistful dreams of his innermost psyche in its revisionist aims. But as we will see, its popularity also bespeaks the ability to generate cultural memory. Main Street celebrates—and maybe even eulogizes—the midwestern small town. Clearly, its comforts cannot compete with the adventures beckoning up the boulevard, where Cinderella's Castle offers a glimpse of what else life might have to offer. As the only way into and out of the Magic Kingdom, Main Street is both a destination and a conduit to the other lands. Its promenade encourages business transactions and social interactions, and not so subtly circumscribes shopping as the first and last activity of the day.[74] Yet even the most traditional pilgrimage centers, as we have seen at Compostela, did not necessarily hide the overt commercial agendas that accompanied their spiritual ones.

Disney's Main Street is a nostalgic symbol for both America's shared past and Walt's personal childhood, making it key in understanding the theme park's function as a pilgrimage center. David Wright and Robert Snow contend that Americans have "reinvested our religious energies in a reified and deified technology."[75] Disney World was consciously developed for this increasingly commercial and technologically advanced culture, helping us adapt to social change while simultaneously preserving national and cultural ideals as a form of civil worship. Combining nostalgia (for small towns, pedestrianism, and vernacular architecture) with technological innovations, Disney encapsulates so-called traditional values through futuristic means.[76] Cultural geographer Richard Francaviglia believes that Disney's Main Street (first at Disneyland, subsequently "perfected" and restaged at Disney World) was conceived by Walt to improve upon his flawed childhood. The main source for Main Street was Marceline, Missouri (about one hundred miles northeast of Kansas City), where Walt spent some of his boyhood.[77] Although the Disneys were only in Marceline about five years (having moved there in 1906, when Walt was still very young), these were developmentally essential ones for Walt, who romanticized them as particularly happy, especially compared to the hard life his family later faced in Kansas City and Chicago. He proclaimed that "more things of importance happened to me in Marceline than have happened since—or are likely to in the future."[78] On his theme park Main Street, only pleasantries are encountered: an ice cream shop, a bakery, the general store–like Emporium, a barbershop quartet, and the like. (The absence of a standard feature on midwestern Main Streets, a church, is attributed to Disney's dislike of organized religion and the notion that "one sect has the monopoly on morality.")[79] Walt said he wanted Main Street to be a Norman Rockwell painting come to life. And it is, both in its longing for a time past and its tendency to ignore the hard facts of history.[80] Robert Neuman suggests Depression- and World War II–era films idealizing small-town life also prompted Walt to model his Main Street after their happier depictions.[81] Here Walt remained blind to American adversities and instead emphasized the circulation of consumer goods and evolution of communal life.[82]

Main Street gently transitions pilgrims from the outside world into the Magic Kingdom's fantasy. The period it conjures is purposefully unspecified, likely somewhere between 1890 and 1910, when electricity and the automobile would forever change American life, a moment most visitors did not live through themselves. With its quaint shops and Victorian architecture, Marceline's Main Street offered a basic pattern for the Imagineers to follow. But instead of making detailed copies, they synthesized elements from different sources, fashioning Disney's Main Street as a decidedly symbolic place, not a re-creation of any particular location.[83] Detractors complain this "filtering and packaging operation" eliminates the "unpleasantness of tragedy, of time and of blemish," which is absolutely true.[84] Historian Michael Wallace notes: "The Disney people don't consider this retrospective tidying up an abuse of the past; they freely and disarmingly admit its falsification. . . . But they also insist they are bringing out deeper truths."[85] These "truths" present the Victorian era as optimistic, prosperous, and progressive, an image emphatically more reassuring than that of immigrant poverty, social protests, and lynchings. For Disney this depoliticized past symbolized "the real America," or at least presented the United States in its most luminous form.[86] The issue is not that Walt created an entirely untrue historical picture, but that it is only a partial view from a much wider, more complicated panorama. In her studies of cultural memory, however, Sturken argues that such memory hinges not upon its "wholeness" as an accurate "recollection" but upon its power to function as a "fluid" and "cathartic" "reenactment." "Mnemonic aids" such as photographs and film are used as "screens, actively blocking out other memories that are more difficult to represent." It is likely, whether he was fully aware of it or not, that Walt conceived Disney World in general and Main Street in particular as such "screens." Yet Sturken is quick to add that American culture is not "amnesiac" or "forgetful" as it is often dismissively portrayed; instead, it produces memory in new ways, especially in the aftermath of tragic events and unhappy circumstances. She concludes that memory is a "form of interpretation" that tells us "as much about desire and denial as it does about remembrance."[87]

Years before embarking on his Florida project, Walt built an apartment for himself on Disneyland's Main Street, just above the firehouse and adjacent to City Hall. (A similar one planned for Cinderella's Castle was not realized until 2007, when the "Year of a Million Dreams" gave prizewinners access to a "Dream Suite" that remains otherwise off-limits to the public.)[88] Like the parent of a new baby, Walt wanted to be near "Disneyland when it sleeps" and increasingly isolated himself in his apartment.[89] Its decor of flocked wallpaper, red rugs, and Victorian furniture, which Marc Eliot quips "gave the impression of nothing so much as the anteroom of a New Orleans whorehouse," was personally chosen by Walt and inspired by his family's living room in Marceline.[90] Disney's public persona as a gentle, "folksy" fellow was sharply contrasted by the private life of a reputedly "grouchy, inarticulate, withdrawn man" with an egocentric need for control. Despite leaving behind an estate worth $20 million (and additional deferred payments and royalty agreements of untold value), Disney was haunted by self-doubt and uncertainty.[91] At the dedication of a Marceline school named after him, Walt revealed a penetrating psychological truth in the guise of humility: "I'm not modest. I'm scared. I'm not funny. I hide behind the mouse, the duck, and a lot of other things."[92]

Francaviglia raises important issues about Disney's Main Street, wondering how accurately Walt had remembered Marceline and how much history may have been altered to match his memories. But he concedes that "Disney masterfully abstracted his experiences in Marceline . . . to produce a small-town image that has nearly universal appeal . . . Disney either knew more about image building than given credit for, or . . . was a pioneer in shaping values."[93] Walt was an enterprising capitalist (and a better businessman than his father) who made images into commodities, but he also wished to foster civic responsibility and inclinations toward the common good. On Main Street, Disney selectively isolated what he considered to be the United States' best qualities, embodied in the midwestern town. His vision was hampered by bouts of insularity and insecurity, but for many pilgrims, Main Street remains a cleverly reworked presentation of the past that delights and reassures them.[94] Architectural critic Dolores Hayden decries Disney's Main Street as a contemporary shopping mall cloaked in small town colloquialisms. A sense of place, she asserts, cannot be willed through a regurgitation of styles.[95] Yet I would counter that Walt's Main Street is an evocative place for many people, including those who acknowledge its obvious editorial idealization of the past. As Richard Snow wrote: "Sinclair Lewis found his Main Street foul with hypocrisy . . . and blighted aspirations. He wasn't wrong. But neither was Walt Disney."[96]

Speaking of the Disney parks before his death, Don Jackson, professor of psychology at Stanford University, attested: "I felt a great sense of awe, wonderment, and reverence . . . as I have experienced in some of the great cathedrals . . . Chartres, Rheims, and Notre Dame."[97] I acknowledge that not everyone will have a religious (or even special) experience at Disney World, but I want to allow for the possibility and intentionality. Disney World's visitors are really participants who imbue the site with significance, and participants can sometimes become pilgrims in an "empowered pursuit of meaningful answers" to life's questions while there.[98] I have made a conscious choice to be a participant and willingly immerse myself in Disney World. Given how many times I have been there, I must be a pilgrim, too. But I did not choose that role with the same self-awareness as I did that of participant. I came into my pilgrimage gradually, converted after years of being entertained, enlightened, emboldened. Pilgrimages are acts of faith, undertaken to renew spirit, regain health, or enlarge perspective. To find magic in Disney World's simulations is also an act of faith. Walt intended to do more than amuse his Guests—he wanted Disney World to fortify and sustain us.[99] After a trip there I may be physically exhausted, but I am also recharged with wonder and even optimism, feeling more composed to deal with whatever problems wait for me outside of Walt's World. As Moore writes, "to visit Disney World is to play, but it is also to bear witness."[100]

three  Swampland

Walt Disney Builds Paradise

For there is literally no limit to the things [Walt] can create. . . . He can make a mouse talk and an elephant fly, and bring a puppet to life.

—"Walt Disney: Great Teacher," *Fortune*, August 1942

People who have worked with me say I am "innocence in action." . . . I still look at the world with uncontaminated wonder, and with all living things I have a terrific sympathy.

—Walt Disney, *Walt Disney: Famous Quotes*

Walt designed Disney World as a personal paradise, believing others would share his vision. His intention was to provide a refuge from the messes of daily life, a place where he could continually tinker with his notions of an ideal society. In his worldview, the United States was the most noble of nations, unified by God-fearing, hardworking, and optimistic citizens. The virtues Walt perceived in his country were the same that he sought to foster at Disney World—freedom, ingenuity, bravery, and contentment. The public quickly responded to his concept: nearly 11 million visitors passed through Disney World's gates in 1971, its first year of operation. Clearly, Walt's vision of paradise resonated with many people.

In the Bible, Paradise is an actual place presented as an "opposition-parallel" with everyday experience.[1] The book of Genesis introduces Adam and Eve as caretakers of the Garden of Eden, and contrasts the symbolic harmony of the Garden to the chaos and disorder of daily life. Yet few physical details are offered about Eden, and many questions remain: Was it more like a garden, or a park? How formal was its arrangement? What role did animals play there?[2] Answers to such queries about this biblical place will likely continue to elude us, but if we turn to other paradisal archetypes,

Disney World included, we can gather more information. In this chapter I trace Disney World's, particularly the Magic Kingdom's, explicit connections to paradisal traditions. Authors, artists, architects, and visionaries of all kinds have evoked earthly Paradise as a place not totally unfamiliar yet unlike anything we have experienced before—a decisive fusion of observed fact and imagined fancy. After briefly considering literary and artistic prototypes that helped establish and propagate images of Paradise, we will consider how the landscape has been consciously cultivated throughout history to accommodate varying paradisal visions, seen at sites such as nature parks and formal gardens. Disney World sits well alongside these models for Paradise, as their designers aimed to foster communities of like-minded people, improve upon everyday existence, and intensify our feelings of aesthetic pleasure and moral fulfillment, as did Walt. These goals noticeably overlap with those we have already encountered at pilgrimage centers, once again demonstrating how Disney World is firmly rooted in the ongoing themes of our built environment and human creativity. As in the case of pilgrimage, sometimes the paradisal prototypes for Disney World were more correlative in nature, such as Yosemite and Boboli Gardens, both of which are discussed here to combat the cultural assumptions that continually undervalue Disney World. Yet we will also find a direct source for Disney World in the designs of Ebenezer Howard, who dreamed of a utopian Garden City.[3] Over the centuries, numerous urban planners have proposed schemes for ideal cities (we will encounter these again in chapters 4 and 5), but Howard's work was known to and studied by Walt, making it particularly helpful in discerning Disney World's paradisal context. I want to note that I will use both the terms *paradisal* and *utopian* in this chapter, with the understanding that although they are not strict synonyms, the concepts they convey are deeply intertwined. Paradise is "a place of extreme beauty, delight or happiness," while a utopia is "an ideal place or state." Walt envisioned Disney World as a beautifully ideal place and a constant source of pleasure. But given that much of it was completed after his death, it is also important to think about how Disney World might have fallen short of Walt's expectations. In the paradisal context of this chapter, these shortcomings are most clearly seen at Animal Kingdom, which we will also consider.

As theologian Carlos Mesters explains it, "Paradise is . . . the mock-up of the world. It is the construction plan to be realized by the contractor who is man."[4] I believe Walt Disney saw himself as such a "contractor"—a post-industrial Adam who would get things right the second time around in Florida. Disney World is more than a themed resort: it is a deliberately conceived, rationally planned, and meticulously executed attempt to restore order to the world. It is also an insular greenhouse where Walt cultivated nostalgic Americana as a sort of escape valve from modern society. He tried to prescribe moral conduct within Disney World's precincts, as his individual values were echoed "through recurring characters and familiar, repetitive themes."[5] Consistent messages praising the merits of hard work, inventiveness, and various forms of abstinence are delivered through attractions that draw upon a network of morality tales. But Walt was also a shrewd businessman who marketed his vision of Paradise as a place where we can recapture innocence and youth. At their worst, attempts to build Paradise sanction exclusionism; at their best, though, these represent humankind's "enduring quest for utopian living," grounded in optimism and hope.[6] Walt pursued such a quest with his Disney World, striving for nothing less than to "set the global standards for imagining happiness."[7]

Words and Pictures

And the Lord God took the man, and put him into the
Garden of Eden to dress it and to keep it.

—Genesis 2:15

Generations of visionaries have attempted to design and even build their own versions of Paradise, but these efforts were preceded by descriptions in words and pictures. Tracking the history of paradisal literature and art is not my intention here, but I do believe that briefly considering representative examples of each illuminates how Walt's ideas align with such longstanding traditions. The most famous literary example is John Milton's *Paradise Lost*.[8] Although I am not suggesting that Walt used Milton's work as a direct model for Disney World, there are compelling similarities between their respective visions of Paradise that ascribe both to the larger paradisal framework. Disillusioned with institutional Christianity, Milton developed his own concepts regarding the nature of man and God.[9] (Likewise, Walt was not a churchgoer but a self-styled "devout Christian," who also drank alcohol, smoked heavily, and cursed frequently.) Milton conceived Eden as a luxuriant place lacking the formality of his age's pervading garden trends. His Paradise, however, did mesh with prevailing conceptions of landscape as instilled with social significance: it could evoke moods, enhance states of reverie, promote contemplation, or delight the senses. Furthermore, his

Paradise marks a clear departure from daily life, reverting to a moment before the "fall" of man.[10] Thus Milton's Eden transcends the familiar, temporal world: it is not a landscape drawn from an extant model but rather a "prospect"—a product of the imagination, influenced by various artistic depictions of Paradise.

As was common of paradisal constructs since antiquity, a wall encloses Milton's Eden, defining it as a protective camp for nature and virtue that "cannot admit within its confines that which will defile it."[11] His Eden is described as a "tableau of frozen movement in a timeless spring landscape," where Adam and Eve meander without fear of getting lost.[12] As already seen in our discussion of pilgrimage, Disney World also demarcates its sacred space with distinct borders, though it seems to defy the boundaries of time as we are whisked from the nostalgic past to a hopeful future in a few steps between themed lands. Walt, too, was concerned that we feel well oriented there, plotting clear routes for us to travel. Milton chronicled the various flora, fauna, and topography of his Eden in great detail.[13] This Garden, tended by man, is an analogy for controlled passions and moral labor. Disney World set new standards for cleanliness, scope, and attention to detail in the built environment. But Walt also believed in the place's restorative powers and ability to coax Guests into exemplary behavior. Milton's epic poem, through which he is immortalized, was written when his health was ailing. The night before he died, Walt plotted Disney World's layout on the ceiling above his hospital bed. His body racked by cancer, Walt determined his last work would be his best.

Many landscape painters have looked to paradisal traditions for inspiration, particularly in the nineteenth century. Among them is Thomas Cole, who painted *The Garden of Eden* in 1828 (fig. 2). Cole's work was greatly influenced by aesthetic theories imbuing landscape with moral purpose, especially Edmund Burke's *Philosophical Inquiry into the Origin of Our Ideas of the Sublime and Beautiful* (1757). Burke's "sublime" and "beautiful" were subjective concepts, in which things were not as important as the states of mind they awakened.[14] Cole painted his *Eden* to evoke both the "beautiful" and the "sublime": bathed in golden light, with a temperate climate and harmonious environs, yet punctuated by dark shadows, swampy forest, and a rocky grotto. *The Garden of Eden* was one of Cole's first attempts to elevate landscape to the hallowed level of historical and religious painting. Likely influenced by the rise of "prospect" painting in which the landscape was invented, Cole did not portray a single specific place but synthesized empirical observation and fantasy.[15] Satisfied with his ingenious amalgam,

Cole wrote of the painting in terms one could imagine Walt would have used to described Disney World: "In this I have endeavored to conceive a happy spot wherein all the beautiful objects of nature were concentrated."[16]

The Garden of Eden's provenance is telling of its importance for Cole. Though "rediscovered" around 1990 and now in the collection of the Amon Carter Museum (Fort Worth, Texas), before then it had not been publicly exhibited since 1831. Art collector Samuel G. Goodrich wished to purchase the work and show it at the Boston Athenaeum, but Cole was intent on exhibiting it at the National Academy of Design to make a reputation for himself in New York. Since Genesis provides only a short account of Eden, Cole turned to other sources for inspiration, including Milton. In a letter to his friend Daniel Wadsworth, Cole describes the painting in phrases lifted nearly verbatim from *Paradise Lost*.[17] And when *The Garden* was finally displayed at the National Academy in May 1828, lines of Milton's prose accompanied its image in the catalog. Regarding artistic prototypes, Cole admitted to using Jan Brueghel (probably the Elder) for models of birds

Figure 2. Thomas Cole, *The Garden of Eden*. 1828. Oil on canvas. Accession No. 1990.10: Amon Carter Museum of American Art, Fort Worth, Texas.

and animals. He also included imagery that was already established in the Paradise tradition: a banana tree symbolizing the Tree of Knowledge of Good and Evil; palms, representing the Tree of Life; and water, alluding to the Four Rivers of Eden. Yet *The Garden* prompted controversy when Cole was accused of plagiarizing Richard Martin. Devastated, Cole hung a print of Martin's *Paphian Bower* (1823) next to *The Garden*, but some skeptics remained unconvinced, and *The Garden* did not sell at the exhibition.[18] It may be a stretch to align the detractors who dislike Disney's simulations with Cole's critics, who decried that his painting remained too close to its sources. But I do believe that both men tried to combat the chaos they perceived around them. When Cole painted his *Eden*, Jacksonian America was in a state of civil unrest, insinuating the Union's demise.[19] Cole undertook *The Garden of Eden* without any patron or commission, and painted a fantasy world that transcended the disorder and confusion of his day.[20] For Walt the 1960s must have been an uncertain time, as free love, no-nukes demonstrations, and the civil rights and feminist movements rankled his quaint ideal of America. At his Florida retreat he could foster cultural memory of supposedly more peaceful times, blissfully removed from any outside turmoil.[21] Social and moral order reign in *Eden* and at Disney World, as Cole and Walt both offered not only beauty and comfort but also reassurance when, to them, their nation seemed unstable.

Parks, Gardens, Cities

It is our shaping perception that makes the difference between raw matter
and landscape.
—Simon Schama, *Landscape and Memory*

For millennia, the landscape has been framed and marketed as a place for enrichment and entertainment. From Eden's "tamed nature as opposed to unkempt wilderness" to Disney World's tidy microcosm—and many points in between—purposeful cultivation has long shaped the land for our enjoyment.[22] Although in recent generations our interactions with the environment have often been viewed as lamentable interference, these exchanges do not necessarily equal exploitation and depletion. Landscape is wrought not just by geology and vegetation but also by human intervention, as witnessed in the widespread rise of landscape tourism.[23] Here I will consider the nature park and formal garden as physical prototypes of paradisal models and show how Disney World fits within this larger tradition.

The royal forest of Fontainebleau was the first arcadia consciously marketed for popular consumption. Former hunting grounds for the monarchy, it became accessible to the public in the nineteenth century as a nature park, a transition greatly enhanced by Claude François Denecourt's plotting of its first trails. Denecourt knew city folk would flock there to commune with idyllic nature, but first he had to contend with the forest's imperial legacy (particularly Louis XIV's "revisions" that had straightened avenues and paved roads). The few maps and guides that existed to Fontainebleau were "absurdly rudimentary," presenting it as "a rustic annex of the palace." Denecourt resolved that the forest would be "penetrated, measured, surveyed, mapped . . . not . . . statistically . . . but descriptively, even poetically." He acted as the forest's scenic engineer, charting specific routes for pleasure and solitude and digging crevices to encourage the growth of moss and mushrooms for "picturesque improvement." He also published an *indicateur* to the forest that included walking paths, interesting sites, and a detailed topographical map (such guides were eventually published in English as well as French). During France's democratic Second Republic, a new railway from Lyon to Paris made Fontainebleau more popular than ever. Denecourt capitalized on the crowds: he provided carriage tours, "all-inclusive" lunch packages, and a viewing platform to survey the entire wood. Unfazed by state officials blaming him for turning the forest into "one enormous open-air resort of public amusement," Denecourt maintained that Fontainebleau had been returned to the people. Simon Schama aptly notes Denecourt's "promotional genius" in supplying "just enough remoteness for the illusion of wilderness, without any of the danger of real disorientation," thus forecasting "the great business principle of mass popular recreation."[24] Walt did much the same in Florida, sharing with Denecourt an obsessive eye for detail and knack for publicity.

During the nineteenth century, nature tourism also became fashionable in the United States as a newly moneyed middle class sought escape from the burgeoning industrial centers. The vast landscape offered not only diversion but also a sense of cultural identity beyond Europe's shadow. John Sears proposes that the sites of American landscape tourism were both "sacred places" and "arenas of consumption," inducing "many tourists to approach them with a double consciousness, with religious awe or poetic rapture on the one hand and a skeptical, sardonic attitude on the other."[25] I experienced such a double consciousness when visiting Yosemite, another nature park purposefully framed and marketed as an earthly Paradise (fig. 3). In 1864 Congress established Yosemite Valley as "a place of sacred significance for the nation," no doubt in recognition of its great natural beauty.[26] But the site required systematic development to transform it into a cultural icon, with promotional efforts ongoing to this day. Words and images endorsed Yosemite as an outpost of national pride, highlighting its awe-inspiring features such as Cathedral Rock and the *Sequoiadendron giganteum* (giant sequoia). Meanwhile, the Ahwahneechee people, whose fire clearances of the valley floor enhanced its Edenic beauty, were "evicted" to a reservation. The scant opposition to Yosemite's preservation as a national park is attributed not only to environmental awareness but also the land's unsuitability for agriculture or mining: its redeeming economic value was understood to be in tourism.[27] Today, Yosemite's parking lots are almost as large as the park and bears riffle through fast-food cartons, though I doubt most visitors would wish that it had remained undeveloped as a tourist site.[28] Nature does not locate, name, or venerate itself. Humans define and determine its beauty in context to—and even as part of—our built environment, which is precisely what Walt set out to do at Disney World.

Walt's impulse to "improve" upon nature is also akin to the evolution of the formal garden. Historically, enclosed gardens served as metaphors for

Figure 3. El Capitan and Yosemite Valley, Yosemite National Park, California. Photograph: Brooke A. Knight, 2008.

ideal realms, designed to amplify nature's underlying regularity while re-creating Eden's botanical variety.[29] European gardens, especially during the Renaissance, used Eden as a source for their isolated precincts where human ingenuity would overcome nature's imperfections. Although Disney World is related to the general tendency of these gardens to treat landscape as spectacle, the processional organization of sequential spaces at the Boboli Gardens in particular make them an excellent comparison for Walt's Florida retreat.[30] Begun by Tribolo (Niccolo di Raffaello) in 1550 and completed by Bernardo Buontalenti in the second half of the sixteenth century, the Boboli Gardens are laid out around the Pitti Palace in Florence.[31] Eleonora of Toledo had bought the villa in 1549 as a wedding gift for her new husband, Duke Cosimo I, a member of the powerful Medici family. The couple wished to construct the greatest gardens of all time not only for their own enjoyment but also for the pleasure of their many privileged guests.[32] Similarly, Walt conceived Disney World to exceed all previous amusement places and to entertain and instruct his targeted public. Both sites were intended to function as larger backdrops for the pageantry staged within their grounds.[33]

In its tightly controlled layout (previously encountered in chapter 2), the Magic Kingdom is much like the Boboli Gardens. The Medici sited their Gardens on the slopes and at the foot of the Boboli hill. The Boboli's design is formal and geometric, but when experienced by foot it has many carefully plotted twists and turns not suggested by the plan (fig. 4). Paths were laid out to optimize visitors' experiences and keep them moving, though not necessarily on the shortest routes. Likewise, Walt and his Imagineers felt that pedestrian movement would set the Magic Kingdom's rhythm, and plotted a clockwise circuit passing as many different attractions, restaurants, and merchants as possible.[34] Tribolo's plan for the Boboli put a colossal fountain in the center of its *prato*, or lawn, as a "visual magnet" to entice visitors onward into a planned sequence of events.[35] At the Magic Kingdom, Cinderella's Castle is the largest "magnet," sitting at the heart of a radial plan with paths to each themed land converging at its traffic circle. The castle is also a point of orientation, easy to visually locate and reach by foot.[36] Walt proclaimed, "I don't want sore feet here. They make people tired and irritable,"[37] and thus endeavored to build "a place where you can't get lost or tired unless you want to."[38]

Boboli's designers conceived of the Gardens as a series of interrelated outdoor rooms, where straight lanes gave way to intimate grottoes. The first "room" was the courtyard, closed off by the Grotto of Moses and a terrace

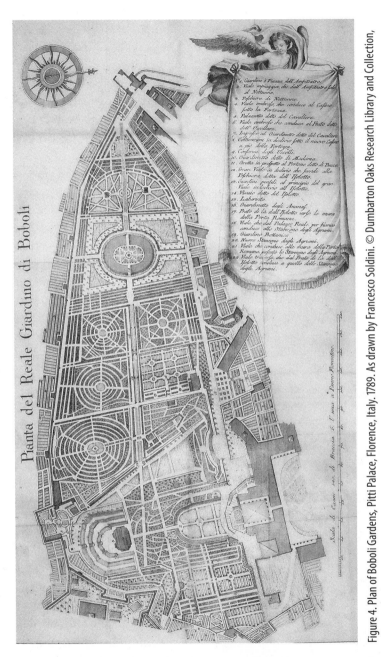

Pianta del Reale Giardino di Boboli

and adorned with Francesco Susini's Fountain of the Carciofo (artichoke). Other "rooms" include the Rondo of Bacchus (named for Valerio Cioli's statue of the god of wine) and the hilltop Giardino del Cavaliere (Garden of the Knight). The father-and-son architect team of Giulio and Alfonso Parigi, working from 1631 to 1656, finally completed the Gardens with an amphitheater, an alley of Cypresses (the "Viottolone"), and a square and pool for the Piazzale of Isolotto. Views were limited throughout the Boboli so that only one section was revealed at a time, framing interesting perspectives and picturesque vistas. Similar to Boboli's serial rooms, the Magic Kingdom's spaces are treated as successive "scenes" in a linear narrative. Imagineer John Hench described the park as a three-dimensional extension of Disney's films: "The visitor is taken, step by step, through a sequence of related experiences. We never jar him—we just lead him along, making the trip as interesting as we know how."[39] He elaborated, "Main Street is like Scene One, and then the castle is designed to pull you down Main Street toward what is next, just like a motion picture unfolding."[40] The transitions between lands are graduated like cinematic cross-dissolves: foliage, color schemes, music, and architecture deftly shift to accommodate different themes, and the lands are visually blocked from each other as much as possible to preserve conceptual unity.[41] Although visitors have the freedom to choose where they will go next, they are always guided by preplanned elements and mapped routes.[42] The Boboli's grottoes were among its most fantastic rooms, evoking a subterranean world that blurred the boundaries between the corporeal realm and what might come beyond it.[43] Their effect is similar to Disney's "dark rides," in which visitors are plucked from daylight and thrust into darkness to encounter the miraculous, emerging afterward as both literally and figuratively enlightened (see chapter 2).[44] The rides re-create the intimacy of a darkened theater, moving us through bounded spaces and past edited vignettes from Disney tales, presented to smaller groups or individuals. Each person's trip is an equal length of time as ride vehicles pivot and turn in the same patterns and directions, to make sure everyone has the same view.[45] The goal is to place the riders "right in the middle of the action, for a total, themed, controlled experience."[46]

Water also played a pivotal role in gardens as a symbol of personal illumination. Fontanieri (fountain masters) such as Buontalenti were sought after to craft magical effects: automata, organ pipes, fountain statuary, and giocchi d'acqua (water jokes, triggered by unsuspecting footsteps). But such playfulness masks underlying themes of hierarchical domination and spiritual mystery as the designers exercised "God-like control" over visitors unable to anticipate what would come next.[47] The fontanieri were like

Renaissance Imagineers, maximizing the level of participation one could have in their magnificent gardens but always working to frame and predetermine visitor experiences. Nothing happens haphazardly at the Boboli or the Magic Kingdom. Movement through their spaces parallels our journeys through life, encountering many joys and challenges along the way.[48] Garden historians J. C. Shepherd and G. A. Jellicoe maintain: "The pathological purpose of the garden was to give pure contentment to its owner."[49] But neither the Boboli nor Disney World was conceived for solely private pleasures—each was designed with a public in mind to bring their respective delights to life.[50]

Although Disney World is clearly part of the same history of the built environment as manifested in the parks and gardens discussed above, there is an even more specific source for it in ideal city or utopian planning. *Utopia* literally means "no place," an idealized fictional construct seeking to exceed its present-day limitations and structures.[51] Renaissance writings, especially Thomas More's *Utopia* (1516), popularized such ideal city schemes, but these literary accounts were rarely intended for practical application. The more immediate effects of the writings were first felt in gardens such as the Boboli, which impressed visitors with their directional orientation, elaborate planning, and consummate organization. Not surprisingly, many of their features were soon incorporated into city plans: axes and geometric forms provided movement and focus, fountains and statues marked terminal points, and open spaces lent variety and interest.[52] Later designers, such as Ebenezer Howard, eventually sought to resolve the garden and the city as a single entity.

The ideal city usually rebukes customary urban planning to protest "a specific order found intolerable" in pursuit of a better system and nobler world. The Industrial Revolution, with its polluted and overcrowded cities, fostered some of the grandest schemes for ideal ones. Englishman Ebenezer Howard (1850–1928) maintained that it was feasible to build sanitary and equitable places "where the social classes would live in harmony and the bond with Nature would be reaffirmed." Although other ideal cities can provide useful comparisons to Disney World, I have chosen to look at Howard's Garden City, which was not only a great influence on other important urban designs (such as Frank Lloyd Wright's Broadacre City) but also a direct source for Walt as he planned his own ideal city for Florida. Purposely folksy, nostalgic, and even regressive, with a "clean, pleasant, timeless look," the Garden City was designed as a physical manifestation of mental well-being, set away from the bustle of metropolitan London.[53] Howard wished to isolate the best of the urban environment and surround

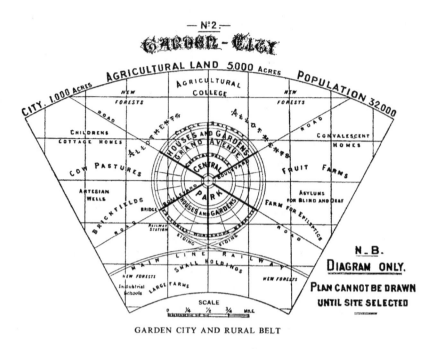

Figure 5. Ebenezer Howard, Plan of the Garden City. 1902. From Ebenezer Howard, edited by F. J. Osborn, *Garden Cities of To-Morrow*, published by MIT Press in 1965.

this with a rural greenbelt for agriculture and recreation. A greenbelt (the concept dates back to ancient Rome) functions as a defensive wall limiting the city's size and discouraging haphazard growth, as Walt attempted to do with his buffer zone in Florida. Howard intended his Garden City to accommodate a population of about thirty thousand residents: big enough to enjoy the "advantages of intensive urban life," but small enough to preserve the "beauty and pleasures of the country."[54] Carefully defined, its plan reveals a park and large public buildings at the center, encircled by the Crystal Palace, a weatherproof enclosed glass arcade (fig. 5). Six wide boulevards bisect the city into equal pieces, offering a striking similarity to the Magic Kingdom, as well as Walt's original plans for Epcot, addressed in chapter 5. (The Celebration community, discussed in chapter 4, is also related to ideal city planning, but all of its design and construction occurred nearly thirty years after Walt's death.)

In his careful design, Howard sought to bring the country and city closer together and to reintroduce the ancient concept of managed growth in his town's physical size, density of habitation, and population. Critic Lewis

Mumford offered high praise for this Garden City, noting that its limited scale regulated essential functions while promoting a vital social life.[55] Walt wished to do much the same at Disney World, and in fact read the 1902 edition of *Howard's Garden Cities of To-morrow*. Urban planner Sam Gennawey describes the "clear simple graphics" of this book, which made Howard's ideas highly accessible to Walt. The evidence of Howard's subsequent influence on Walt is still visible today, from Disney's transportation and land use practices, to the radial planning of the theme parks.[56] But detractors complained that Howard's city was too limited in size and static in growth to address urbanization's larger challenges. Howard preached self-sufficiency, yet the Garden City was a satellite, reliant upon the "big city" for many of its needs. Though the Garden City was meant to be "the closest we came to paradise on earth," cities are rarely so single-minded in their usage, no matter how rationally planned or politically unified they seem. To enjoy the richness of the urban fabric is also to encounter the problems ensnared in it. Architectural historian Spiro Kostof found plans for ideal cities to be ultimately "dehumanizing": "Life cannot be regimented, it seems . . . except in totally artificial units like monasteries . . . and concentration camps where inhabitants submit willingly or are constrained without choice."[57] Howard realized that goodwill could not be imposed via stringent planning just anywhere, noting on his Garden City diagram that a site must be determined before the plan was executed (though he did envision it as an archetype to possibly emulate elsewhere).[58] Howard's Garden City also required the land to be owned by a municipality, a premise Disney rejected, unwilling to give up that much control. Thus on the point of landownership Walt could no longer follow Howard's "peaceful path to real reform" and instead charted his own way, stubbornly on his own terms.

Paradise Lost and Found, in Florida

Here in Florida we have something special we never enjoyed at Disneyland: the blessing of size.

—Walt Disney, *Project Florida* (also known as the "EPCOT Film")

Had Walt been happy with Disneyland, perhaps he would not have pursued building Disney World, or at least he would have done so less zealously. Initially, Disneyland's site of Anaheim, California, about twenty-five miles outside Los Angeles, pleased him. Still largely undeveloped (as Walt described it, "just orange groves and a few acres of walnut trees"), with good weather year-round and the new Santa Ana Freeway system providing easy access, it seemed like a perfect location.[59] During Disneyland's design, Walt commissioned surveys of what he considered to be successful themed environments, including Greenfield Village in Dearborn, Michigan, and Colonial Williamsburg in Virginia. He also studied places closer to home, such as Knott's Berry Farm in Buena Park and the Los Angeles County Fair in Pomona. These reports were quite detailed, examining issues such as traffic flow by measuring the walkways at Knott's Berry Farm. Walt also visited Copenhagen's Tivoli Gardens in 1952—a seminal year in Disneyland's planning—greatly admiring its ability to attract families. Though built in 1843, Tivoli Gardens was in no way dilapidated, and Walt marveled at its clean and orderly microcosm. As he toured the place, he made notes on all of the elements (such as lighting, seating, and food) that contributed to its ambience and utility, thinking about how Tivoli's lessons could be applied to his own park.[60] Disney thought it was also essential to study what he found to be poorly themed places, including New York's Coney Island and Severton Village in Connecticut. From his research, Walt concluded that his park must emphasize quality at any cost: attractions had to be unique, settings must be easy to navigate, and all of it needed to be spotlessly maintained. He also employed tactics to weed out the less-affluent and more unruly crowds who flocked to places like Coney Island. By siting his park away from mass transit systems and charging higher admission prices, Walt catered to a fairly homogeneous audience.[61]

Eric Avila aligns Disneyland with the "utopian aspirations" of Southern California's development at the time and views it as a response to the uncertainties of postwar American culture, especially in terms of race relations. It is true that Disney built his park "removed from urban concentrations of racialized poverty" and marketed it to upwardly mobile suburbanites, many of whom were white and then fleeing cities. But I do not agree with Avila that Walt "remained suspicious of cities and their culture throughout his life."[62] In fact, as we will see in the subsequent chapters, Disney spent much of his last years engaged with urban design and planning, appreciating the variety and excitement to be found in cities. Admittedly, in these endeavors Walt was too often a victim of his own naïveté and hubris, believing a "better" city would certainly result if he were to build it from the ground up and administrate it, too.

Gary Cross suggests that Coney Island, an "industrial saturnalia" from an earlier time, was displaced by Disney's modernized "commercial saturnalia." Walt did not entirely reject Coney Island, however, but "selectively imitated" its scenic dioramas, thrill rides, and dramatic reenactments. Instead of freaks, Disney offered huggable characters; sideshows were supplanted by elaborate attractions; and carnies were replaced by clean-cut Cast Members resembling the Guests. Thus Disney revived "genteel ideals of the sublime," making a decisive break with the seedier entertainments of the first half of the twentieth century. Walt also reconstituted the notion of the "playful crowd" by focusing on cross-generational families, emphasizing the "wondrous innocence" of kids, and encouraging adults to reawaken their "inner children."[63] During its construction, Walt began talking of his park as a sort of a panacea, encompassing all that was "good and true in American life": "It would reflect the faith and challenge of the future, the entertainment, the interest in intelligently presented facts, the stimulation of the imagination, the standards of health and achievement, and above all, a sense of strength, contentment and well-being."[64] Despite such optimism, Disneyland quickly fell short of Walt's lofty expectations. Soon after the park's 1955 opening, visitors started to flock to Anaheim. A multitude of motels, parking lots, cheap souvenir stands, and all-you-can-eat buffets sprang up almost overnight, ready to accommodate the throngs of vacationers, but such congestion and "low-brow" commercialism did not coincide with Walt's vision of Paradise. Insisting he would not construct a second park merely for money, Walt scouted locations as early as 1959, declaring that "if I ever built another Disneyland, I would make sure I could control the class and the theme of the enterprises around it."[65] If he could secure management of the surrounding natural and built environment, Walt knew he would then be able to maintain his aesthetics and quality standards, keep neighbors at bay, and reap more profits rather than have these siphoned off by competitors riding his coattails.

Florida (Spanish for "feast of flowers," alluding to Ponce de León's "discovery" of it on Easter Sunday, 1513) was considered a Paradise from early in history. De León went there in search of the Fountain of Youth but instead found fantastic flora and fauna, since connecting Florida with Edenic traditions.[66] Beheld as virgin land, untouched and unspoiled, Florida was a place of breathtaking beauty and soon tempted visitors with promises of restored health, hedonistic pleasure, and business opportunities.[67] By the end of the nineteenth century, Florida was regarded as an exotic though welcoming place, and numerous guides were published to promote travel there.[68] Although Walt considered thirteen other sites for his new project (including St. Louis), Florida had appealed to him early on.[69] In 1959 Disney was in discussions with RCA, NBC, and multimillionaire John D. MacArthur to build "City of Tomorrow" on more than five thousand acres north of Palm Beach owned by MacArthur. The idea was to construct a "recreational paradise," and there was even talk of including a theme park.

Though the deal never materialized, an interest in urban planning and the benefits of Florida's hospitable climate stuck with Walt.[70] While scoping out potential sites in the state, he commissioned feasibility studies in which central Florida emerged as the best contender: it was within driving distance of the Northeast and the Midwest; it boasted cheap land and a network of developing highways; it did not have any nearby beaches that might compete for tourists' attention; and it had an aura of romanticized remoteness that suited Walt's purposes perfectly.[71] Furthermore, Florida held personal meaning for him. Walt's father, Elias, had gone there in the late nineteenth century to grow oranges and later run a Daytona Beach hotel (though he failed at both), and his parents married in Kissimmee, just miles from Disney World.

As noted in chapter 1, Disney was able to secure 27,443 acres (nearly forty-three contiguous square miles) of mostly swampland about fifteen miles south of Orlando. On 22 November 1963, Disney and his team flew over this swath of land, and Walt confirmed that this was indeed the place for his "Project Florida" (sadly, this was also the day President Kennedy was assassinated, which remained unknown to Disney and his cohort until after they had landed). Though some of the team was concerned about the location, Walt noted how Interstate 4 (then still under construction) and the Sunshine State Parkway intersected, assuring the others that people would come from all directions to this spot in the middle of the state. Disney's pilot, Kelvin Bailey, remembered Walt's excitement about the property: Disney could envision its transformation from a "nasty wasted country" of alligators and swamp, pointing out where each of the Magic Kingdom's themed lands would reside.[72] Beginning in 1964 and for a period of approximately eighteen months, the land was acquired in a complex and clandestine manner, with only nine people in the Disney organization—including Walt and Roy—being in the know. The acquisition required forty-seven different land transactions made through five dummy corporations (their names are inscribed on the windows above the Crystal Arts shop on Main Street), as Walt was rightfully convinced that sellers would drive up prices if they knew the land was for him.[73] Bob Thomas, Disney's official biographer, reports: "A conference room in Burbank contained a huge map . . . and each day the state of acquisitions was plotted, like territory won by troops in a war." In Anaheim, Walt only acquired about 180 acres; in Florida he would own enough land to accommodate a much grander vision, while keeping unwanted neighbors further away.[74] Emily Bavar, a journalist from the *Orlando Sentinel*, eventually discovered it was Disney who had bought the land, though by then most of it was already accumulated. With his secret out, Walt held a press conference on 15 November 1965, and declared that Disney World would be "the greatest thing to happen to the state of Florida since Ponce de León."[75]

Chad Denver Emerson aptly notes that Disney World was "built less on pixie dust than on a determined, clever effort to turn an isolated piece of Central Florida" into the "Vacation Kingdom of the World."[76] In this process, Walt also aimed to demonstrate that private industry could be socially responsible, hiring environmentalists to consult on Project Florida's development and ecological impact. A forty-four-mile-long system of canals, levees, and flood-control structures was required before park construction could even begin on the land nestled between the Reedy Creek and Bonnet Creek wetlands. Over time, Disney's land was equipped with water-treatment facilities, conservation zones, underground utility lines, extensive recirculation systems to replenish waterways, and manmade drainage channels and lagoons with natural-looking contours. Instead of lowering the water table, construction area elevations were raised. Throughout the property, transitional spaces and buffer zones (Jeremiah Sullivan dubs these "manicured emptiness") were established.[77] Gardeners propagated plants in Disney greenhouses, and whenever possible trees were moved instead of cut down. Contained in the acreage was the polluted 450-acre Bay Lake, which was entirely drained, cleaned, refilled, and restocked with fish.[78] Disney World's environmental mandate was "observed to an extent almost unheard of in its day" as Walt and his team labored to avoid all that had gone wrong in "Eisenhower-boom California."[79] Such green efforts did not go unnoticed, and in 1981 Disney World received the Urban Land Institute Award for Excellence in recognition of its thoughtful land use. But Walt's process of obtaining and cultivating this property also tipped his hand, as did his resolve not to repeat the same "mistakes" of Disneyland. A tabula rasa was needed because he planned to do more in Florida than build another theme park—Walt was conceiving a new arcadia. In his Seventh Preliminary Master Plot Plan (1965), he personally sketched what would hold as the basic pattern of development for Disney World, marking features like the "Main Entrance" and "Park-Hotels" and stipulating a separate "Industrial Entrance." He enthused: "Why, we could not only have our own Disneyland, but our own Sea World, our own Knott's Berry Farm, as well as a couple of cities. And we'll run it all the way it should be run."[80]

Disney World's deftly controlled landscape reminds us of the company's wealth and power: money is required to maintain such fastidious environs, as are the desire and ability to create and preserve order. In the history of landscaping, a carpet of green turf became the ideal—a symbol of good taste and elevated status that set an example for others. Even today, how one keeps a lawn supposedly suggests something about "being a good neighbor."[81] At Disney World, maintenance standards are fanatical: faded blooms are picked and trampled plants replaced at night; gallons of insecticide are sprayed to fend off bugs; sweepers constantly collect rubbish, though each Cast Member works "custodial," picking up errant debris; trashcans are set no more than twenty-six paces apart (according to research indicating that was how far Guests were willing to carry garbage), thus hardly any visitors litter while in the parks; and the Swedish AVAC (Automated Vacuum Assisted Collection, the first in the United States and the largest in the world) system whisks away up to eighty thousand pounds of trash a day at sixty miles an hour.[82] The Magic Kingdom was constructed on top of a utility basement containing acres of corridors ("utilidors"; see the conclusion) housing service and repair facilities, thereby reducing eyesores while maximizing the infrastructure's cleanliness and efficiency. Since the utilidors provide inconspicuous access to move people and goods throughout the park, they help maintain thematic continuity: here, costumed Cast Members can travel to their respective workplaces without passing through the other lands. Anything—from visible signs of hard labor to Cinderella smoking a cigarette on her break—that might break the magic above ground is relegated to the utilidors' "fluorescent maze."[83] Sociologist George Ritzer contends that all of Disney's tidying up has produced "a world of predictable, almost surreal, orderliness."[84] But despite complaints that Disney World is too sterile, many people, including prominent urban planners, remain impressed with its immaculate upkeep. Walt had been determined that his parks would not lapse into the filth and grime of other amusement places, insisting: "If you keep a place clean, people will respect it; if you let it get dirty, they'll make it worse. . . . Just make [the park] beautiful and you'll appeal to the best side of people. They all have it; all you have to do is bring it out."[85]

At Disney World, Walt could make life manageable, editing out its "flaws" and enhancing its "virtues." He had long been occupied with creating his own perfected microcosm, engaging in hobbies such as model railroading and handcrafting tiny objects. On his European travels he visited places such as Madurodam in Holland, where he saw miniature villages offering evocative prototypes for an enclosed realm. Disney wanted to build such a containable world, but he also needed it to be large enough to accommodate the fullness of his vision. Project Florida was Walt's dream of what the world should and could be. It also gave him a chance to rework a less-than-happy childhood, growing up with a father whose discipline allegedly "bordered on brutality," into a charmed one.[86] Walt's happiest days as a boy were the few years spent in Marceline, Missouri, before his family's relocations to Chicago and Kansas City. As discussed in chapter 2, Marceline inspired Disney's theme park Main Streets, though the Imagineers evaded the hardships of small-town life such as Walt's father auctioning off the family farm. Michael Wallace calls this process "Disney realism," in which any undesirable elements are edited out and only positive ones are programmed in.[87] Unsatisfied with his past, Walt simply invented a new, happier one for himself and for any of his Guests who might be in need of similar comfort. At Disney World there would be no demoralizing messages, bad customer service, or gloomy gloved mouse, anywhere. If Paradise could not be found, it would be fabricated.

At the heart of Walt's conception for Project Florida was a utopian desire to instill "proper" moral behavior in his captive audience. Disney World's well-defined boundaries ensure order, provide security, create continuity, and even promote conformity. Walt believed that once Guests and Cast Members were inside this secured territory, its meticulous surroundings and wholesome atmosphere would prompt them to hold themselves to higher standards of conduct. In this way Disney not only groomed the land but also tried to groom people. The "Courtesy" disclaimer that appears on Disney World park maps reveals the aspiration to set conduct: "We work hard to offer a comfortable, safe and enjoyable experience for all our Guests. Please assist us by showing common *Courtesy* to fellow Park Guests. Please be respectful of others. Do not use profanity or engage in unsafe, illegal or offensive behavior. Proper attire, including shoes and shirts, must be worn at all times." While "offensive behavior" is a vague term, most of us probably agree that in a crowded environment with many children present, it is best to use "common *Courtesy*" (Disney's emphasis) toward others and have them behave in kind. Many Cast Members seem deeply invested in this courtesy creed, "genuinely convinced that they are the fortunate few especially chosen to work in paradise on earth."[88] Disney employees are polite and exceedingly friendly, and as if by osmosis, park visitors are especially pleasant and kind to each other. As Imagineer John Hench noted, Disney elevates our sense of comfort so that we are more likely to engage with strangers without any sense of fear.[89] But just in case "common *Courtesy*" does not prevail, Guests are kept in check by Disney's formidable security force, some of them dressed as tourists. A screening process occurs when Guests come into the parks, as guards stand at the entrance gates profiling people to see who might disrupt Disney's atmosphere.[90] Costly admission prices provide a further level of screening, selectively pruning out those more "likely to cause problems."[91] Meanwhile, the Total Systems/Integrated Electronics Approach, pioneered by the Radio Corporation of America (RCA), secures operations at Disney World. Developed while RCA was also working on military projects such as early warning missiles, it monitors everything from rides to energy consumption at a centralized computer system, automatically shutting down any malfunctioning equipment.[92]

To maintain the desired ambience of Disney's parks, no smoking is allowed in any building, indoor dining area, or waiting area, and no alcoholic beverages are served in the Magic Kingdom, though Walt had been a heavy smoker and an avid drinker.[93] (Had Walt lived to see the other Disney World parks, he likely would have disallowed their sale of alcohol, too.) Initially, Disney visitors were held to specific standards: women could not wear anything that was "too revealing," clothing with controversial political messages or drug references was banned,[94] and behavior "suggestive of homosexuality was also taboo."[95] (Disney has since become much more welcoming of gay patrons, as we will see in the conclusion.) Cast Members not only had to adhere to strict dress and behavior codes, as described in chapter 1, but were also expected to manage their emotions and make work seem playful for the Guests' watchful eyes.[96] Of course, Walt's grooming of people does not always work as he intended, as compliance to behavioral expectations and any obligations to maintain harmony are ultimately tenuous, even at Disney World. In 1997, while waiting to get into the Haunted Mansion, I heard a boy who spied fellow Guests cutting the line ask his mother why they did not do the same. "Because," she replied, "all these other people have to wait, and if everyone started doing that we'd have fistfights." But sometimes self-control does not prevail. For example, had Walt lived to see the Splash Mountain attraction, he would have surely lamented Flashmountain.com (a website with no relation to the Disney Company). Here pictures and videos of "free flashers flashing public nudity" are posted, showing women baring their bodies while on the ride, often timed to the souvenir photos Disney takes.[97] The pedophilic predators and other criminals who allegedly roam the parks pose far more dangerous problems, particularly as some critics claim Disney is largely unresponsive to these threats in order to maintain its safe image.[98]

Fairy tales provide much of Disney's content, addressing challenges of the universal human condition in a manner that is comprehensible, even to kids. Since life is not always happy and people are not always good, neither are Disney's tales nor the characters that inhabit them. But any such negativity serves to thicken the plot, making the triumph of goodness sweeter when a character chooses the most honorable path.[99] Mark Pinsky suggests that Walt's personal values constituted the foundations of a "Disney Gospel": the good will be rewarded and the evil are punished, as long as one is faithful, works hard, and remains virtuous.[100] Walt carried over the morality themes of his films to his parks, where virtue and vice are easily identified and separated and innocence and kindness always win, leading to certain happiness. Disney's tactic in both the films and theme parks was to teach audiences while they were being blissfully entertained.[101] Though the relationship between education and entertainment remains suspect to Disney's detractors, the company continues to cast Walt (who never graduated from high school) as a supremely talented teacher, able to combine history, technology, and adventure in powerful educational experiences. Indeed, Walt viewed himself as an accomplished educator, and by 1948 he coined the term "edutainment" to describe films designed to simultaneously educate and entertain.[102] Ranging from live-action documentaries to animations about scientific or political concepts, the messages of these films were consistent with those in Disney's fantasy blockbusters, but they had the additional obligation to "actively convey factual information about the real world" in a "lively and engaging" manner.[103] Over the years the company expanded this educational agenda in various ways, including the development of a traveling exhibition, Disneylandia, which used miniature scenes to teach about American folklore and history; and producing viewers' guides on its television shows for teachers and parents, bringing Disney's lessons into classrooms and homes.[104] But Disney's most interactive educational efforts occur at the theme parks, where Guests literally inhabit Walt's morality plays.

Warding off criticism by focusing on widely shared values such as family and freedom, Walt targeted the audience most likely to accept his parks—the American middle class.[105] (As famed Mouseketeer Annette Funicello once gushed: "Mr. Disney knows what *he* wants and it turns out that that's what the people want, too.")[106] It is possible to read Disney World as its own moral universe, one in which the American system of democratic capitalism is blatantly endorsed and presented as "natural," "intrinsically progressive," and beneficial for all. The principles of determinism, pragmatism, and collectivism (balanced by personal fortitude, of course) are all celebrated, as are their manifestations in science and technology. But despite such a forward-looking agenda, Disney's paternalist approach also encourages us to look back at our "individual childhoods" and the "childhood of the nation," evoking "the pleasure of memory without the pain and disillusionment of actual return."[107] John Hench argued for the merits of such optimism, asking: "How do you abuse harmony? How do you give people too much a sense of well-being?"[108] But Warren Susman believes that Disney was responsive to the cultural zeitgeist of the Cold War, and that any such hopefulness was tempered by alienation and anxiety, subsequently glossed over in a "collective representation of a utopian and ideal American world."[109] Yet Walt believed in his ability to craft a perfectible place, claiming that his theme park would be "among the few things in this world that people of all ages, races, creeds, convictions, languages and physical capabilities can all enjoy at the same time together."[110] But although discordant sites, eras, and themes can be harmonized at Disney World, cultural tensions and social ills cannot be completely banished, and so the best Imagineers can do is try to trump them.[111] Walt remained firmly committed to this program, however, declaring: "There's enough ugliness and cynicism in the world without me adding to it."[112]

Before arriving in Florida, Walt had already pursued landscape tourism on an ambitious scale. His unrealized Mineral King project sought to develop twenty square miles in a valley of the Sequoia National Forest, abutted by the Sierra Nevada Mountains and conveniently located between Los Angeles and San Francisco. Mineral King was to be a year-round resort, including an Alpine Village, lodges, restaurants, and ski lifts, "all designed to blend unobtrusively with the valley's natural contours." The proposal called for cutting down about forty-five giant redwoods to accommodate a road, drawing opposition from environmentalists (especially the Sierra Club, which had honored Walt in 1955) who successfully blocked it.[113] But now the company markets nature more skillfully. Consider that Disney purchased Gorda Cay, a secluded Bahamian island with an unpatrolled airfield used for drug trafficking in the 1970s and 1980s, as a destination for its cruise ships. Deftly eradicating its problematic past, Disney renamed the island Castaway Cay and provided a more acceptable history for it, focusing on exiled European settlers in that region during the American Revolution.[114] The company proudly boasted: "More than two centuries later, Disney purchased the island—used as a location in the classic 1984 Disney film Splash—to create a private paradise for Disney Cruise Line Guests. It took builders 18 months to perfect the rustic, 'castaway' landscape and motif that lend the pristine scenery additional charm. Of the island's 1,000 acres, only 55 have been developed . . . leaving the remaining land unspoiled and untamed."[115] To the company, Gorda Cay was a fixer-upper, not "rustic" enough on its own until Disney's magic enhanced its "charm."

It is fair to say that efforts to actualize Eden throughout history have been spotty. This is particularly true of zoological models as opposed to botanical ones, likely because we have less information about the fauna that supposedly inhabited Eden than we do of its flora. For instance, London Zoo in Regent's Park (founded 1826) used the nineteenth-century innovations of steel and glass to put visitors face-to-face with "untamed beasts." Here the creatures' exoticism was tempered by fanciful domesticity: animal houses were designed to look like Victorian, Gothic, or Beaux-Arts buildings; and apes were dressed in clothes and made to have tea parties.[116] (One might think of Walt here, who cast animals as good citizens living in homes like our own.) Certainly the difficulties in marketing a zoo as Paradise are considerable, especially when compared to the relative ease of attaining botanical harmony, which sidesteps many of the practical problems of wildness. Walt quickly apprehended this fact, dispensing with initial plans to include live animals at Disneyland as he realized how challenging it would be to regulate them within his "wholesome" family environment. Not only do animals keep inconvenient hours for a theme park, but they also engage in all kinds of "rebellious" behaviors such as defecating or copulating as tourists trundle past them. Walt came to favor mechanical animals, which ensured a standard of quality for his attractions: each visitor would see exactly the same thing as the automata performed their routines over and over again.[117] Thus if Walt had lived to see Animal Kingdom opened, I am convinced he would have taken issue with it.

Animal Kingdom is Disney World's most recent (1998), costly (nearly a billion dollars), and largest (540 acres) theme park. Although Animal Kingdom welcomed 6 million visitors in its first year, the Disney Company had been unsure of such a park's appeal, taking five and a half years to decide whether or not to build it. Wary of creating a "smelly," "depressing" zoo, Disney opted to combine educational elements with themed entertainment. Here the company presents itself as visibly eco-conscious, touting the Disney Worldwide Conservation Fund, handing out "I'm a Conservation Hero" badges to Guests, and celebrating its own environmental efforts. Visitors are urged to volunteer, recycle, conserve—"We Can All Make a Difference!"—and learn more about wildlife. Ironically, not long after Animal Kingdom opened, a nature preserve on Disney's property, Discovery Island, was closed. Now abandoned by the company, the island still teems with wildlife as it reverts to nature.[118] (Meanwhile, the Animal Kingdom sector with an attraction based on the popular animated film, *A Bug's Life*, became the new "Discovery Island.")

Throughout the park we encounter "real, imaginary and extinct" animals, including live ones during a mock safari, costumed Disney characters, and animatronic dinosaurs. There was a plan to expand Animal Kingdom's offerings even further with Beastlie Kingdomme, a zone themed to feature mythical creatures such as unicorns and dragons, though this was subsequently abandoned and replaced by the character greeting station of Camp Minnie-Mickey.[119] Interactions with live animals are as controlled and predictable as possible: "captive-bred" creatures, "showcased in a spectacular setting" as part of a larger "conservation theme," are coaxed into photo opportunities through "stage directions."[120] The animals are confined behind well-disguised moats and fences so that they do not attack each other or visitors, and they evacuate their "savannah" each night for holding pens. Although Animal Kingdom does not possess the biggest collection of animals, Disney does create "intensive theming" absent from conventional zoos,[121] thus articulating "a holism in its nature park that other venues rarely matched."[122]

As a Disney resort Guest in early April 1998, I was able to preview Animal Kingdom before its official opening on 22 April. Clearly, there were all kinds of kinks still to be worked out, indicating that Animal Kingdom was not really ready for its debut and thus making the preview visit an unsettling experience. Walt would have been unhappy with its rough state. Only weeks before, there were hardly any trees on the park site, and forty thousand of them had to be dropped in by cranes at night to produce an instantly "exotic" landscape. Sprinklers with automatic timers set for 7:00 p.m. threatened to douse us and the other last visitors out of the park. A geyser meant to be a main feature on the riverboat tour (now defunct) malfunctioned pitifully. For me the most egregious ride was the Kilimanjaro Safaris, during which our driver, "Ruth," spouted a script about Disney's savannah as a representation of the "wild Africa we're all working to save." She pointed out a "thousand-year-old" tree, proclaiming the "local people" make a drink from its fruit. Who are these local people? I wondered. Floridians? At the trip's end "Ruth" implored us to "Come back to Africa real soon. The animals will be waiting for you." Of course, this is not Africa, and certainly the animals are not "waiting for" us. My preview of Animal Kingdom confirmed, at least for me, that the Disney formula does not translate to all contexts. Here the mingling of simulations with real animals creates an environment that cannot be managed to Disney's exacting standards. Biographer Gerald Kurland notes that in pursuit of "wholesome family entertainment," Walt often glossed over nature's more complicated aspects "to make its workings neater and cleaner" than they are in reality. After all, he was the kind of man who had a tiger propped up on his desk for a publicity photo, stroking it as if petting the family cat.[123] Walt may have admired the ambition of Animal Kingdom, but he would have lamented Disney's lack of full control over the park.

If the Disney parks are utopian, Louis Marin insists they are degenerately so, arguing that Disney does not permit genuinely free play or association but relies upon controlled spaces to deliver its predetermined meanings. A map, Marin offhandedly proposes, can substitute for a park visit![124] While overstated, such complaints have their merits, though these rarely take into account the social critique implicit in Walt's desire to build his parks.[125] While we may disagree with his methods and even their results, Walt's re-formist aspirations were guided by a sincere hope to make life more hospitable. Driven by "forces that were at once Victorian and progressive," Walt demanded cleanliness and precision as "an antidote to the degradation he saw in the urban environment."[126] In 1966 he announced on his *Wonderful World of Disney* show that he was designing Disney World as "a real city of the future, where everything would be perfect."[127] Here, he assured, every measure would be taken to combat pollutants, adopt efficient transportation systems, and preserve the land's ecological balance. As built, Disney World is a testament to careful planning, its disparate natural features and man-made facilities being integrated into a cohesive environment where the ideal meets the practical. No doubt the question of who can afford and is thus welcomed into this Paradise "can be highly contentious," but even Heaven is reputed to have a gate.[128]

Alex Michalos once observed, "there is no trick in designing one's own view of utopia. . . . The real trick is to bring the rest of the world along."[129] Unlike most of his predecessors, Walt was able to bring so many of us along on his pursuit of Paradise. At Disney World our fantasies are actualized and our potentialities can be realized: we are brave heroes and dashing adventurers—even if only for a little while. As journalist Eric Sevareid eulogized Walt: "He probably did more to heal or at least sooth troubled human spirits than all the psychiatrists in the world. There can't be many adults in the allegedly civilized parts of the globe who did not inhabit Disney's mind and imagination at least for a few hours and feel better for the visitation."[130]

four  Fantasy for Sale
Living Large at Disney World

Here we have the principle of commodity fetishism. . . . This principle is absolutely fulfilled in the spectacle, where the perceptible world is replaced by a set of images that are superior to that world yet at the same time impose themselves as *eminently* perceptible.

—Guy Debord, *The Society of the Spectacle*

Fantasy, if it's really convincing, can't become dated . . . it represents a flight into a dimension that lies beyond the reach of time . . . nothing corrodes or gets run down at the heel, or gets to look ridiculous. . . . And nobody gets any older.

—Walt Disney, *Walt Disney: Famous Quotes*

Guy Debord and Walt Disney both thought a lot about the function of simulations. Debord believed simulation was a by-product of the social and political turbulence of the 1960s, which created a breakdown in the primacy of lived experience. Though Walt was also disillusioned by the cultural chaos of the 1960s, he wanted to do more than lodge his complaints in a manifesto, as Debord had done in *The Society of the Spectacle*. Instead, Walt tried to overcome the unruliness of contemporary life in the physical form of Disney World, laboring on its plans until his death. While Debord feared the commodification of fantasy, Disney embraced such. As Debord urged his readers to shake off the dream world of spectacles, Walt convinced his followers that there is no better place to reside—if only for a little while—than in a themed fantasyland. When examining the production of fantasy for sale, especially in the United States, several places emerge as worthy of comparison to Disney World. But the founding and development of Las Vegas in particular offer striking similarities to Walt's Florida resort. Both were remote, inhospitable locations subsequently transformed into thriving tourism sites. Each utilizes themed attractions and spaces, with an intensity of showmanship elevated far beyond most other American amusement places. Furthermore, both Las Vegas and Disney World are firmly embedded in our collective consciousness as benchmarks for escapist fantasy. A comparison between them reveals much about evolving notions of "public" space, community, and spectacle in American culture.

Connections have been made between Las Vegas and the Disney parks since Disneyland was built. In 1958 novelist and screenwriter Julian Halevy, an American expatriate in Mexico, published a scathing review in *The Nation* dismissing both Vegas and Disneyland as feeble attempts to relieve the daily tedium and "social anxiety" of American life.[1] In response, science-fiction writer—and self-proclaimed "Disney nut"—Ray Bradbury retorted that critics like Halevy were just "Cool people with Cool faces pretending not to care, thus swindling themselves out of life or any chance for life."[2] Another writer for *The Nation*, John Bright, argued that Halevy's comparison was "ill-conceived": Vegas was "dirty" and "cynical," but Disneyland offered its "fantasy" with "aggression"-free sincerity.[3] Rather than discredit the analogy between Las Vegas and the Disney parks as Bright had done, I focus here on a fuller understanding of their relationship to each other. Of course, there are essential distinctions between Disney World and Las Vegas. The most apparent difference is that Vegas is targeted to adults, while Disney World is geared especially toward children. The gambling and prostitution of Vegas are absent (one would assume) from the Disney parks. Even when Vegas attempts to lure family vacationers with rides and amusements designed with kids in mind, it remains clear that adults constitute the city's primary audience. Disney tries to cross generations, too, with marketing pitches for the "grown-up" fun to be had at its parks (spas, celebrity chefs' restaurants, shopping, golfing, and babysitting services to keep the kids busy while their parents are out and about).[4] Ultimately, however, adults are still expected to surrender to Disney's magic with childlike wonder. But a less obvious distinction is found in the way each place reckons with its historical and cultural identity. As we saw in chapter 2, the history of Disney World's attractions and the people who created them is literally inscribed into the parks for attentive visitors to find, attesting to the company's commitment to remembering its own past. Meanwhile, Vegas suffers from an identity crisis. Can it be both a "family-friendly" destination (as it was restyled in the late 1980s) and a place where "What happens in Vegas stays in Vegas" (as promoted in its recent marketing campaigns)?[5]

As theming shifted from the private garden (see chapter 3) to the public street, Las Vegas and Disney World forecasted how pervasive themed environments would become. Today, we are hard pressed to escape them: restaurants, retail stores, even entire neighborhoods are themed. Some critics view theming as a troubling symptom of the corporatization of public space, and certainly there is some truth in this contention.[6] But it is important to ensure that such protestations against Disney World and Vegas do not overwhelm our recognition of their implications for and influences upon urban design and planning. Each is a consumption center that relies on technology and on cultural clichés with broad appeal. Their familiar modes of visual communication allow us to navigate spaces of potential cognitive overload, inducing insular frames of mind to banish everyday worries. And in so doing, they temporarily suspend our disbelief, along with the limits of time and economics. In short, both Vegas and Disney World are much like the pilgrimage centers and paradisal prototypes we have already encountered. Each provides comfort and enjoyment amid the company of others seeking escape from daily routine, while intensifying our experiences so that we somehow feel more alive.

Not coincidentally, each place also enjoys some level of political autonomy. Disney World became its own governing entity through the establishment of the Reedy Creek Improvement District (see chapter 5 and the conclusion), as the company openly pushed for improved highways, tax concessions, affordable financing, and community support with the promise that it would stimulate mass tourism and provide extensive employment.[7] The Vegas Strip, another tourist mecca, is conveniently located in an unincorporated part of Clark County. Thus governance of it sidesteps the jurisdiction of city officials more likely to worry about water supply and schools than the county's pro-growth commission.[8] When the service economy overtook manufacturing and agriculture in the United States, Vegas became both an economic and cultural model—a "vast laboratory" for "experimenting with every possible combination of entertainment, gaming, mass media, and leisure."[9] Hal Rothman has serious misgivings about such touristic spaces that use "artificial controls," which seem "natural and ordinary," to distract and pacify us. But he also acknowledges that Vegas functions as a contemporary rebuke to the elite tourism traditions of the late nineteenth century. At Vegas, the "stigmatized activity" of gambling is embraced and made available to a broad populous, transforming its casinos into "shared spaces" of classlessness in which everyone "was on the same side . . . someone else's victory only anticipated your own." Disney World operates in much the same way, drawing together its widely constituted audiences through immersive attractions and settings intended to create a "complete experience." The ability to situate visitors "at the center of the story," whether they be in Las Vegas or Disney World, remains a winning formula.[10]

Strip Tease

Less is a Bore.

—Robert Venturi

Like Disney World, Las Vegas was a product of optimistic vision and ambitious planning. When Spanish explorers discovered an oasis-like respite in the desert in 1829, they named it Las Vegas, or "the meadows," being seduced by the temperate climate and unusual beauty of the place, as would be successive generations of settlers. Similarly, Walt had chosen Florida for the site to construct his paradise because it offered natural splendor, good weather, a central location, and ample land. Even before Nevada had legalized gambling in 1931, Vegas was marketed for public consumption. The first real estate lots were auctioned in 1905 as part of Senator William Clark's idea for a "Townsite," which also included linking the Pacific Ocean with Great Salt Lake via a railroad.[11] Clark's scheme incited the first land boom in what would become the largest city founded in the twentieth century. By the 1990s both Las Vegas and Orlando experienced massive surges in their resident populations, while remaining leading vacation destinations in the United States. But as the first decade of the twenty-first century ended, American economic woes and recessionary austerity dampened profits at entertainment destinations throughout the country. Though Disney World and Vegas still attract many annual visitors, their promoters have to work harder than ever to distinguish them from the competition. For example, gambling has become increasingly widespread in the United States, at other resort cities such as Atlantic City, and on Native American reservations like Foxwoods in Stonington, Connecticut (built by the Mashantucket Pequots). The pressures of such rivalry are reflected in the changeability of Vegas's reputation over the years: first celebrated as a rowdy outpost for illicit adult pleasures; then as a family-friendly vacation spot; and now as a resort town for upscale and decidedly grown-up indulgences. Regardless of these shifting identities, however, casino owners and real estate developers have learned that Vegas must function as a conglomerate of "helpfully competitive" entities if the city wants to survive.[12] A single resort does not expect to keep visitors within its compound—no matter how expansive and magnificent—during their entire stay. On the contrary, business collaboration is made easy in Vegas by the uniformity of most gambling games so that everyone can share in the wealth. Disney World operates differently, trying to distract its Guests from other nearby attractions (especially Universal Studios' two theme parks, built to skim some of Disney's Orlando-bound tourists), and it does a better job of maintaining their captive attention. This distinction seems to be a matter of perspective, quite literally: at Vegas, multiple thrilling locales are always within view of each other, but Disney World's buffer zone effectively blocks out anything that is not Disney's.

Though Vegas has been long derided as lowbrow and uncouth, the publication of the wildly influential *Learning from Las Vegas* (1972) by practicing architects Robert Venturi, Denise Scott Brown, and Steven Izenour helped change things. The three colleagues took fifteen Yale University graduate students to Vegas in 1968, touting the city's populist approach as a welcome antidote to rampant modernist pretensions.[13] Izenour reflects: "To architects like us, who had been trained in the hermetic, hard-edged, black-and-white, concrete-and-steel vocabulary of Modernism, downtown Las Vegas was liberating. It became our classroom."[14] If pop art, rock music, and McDonald's hamburgers were at least partly indicative of American culture, they argued, than Vegas had something to teach "serious" architects. *Learning from Las Vegas* blatantly proclaimed what many architects did not want to hear: that they had selfishly indulged their egos, neglecting public needs and desires. To correct this situation, the trio adopted an experience first, analyze later attitude, privileging Vegas's architecture as one of inclusion and allusion. Although the lessons codified in *Learning from Las Vegas* were not universally embraced, the book was a wake-up call for the architectural establishment, and its publication coincided with the rise of postmodern architecture.[15] Such architecture, typified by Vegas's Strip, counters modernist asceticism with its more democratic methods, mixing multiple styles and using familiar forms to communicate with wide-ranging audiences. As noted in chapter 1, postmodern architects often adopt collage-like techniques to fragment structures and spaces, rummaging through historical styles for possible sources.[16] Disney's design approach is in sympathy with postmodernism, as the goal is to create well-loved, amenable places that draw upon collective memory and make us feel more connected to each other. Of particular interest is the practice of "plussing," through which Imagineers enhance Disney's simulations of remote and fantastic locales with precise architectural details.[17] Although the advent of such "entertainment architecture" (as it is dubbed in Disney Speak) has been received with critical hesitations, we must become aware of how these places can satisfy our needs for urban "communion."[18] Disney World and Las Vegas are ironic and lively sites that prompt all kinds of sensory and emotional responses.[19] Venturi once claimed that Disney World is "nearer to what people really want than anything architects have ever given them," and I am becoming convinced that he is right.[20] When I am at Disney World I feel happy, safe, and convivial, far more good-natured and optimistic than in daily life. I am not as annoyed by other people, in fact, I seem to appreciate them more. I am less rushed, though not any less organized. And I have noticed over my many visits that Disney's carefully crafted environment has the power to similarly alter many other people's moods and frames of mind.

Critics, however, remain troubled by the "hyperreality" of Disney World and Vegas, noting how their "enchanted" environs are used to coax us into buying goods and services. In our image-laden society we are conditioned to crave increasingly spectacular settings and higher levels of stimulation that, according to George Ritzer, create "a vacuous positivity" to keep us focused on our consumer obligations.[21] But Ritzer does not fully acknowledge our free will and complicity: people choose to play along with simulations—we are not dim-witted or forced into submission. Disney World and Vegas openly celebrate their contrived fantasies, and in doing so they allow visitors to gauge "authenticity" by individual experiences rather than objects for sale.[22] Furthermore, perceptions of "reality" change over time. The nineteenth century gave rise to a "cult of imitation" in which replicas were set off from the world at large, much like Disney World. Miles Orvell identifies a "tendency to enclose reality" in such "manageable forms," concluding that if "the world outside the frame was beyond control, the world inside of it could at least offer the illusion of mastery and comprehension."[23]

Likewise, Scott Bukatman traces a "hyperbole of the visible" back to eighteenth- and nineteenth-century painting, linking contemporary spectacles with older concepts of the sublime. He notes a recurring human desire to experience awe while simultaneously being reassured by the "sense of play" that comes with the apprehension of simulations. Even viewers looking at a panoramic painting centuries ago would have comprehended its imitative functions, enjoying the "scopic mastery" it offered them as a means to counteract the perceptual and visual confusions of an increasingly technological world.[24] Such sublime encounters disrupt the supposedly stabile coordinates of time and space, thus setting the stage for "fundamentally transformative" experiences. These encounters also further our recognition that nature can be neither fully controlled nor fully understood.[25] Although Disney cannot govern natural forces, its ability to create, monitor, and manage the experiences it produces is uncanny. I believe, however, that this overarching control does not endanger Disney World's sublime potential but enhances it, enfolding our awareness of the constructed quality of the Disney phenomenon into our experience of it.

The grand spectacles that reign supreme at Disney World and Las Vegas also have historical precedents in European gardens (for paradisal garden traditions see chapter 3). In the seventeenth century, large "pleasure gardens" combining recreational activities and relaxation within beautifully landscaped surroundings became popular. By the eighteenth century these hosted more varied entertainments, ranging from circus acts and music to gambling and prostitution.[26] The eighteenth century also brought a rise in spectacular private gardens, which had the affectations of natural growth but were actually carefully manicured and often equipped with elaborate simulations. As Simon Schama asserts of these gardens: "If art and artifice had to be used, then why not revel in it? . . . The name *fabrique* given to the synthetic landscapes of terror and sublimity created by these spectacle-machines perfectly captured their air of unapologetic artificiality."[27] In this manner, the *fabrique* anticipated the concept of the theme park.

In England the publication of Sir William Chambers's *Designs of Chinese Buildings* (1757) urged designers to manipulate natural landscape to be "laughing," "enchanted," or "horrible," a recommendation in keeping with the work of Irish political theorist and philosopher Edmund Burke, whose *Philosophical Inquiry into the Origin of Our Ideas of the Sublime and Beautiful* (also 1757; see chapter 3) suggested that the deepest wellsprings of the sublime are tapped when our sense of well-being seems threatened. One of the most elaborate gardens in the tradition of Chambers and Burke was Hawkstone in Shropshire, England, owned by Sir Richard Hill. Its ten-mile tour included a ravine nicknamed "The Dungeon" and scenes representing Switzerland and Tahiti. Hawkstone's exiting visitors were perched on "Raven's Shelf," from which cliffs dropped one hundred feet. In Germany, a garden named Worlitz, owned by Prince Leopold of Anhalt-Dessau, included a mechanical volcano erupting nightly with fire, smoke, and lava (water flowing over illuminated glass panels).[28] The Mirage (1989), a $615 million Vegas resort designed by Joel Bergman, offers its own fifty-four-foot-tall

Figure 6. The Mirage Hotel and Casino, Las Vegas, Nevada. Architect: Joel Bergman. Opened 1989. View of erupting volcano. Copyright: ARTonFILE.com.

volcano amid the lush palms and waterfalls of its South Seas themed property (fig. 6). This volcano used to erupt every fifteen minutes in the evening with steam geysers and flaming gas jets, but now it explodes on the hour (6 to 11 p.m.) and was recently revamped to become more thrilling: "The Mirage . . . joined forces with legendary Grateful Dead drummer Mickey Hart, Indian tabla sensation Zakir Hussain and Fountains of Bellagio design firm WET to create an all-new audio/visual spectacle."[29] Although Worlitz's volcano had an interior complete with labyrinths, catacombs, and mock horror scenes for guests to explore, they had to be invited by the prince to do so. In Vegas, visitors can watch The Mirage's volcano erupt as many times as they like free of charge.[30]

The Strip, a stretch of Las Vegas Boulevard that was once just a vehicular thoroughfare, has become a destination in its own right hosting many resorts and their dazzling spectacles.[31] Its first public art, and icons of 1950s design, were flamboyant neon signs competing for speeding motorists' attention. Bright, colorful, easily seen and understood, they were unapologetically commercial advertisements set next to low-key buildings. While the Strip hotels built in the 1940s and 1950s (such as the Flamingo and the

Sahara) emulated the elegant spa resorts in places like Palm Springs, they were not necessarily spectacular.[32] Today's mega hotel complexes dwarf the size and impact of the older signs, many of which now reside in Vegas's Neon Museum (founded 1996, the museum includes masterworks by Yesco, and a Neon Boneyard where dismantled signs are displayed).[33] Although not planned as a walking promenade, the Strip now has ample pedestrian traffic that is plunged into its sensory cacophony. As David Stratton describes it, "you have the distinctly urban feeling of being onstage or, perhaps, in the midst of a prison riot."[34] The "decorated sheds" and "ducks" described in *Learning from Las Vegas* have given way to what architectural critic Morris Newman dubbed—in an obvious nod to The Mirage—"Flaming Volcano" urbanism. The decorated shed was a workhorse building enhanced with decoration, but the duck's shape was symbolic of its function. By contrast, Newman explains: "In Flaming Volcano urbanism, environmental graphics replace both sign and applied ornament. As a presence on the street, the building virtually dematerializes behind the spectacle . . . the Flaming Volcano is roadside architecture intended to be viewed by pedestrians." Newman perceives this urban model as a revival of Baroque spectacle, employing devices that "tasteful" architects eschew and using these to powerful effect. Its evolution was incited by "friendly" competition between Vegas's casino owners, resort developers, and vacation hawkers, each contending for the same tourist dollars.[35]

Vegas's original budget-priced family resort was Circus Circus, constructed in 1968 for the bargain price of $15 million by Rissman and Rissman Associates (Lee Linton added its enormous porte cochere in 1972). Still in existence, though significantly renovated, Circus Circus now sports a five-acre indoor theme park, Adventuredome, evidence of an implicit imperative to make things ever more grand in Vegas. Although cheap buffets and tacky souvenir shops persist in the city, these are now literally overshadowed by urban renewal projects and hotel-casinos by "designer-label architects and special effects masters."[36] The 1980s and 1990s brought multiple regentrification projects, such as the Freemont Street Experience designed by the Jerde Partnership architects. The Experience suspended a ninety-foot-tall, fourteen-hundred-foot-long latticework canopy above the formerly dilapidated downtown that had been Vegas's original gambling district. By day its canopy provides shade, and at night booming sound accompanies millions of electronic pixels lighting up its "Celestial Vault."[37] At the same time, massive themed complexes that merged casino, hotel, and entertainment facilities sprouted up along the Strip,[38] allowing visitors to casually traverse time and space—ancient Egypt, medieval Europe, Renaissance Italy, present-day New York City—in a few blocks.

Luxor Hotel and Casino opened in October 1993, with Veldon Simpson, who also designed Vegas's Excalibur and MGM Grand, serving as its principal architect (fig. 7). Simpson conceives his buildings as three-dimensional signs, which function as pre-shows to the total experiences available inside.[39] His $375 million Luxor is beleaguered by historical inaccuracies, but one assumes that visitors to a steel-and-glass pyramid are not really troubled by inconsistencies such as the fact that by the New Kingdom, pharaohs were no longer buried in pyramids. Clearly, Luxor's Egyptology is channeled through Hollywood camp à la Liz Taylor in *Cleopatra*. But perhaps Luxor Hotel and Casino is really not that jarring compared to the Temple of Dendur squeezed into Manhattan's Metropolitan Museum of Art, or Luxor itself after Islamic militants bombed tourism and historical sites.[40] Initially, there was an attempt to provide historical context at Vegas's Luxor with an exhibition meant to re-create King Tutankhamen's tomb as closely as possible. A team of Egyptologists consulted on reproductions created with methods and materials dating back 3,300 years, gallery dimensions precisely matched the tomb measurements found by Howard

Figure 7. Luxor Hotel and Casino, Las Vegas, Nevada. Architect: Veldon Simpson. Opened 1993. Overview from Las Vegas Boulevard. Copyright: ARTonFILE.com.

Carter in 1922, and a portion of admission fees went toward archaeological research in Egypt.[41] But ultimately, spectacle won out. As Luxor interior designer Charles Silverman puts it, "This is not the Natural History Museum."[42]

The irony of the above statement could not have been predicted by Silverman; by June 2008 Luxor closed down the exhibition and donated the artifacts to the Las Vegas Natural History Museum, thereby freeing space up for other entertainments. But even before then the Tut Museum had been closed for a renovation in 1996, when it was only three years old. Was refurbishment already needed, or was it another case of Vegas's revisionist flu? In Vegas there is constant change—always in pursuit of the bigger and better, the new and improved. The city's history is that of continual expansion, revision, and even demolition rather than preservation and conservation. Ever since Vegas resorts first sprung up in the 1920s, they have been subject to enterprising developers trying to anticipate what customers will want next. Such a fickle approach to urban planning can be worrisome, but Hal Rothman and Mike Davis remind us that such malleability also allows for timely responses to sociocultural, intellectual, and economic trends: "No city in American history has ever changed its clothes as frequently or as rapidly as Las Vegas. No place has grown so fast in so many ways without allegiance to any of the forms of identity its past fostered. Nowhere had each incarnation of existence been more fleeting, more transitory, less based in anything but the human imagination."[43]

MGM Grand, built for $1 billion (40 percent of which was financed by billionaire Kirk Kerkorian), opened in December 1993, billing itself as the world's largest hotel, casino, and amusement complex (an honor now accorded to Vegas's The Venetian). MGM Grand was originally themed mostly around the classic film *The Wizard of Oz*, but this family-friendly approach has given way to a more sophisticated art deco sensibility evoking Old Hollywood glamour (though the Emerald City's bright-green hue still wraps the facade). MGM once had its own theme park, Grand Adventures, sited on thirty-three acres of prime Vegas real estate. It offered Hollywood backlot themes such as a Moroccan plaza and the Salem waterfront, but all were conjured with less-than-impressive results and the park was officially closed by 2002. Today MGM's sister resort, The Signature (a non-gambling, non-smoking luxury facility), stands in Grand Adventures' place.

Treasure Island has also been subjected to similar revamping and renovation. Built for $475 million, Treasure Island was the brainstorm of mogul Steve Wynn, who has since developed other prominent Vegas resorts, including his eponymous The Wynn. Rothman describes him as a "visionary entrepreneur," able to apprehend a decline in gambling stigma and appreciate the appeal of more "conventional postwar attractions" like theme parks.[44] Built by Jon Jerde Associates as a family-oriented sister complex to The Mirage, Treasure Island takes its pirate theme from Robert Louis Stevenson's novel of the same name, although reputedly Wynn was inspired by a visit to the set of Steven Spielberg's *Hook*. Its theme is carried onto the street in a $32 billion "Old World" sea village, initially named Buccaneer Bay. Here pedestrians used to watch a special effects show that culminated in the sinking of a full-size British frigate by pirates—six times a day.[45] Today, the Bay has been renamed Sirens' Cove; shows occur four times nightly, though now it is scantily clad women who do battle with the pirates, and parental guidance is suggested. TI (rebranded as such along with the Cove), has since adopted a western flavor, though the cowboy culture of its Gilley's club does not mesh well with the remaining vestiges of the pirate theme. Despite any such thematic hiccups, Wynn continues to build "fantasy resorts," insisting it is these and not "little dumps with casinos" that will keep Vegas profitable as "every few years it becomes more fabulous, more outrageous."[46] Emulating Walt's creative vision, Wynn observed: "How could anyone understand Disneyland if all they'd ever seen was the Santa Monica pier?"[47]

Since 2000 the emphasis in Las Vegas has moved from family-oriented theming to a heightened luxe sensibility. Although its more salacious entertainments persevere and have even found homes at some of the nicer[?] resorts, the current focus is on pampered indulgence, or more accurately, overindulgence. If the city has a new theme, it is conspicuous consumption of "the good life." This shift was presaged by the $1.4 billion, all-suite Bellagio, which stands on the former site of the Sands Hotel.[48] Named after a small Italian village on Lake Como, Bellagio covers 120 acres and features a huge man-made lake, sprawling gardens, a luxury spa, chic shops, and its own canals. Other decidedly upscale resorts have since joined Bellagio, including The Wynn and its all-suite Encore, Aria, and "The Hotel" at Mandalay Bay. Each one of these offers designer boutiques, exclusive spas, gourmet restaurants, trendy clubs, and hip poolside scenes. And in some cases, such as at Aria's sister resort, Vdara, the casino is foregone altogether in favor of lavish suites and world-class fine art. Instead of fantasy theming we now find modernist design and high-end finishes, but these newer resorts are as massive as the mega complexes of the 1990s, and sometimes even larger.

With the realization that one can go many places other than Vegas to gamble, city developers have provided alternative diversions while enhancing Vegas's cultural resources. Admittedly, not all art venues have fared well in the city (the Guggenheim Las Vegas closed after only fifteen months, and the Guggenheim Heritage Museum at The Venetian closed in 2008; both had opened in 2001).[49] But other venues, such as the Bellagio Gallery of Fine Art, continue to thrive. Perhaps this is due to Bellagio's reputation as one of the city's most refined resorts with $285 million of artwork throughout its facilities, including Dale Chihuly's *Fiori di Como* (1998), a stunning canopy of glass flowers suspended over the lobby. The Bellagio Gallery is a for-profit space charging world-class museum entry fees for smaller-sized traveling exhibitions, though these usually showcase blockbuster artists. The city now also has a first-rate permanent public art collection at its mixed-use CityCenter. During my last visit to Las Vegas I stayed at the casino-less Vdara, sampling its spa services and touring its art collection (and that of the nearby CityCenter). I still gambled elsewhere, but less than I might have otherwise. I had a good time everywhere I went, but what I appreciated most was my escape from Vegas's relentless escapism—and the knowledge that I could always rejoin the fray in a few air-conditioned minutes.

The Endless Vacation

An interest in speculative social engineering has always been part of the Disney mission.

—David Rakoff, *Half Empty*

Despite the kinds of urban revitalization described above, crime and grime still hinder many cities. The controlled order and pleasant functionality of planned communities aim to provide an alternative to the unwieldy metropolis, with idyllic images that promise a higher quality of life to those with money to buy their share of the American Dream. As we saw in chapter 3, planned communities have their roots in the notion of an ideal city. Spiro Kostof characterizes the ideal city as a reformist enterprise that exists to clarify the ideology of a ruler, its designer, or group of like-minded people who are potential residents. The respective ideology is enforced through various modes of monitoring to ensure that citizens adhere to the codified rules. Yet any city, including an ideal one, rarely retains the single-mindedness of its initial plan and founding philosophy. Over time cities acquire new uses as residents tinker with them and introduce elements unforeseen by their designers. Even the most closely planned community will not be used in strictly predetermined ways.[50]

Architect and planner Peter Calthorpe calls for an urbanism of diversity, pedestrian scale, decentralization, and public identity, suggesting that the "privatization" of postwar suburbs hampered development of "equitable, sustainable and inclusive" communities.[51] In the United States, a more optimistic kind of urbanism was attempted at "New Towns," throwbacks to Englishman Ebenezer Howard's Garden City as a panacea for city sprawl (see chapter 3). Reston, Virginia, was built outside of Washington, D.C., as part of the "Year 2000 Plan" (1961) proposing a managed growth pattern for the region. Developed by R. E. Simon, Reston was conceived primarily as a "leisure society" with "villages" organized around amenities such as a lake and a golf course. A fifth of the town's land was set aside for recreational use, while the rest was planned to house a projected population of 75,000 residents. Unfortunately, Simon did not secure adequate financing, and subsequent architectural clusters, built under the guidance of an oil company, lacked the quality planning of his originals. The Reston Town Center probably comes the closest to what Simon had intended, as many pedestrians gather there to use its varied facilities.[52] The design of Columbia, Maryland, built halfway between Washington and Baltimore, was overseen by James Rouse, who later developed historical properties into "festival marketplaces" such as South Street Seaport in New York, Baltimore's Inner Harbor, and Quincy Market in Boston. Not surprisingly, Rouse and Walt Disney greatly admired each other. In 1965 they spent three days together with their wives in tow, touring east coast developments like Reston and Columbia. (Two years earlier, Rouse had declared Disneyland the "greatest piece of urban design in the United States," citing its profitability, high standards, and significance for visitors.)[53] The planning for Columbia began in 1962, with the intention to house 110,000 people there over a fifteen-year period. Rouse had already developed many shopping centers and thought of Columbia as an "efficient consumption" community, though his publicly stated goal was to provide affordable housing for anyone who worked in the town. Early residents wanted a low-density community, however, which did not allow for a public transit system or the socially and economically mixed population to which Rouse had supposedly aspired.[54] Seaside, Florida, designed by husband and wife Andres M. Duany and Elizabeth Plater-Zyberk, is a more recent "New Town." Developer Robert Davis wanted to build a mixed-use community on his eighty acres, enlisting Duany and

Plater-Zyberk in 1983 to create a coherent master plan and zoning codes that could be followed over the years by various architects. The planners conceived the town as a collective social space, envisioning its streets as "public rooms" for pedestrian interaction.[55] Though Edward Ball complains the aesthetics here recall only "the white middle-class vernacular architecture of the old segregated South,"[56] architect Robert Stern believes Seaside demonstrates the beneficial potential of planned communities.[57]

From early on, Las Vegas has contended with difficult planning issues like any other Sun Belt city, such as how to deal with a dwindling water supply in the midst of a population boom. But these concerns often get lost in discussions of Vegas's fantasy elements, or went largely ignored for decades until the late 1980s, when "carefully studied urban values" were deployed in the city via civic spaces and facilities.[58] Around the same time, planned communities began to flourish not far from the city. One of the best known of these is Summerlin, an ecologically minded town west of Vegas that sits on 22,500 acres of land once owned by Howard Hughes. Developed by the Summa Corporation, Summerlin includes a network of homes, schools, golf courses, shops, places of worship, parks, and 150 miles of trails. Of course, its developers promote it as an extraordinary place: "Summerlin is truly a community master-planned to perfection. . . . Designed to live as good as it looks, Summerlin offers more choices for how and where you want to live. . . . Framed by soaring mountain peaks, woven together by double tree-lined streets, European roundabouts and picturesque streetscapes, Summerlin is unlike any other community in Las Vegas."[59] Such rhetoric suggests that life for someone in Summerlin is unquestionably better than elsewhere around Vegas, or as implied, pretty much anywhere. Furthermore, the existence of such communities in close proximity to major tourist destinations insinuates that vacationing can become a sustainable lifestyle: it is not enough to merely visit a place when one could live there.

As we would expect, Florida also hosts many planned communities designed to extend the vacation frame of mind to daily living, including Celebration, built by the Disney Development Company (DDC). The DDC, established by Michael Eisner and Frank Wells to maximize land assets, is responsible for everything Disney builds other than theme parks. Of the preliminary forty-two or so square miles of Disney's Florida property, thirty-five were intended to remain as an undeveloped buffer. But after a failed attempt by Saul Steinberg to take over the company, Disney began to fortify itself with more vigorous real estate development, though making sure not to encroach upon Disney World's theme parks and resorts. In 1984 Disney acquired the Arvida Corporation (a land development company from Boca Raton) and decided to develop portions of the buffer zone, including Celebration, which would be built just five miles from Disney World. Ten thousand acres were earmarked, and planning began on the $2.5 billion community, to be managed by The Celebration Company. The town would be regulated by codes descended from Walt's values, emphasizing cleanliness, comfort, reassurance, and safety. According to a Disney spokesperson, Celebration would be "a place like Walt Disney always wanted. Where people can go and live and be friendly to each other."[60] As built, it captures some of the spirit of Walt's original idea for a residential community, though not in its appearance (see chapter 5).

Celebration (its name supposedly suggested by Eisner's wife) is both a prototypical and an exceptional example of a planned community. Its highly organized spaces can be translated, seemingly, almost anywhere else. Yet the town was subject to the particular whims and woes of Disney's "magic." Planned for an expected population of 20,000 (who began moving in 4 July 1996), that figure was later adjusted to 12,000 (Celebration currently has approximately 9,000 residents). Its initial plan insulated the 4,900-acre site with a 4,700-acre greenbelt and projected the construction of 8,000 homes (single-family dwellings, townhouses, and rental apartments) over ten to fifteen years. A downtown area, shopping promenade, health center (in conjunction with Florida Hospital), school, lake, nature trails, and recreational parks were also planned, most within walking distance of homes. (Over time, different religious organizations have established places of worship here as well). Fire and police protection and emergency medical services are provided by Osceola County. As noted in chapter 1, Disney had been commissioning high-profile architects since the 1980s, a practice it continued when hiring Robert Stern and Jacquelin (Jaque) Robertson to design Celebration.[61]

Almost immediately a feeding frenzy arose among the town's first prospective residents. With only models, promotional materials, and unquestioned trust in Disney to guide them, people chose from six basic home styles that were designated as especially picturesque (Classical, Victorian, Colonial Revival, Coastal, Mediterranean, and French).[62] A fixed number of sanctioned trees and plantings, as carefully regulated as the housing, produce the effect that "every yard looks as if it were planted by the same compulsive gardener."[63] The entire community was planned to enhance feelings of neighborliness, as indicated in its *Architectural Walking Tour,* which describes Celebration as "a traditional American town built anew . . . a return to a more sociable and civic-minded way of life . . . designed on a computer screen, but with an eye toward the elegance of things past and forgotten about." Celebration even offered an official history course on the town for new residents. Administrator Charles Adams asserted, "We do have some history, really, going back to the original vision from Walt."[64] As an antidote to suburban sprawl and social alienation, Celebration was indeed conceived as a return to the kind of small-town life Walt had idealized on Main Street, U.S.A., as we saw in chapter 2. In Celebration, white picket fences encircle pastel houses, nearly all of which sport a front porch in the hopes of coaxing neighborhood hospitality. Garages are tucked into alleys behind the homes, much like the Magic Kingdom's service facilities are hidden out of sight in utility corridors (discussed in chapter 3 and the conclusion). Axial alignment dominates the plan, but things seem scaled down as they do in the theme parks, enhancing Celebration's "whimsical, toy-like quality."[65] Marissa Marton, an eight-year-old resident, aptly compared her town to the Magic Kingdom, noting, "It's kinda the same, except without the rides."[66]

Disney's attempts to enforce a unified notion of genteel civility and a sense of visual harmony certainly limit choice at Celebration, but such constraints did not hinder the community's public appeal.[67] Demand for the preliminary offering of homes exceeded supply by a ratio of three to one, thus on "Founders Day" (18 November 1995, Mickey Mouse's birthday) a lottery *awarded* opportunities to buy the first 350 houses and rent the first 120 apartments. By the late 1990s, Celebration's Welcome Center was receiving fifteen thousand curious Guests each month, and housing sales remained brisk (the average for 1998–99 was a house sold every other day despite premium prices for Osceola County).[68]

Even though Celebration's planners resist the label of "New Urbanism," the town does adhere to nearly all guidelines prescribed by the Congress for New Urbanism (which include higher-density residential areas with mixed housing, amenities within walking distance, and design elements to encourage social interaction).[69] Subsequently, Celebration won the Award of Excellence for its town center from the American Society of Landscape Architects (1998) and was named the "New Community of the Year" by the Urban Land Institute (2001). As Peter Rummell, former Disney design and development director, bragged: "We decided the only way to encourage better, higher-end development is to do it ourselves."[70]

Initially, Celebration's citizens were similar to theme park visitors, unburdened of many civic responsibilities because Disney made most of the decisions. Since Celebration was first designated as an unincorporated town under Osceola County's jurisdiction, the Disney Company had veto power over its Homeowners Association for forty years, or until three-quarters of master-plan residences were occupied. The association could not change any rule without prior notice to and written consent from Disney's Celebration Company.[71] Wayne S. Hyatt, a lawyer specializing in master-planned governments, served as the primary "framer" for Celebration's "constitution." Despite Disney's top-down system of checks and balances, he described the town as "progressive" and "participatory," focused on community building rather than "people and property management." But critics dismissed Celebration as a democracy based on consumerism, where residents willingly forfeited self-rule in the belief that Disney would take care of their needs while maintaining quality—and property values.[72] Such hollow politics and an absence of meaningful local government did mark the early phases of Celebration's civic life, recalling Walt's original plans for Epcot (that his company would own and rent homes so residents effectively relinquished landownership and voting rights; see chapter 5 and the conclusion). For Mark Dery, a visit to Celebration confirmed the rise of technocratic privatization in a company town "with dark designs." He concluded that its citizens must be yearning "for the lost (and for many of us, largely imagined) community of an earlier America: *Our Town* minus the angst, *Huckleberry Finn* with the slave traders and the lynch mobs left out."[73]

It can be tempting to dismiss Celebration as a squeaky-clean vision of an ideal time that never existed. But the town is a complex and even contradictory place, and clearly there is a significant market for its brand of "themed living." Architectural critic Ada Louise Huxtable decried Celebration's mix of styles and the "simplistic, xenophobic, and exclusionary instincts" from which she believes it originated. But she also admitted that "when you get past the saccharine hyperbole," Celebration "is an example of the wrong thing being done right. Enormously and alarmingly right." Praising Celebration's architects and amenities, Huxtable writes: "Intelligence and taste are in stunning supply; how they are being applied is instructive."[74] John Beardsley also admired Celebration as a "cut above your typical suburb," but he complained that it appeals to a group of "like-minded people within a narrow socio-economic band."[75] His concern is well founded, given that Celebration's original housing stock cost about 15 to 25 percent above that of comparable Orlando developments, and remained about a third higher in 2007.[76] Though great care was taken to build an architecturally diverse community, it is filled with a fairly homogeneous population (more than 93 percent of the current residents are white).

While covering Celebration for the *New York Times,* Michael Pollan perceived a dualism of contradictory forces: the desire to build a real "community" rather than a conventional "housing development," counterbalanced by Disney's tenacious control. He found the level of Celebration's "designed-ness" overwhelming: "Eventually the streetscape began to feel a little too perfect, a little too considered. After a while my eye longed for something not quite so orchestrated." Resident behavior was also tightly regulated, as evidenced in the "Declaration of Covenants, Codes and Restrictions" (Celebration's "constitution," which its initial residents were required to sign).[77] All of this can sound more than a little overbearing, but as Peter Rummell reminded the town's critics, "you are not required to live here. People who come here buy into it."[78]

Andrew Ross, professor of social and cultural analysis at New York University, lived in a downtown Celebration apartment for a year while working on a book about the place. He distinguished the "themed" community from a theme park, noting that many Celebration residents felt little connection to Disney World. Ross instead saw the town as a riskless "kind of pioneer settlement" that engenders a reassuring sense of personal safety.[79] Douglas Franz and Catherine Collins also moved to Celebration temporarily, living there with their family for two years to research a book on it. They found Celebration similar to Seaside (for which it was often mistaken by fans of the film *The Truman Show*) in its attractive order and high-concept social engineering. The couple's initial reservations about Celebration as a "monotonous" place were offset by its plentiful "community spirit." Block parties and town festivities fostered camaraderie, as did a shared belief in the town's five founding Cornerstones: education, technology, health/wellness, community, and place. But what impressed Franz and Collins most about Celebration was its evolution into a town in which the citizens were invested. Although Disney did not create a "perfect" place, it built a genuinely "good" one where communal life does flourish.[80]

Perhaps the most encouraging thing about Celebration is its residents' willingness to become involved citizens, as evidenced by the response to the K–12 Celebration School. For many families, Celebration's "strongest selling point" was the public education it could provide. Parents willingly paid more to live there, believing their children would receive exceptional schooling. But soon after the K–12 school opened in 1996, objections were waged against its progressivism. Although Celebration is in the Osceola County School District, its curriculum was developed at Stetson University and utilized multi-age classrooms as collaborative learning environments. Few exams were given, and "narrative assessments" were offered in lieu of grades. While this may sound like a desirable educational environment to some of us, many parents at the school were unhappy with the arrangement. Disney executives listened to their concerns but disengaged the company's responsibility—after all, it was a public school under the jurisdiction of Osceola County. A majority of teachers left in the first year, and frustrated residents began to speak out to an attentive press. Behind the scenes Disney galvanized support from the "positive parents"; detractors were called "negative parents," though they referred to themselves as "refuseniks." Tensions between the two factions were high: "negative parents" were ostracized, the principal quit, and some parents even pulled their kids out of the school. According to the Celebration contract at the time, citizens who had been there for less than a year could not sell their homes for a profit unless they could prove hardship. Disney utilized this situation to its advantage, offering disgruntled residents an exemption from the regulation in exchange for signing confidentiality agreements.[81] But things did change over time, in large measure through the efforts of engaged citizens. Today there exists the Celebration School (for kindergarten through eighth grade), a separate Celebration High School (for ninth through twelfth grades, opened in August 2003), and private education options via the Montessori School of Celebration.

George Ritzer once proclaimed that Celebration was "a wholly simulated community."[82] Obviously, that is not true: it is an actual town—albeit tightly conceived and carefully managed—where people live year-round. Many residents really do enjoy living there. But it would be naive to assume that everyone finds Celebration's lifestyle appealing, as it would be to assume that Disney is poised to dictate residential development on a massive scale. Sean Helton, an employee of The Celebration Company, observed that while critics crowed about the town's Disney connections, beyond the development of the land and downtown area, Disney's involvement was "nearly non-existent."[83] In fact, the company had an exit strategy in place, with an option to sell the community to another land developer if it became a public-relations liability. Disney had already begun to distance itself from Celebration as early as 1999, after complaints about the school, shoddy building practices, and construction delays. It removed the trademark mouse ears from Celebration's water tower and stopped promoting tourism there. By early 2000 several downtown stores and restaurants closed due to the reduced patronage (though in 2005 Water Tower Place opened, offering a mix of retail shops and services).[84] In 2002 Disney sold Celebration's remaining residential acreage to Arvida, a company it has owned since the mid-1980s. The next year a private corporation bought the town's golf course. By 2004 the downtown center was sold to a New York investment firm, though the buyers had to assure Disney that they would maintain the town's "core ambience."[85] Today Celebration is its own municipality, no longer on Disney property as per the company's plans to divest most of its control over the town after the greater part of residential lots had sold.[86] But I would argue the most significant change occurred in September 2003, when residents gained the three-to-two majority on the Homeowners' Association board. Though Celebration bears the distinctive imprint of its "benefactor and strict parent," it is no longer, really, a Disney town.[87]

In 1972, not long after Disney World's opening, architectural critic Paul Goldberger noted that the resort was distanced enough from reality to make its smooth functioning a finite, attainable goal.[88] At Disney World, millions of vacationers spend their time and money in pursuit, if only temporarily, of the "good life" according to Disney. Celebration offers a daily supply of the "good life" for its townspeople, but increasingly this is found without adhering faithfully to Disney's script. Catherine Ryan Howard contends that to this day Celebration remains "beautiful and quiet," boasting "a great sense of community amongst the majority of its residents."[89] Helton, too, has faith in Celebration's citizens, both in their desire for kinship and their understanding that the town "is not utopia." He queries: "Will new urbanism work? I have no idea. Will Celebration work? Yes."[90] Shortly after Celebration opened, my husband and I visited the town to check it out for ourselves. We stopped by the Welcome Center, and since it was assumed that we were potential buyers, we were encouraged to tour several model homes. Surely any model home is a clean slate, but I was struck by how orderly Celebration's models were, somehow more pristine than it seemed fair to expect. They were noticeably close to the neighbors and the rooms seemed kind of small, but these things did not really bother me. Yet, despite how pleasant Celebration was and its proximity to my beloved Disney World, I would not want to live there. This is due partly to my dislike of hot climates and the pests they attract, but mostly because Celebration still felt too generic for me. Although there were multiple housing styles from which to choose, their execution and finishes were too similar, as I might complain of any subdivision. If I am honest, though, what I remember best of my time at Celebration was a (surprisingly?) good meal we ate at a Cuban restaurant in its downtown. The restaurant is no longer there, but the community continues to thrive.

Fantastic History/Historical Fantasy

Better a misinformed enjoyment of history than none, a lighthearted dalliance with the past than a wholesale rejection of it. Our heritage is amusing as well as serious, incongruous as well as harmonious.

—David Lowenthal, *The Past Is a Foreign Country*

Themed environments re-stage history to entertain and enlighten us. While monuments and events of the past may be referenced with little regard for their original contexts, the results of such rummaging through history can be provocative and informative. Sometimes this sampling of history is delightfully ironic: the use of Neuschwanstein, a Gothic Revival building, as a model for Cinderella's Castle. Other times it is too derivative: both Las Vegas and Epcot sport their own scaled-down Eiffel Towers. Of course, it can even be disastrous: Disney's failed attempt to build a Civil War theme park down the street from the actual Manassas battle site. Undeniably, the use of historical replicas has flourished because they are so successful at stimulating our consumer impulses. In contemporary society it seems that everything has become a commodity, even time. Time is something we are obligated to *spend*.[91] Historical time, or rather a convincing attempt at recapturing it, is a particularly precious commodity, somehow putting the past within our reach while simultaneously keeping it at a safe distance from our present. We have learned to shop for nearly everything, including reassuring images and re-created experiences of the past. Yet it is important to recognize that replicas and re-stagings are not meant to genuinely trick us: we apprehend their illusions and enjoy our ability to do so. The sites of historical re-creation are pleasurable for many of us because they are, so obviously, fantasies constructed for our consumption.

In the United States the Cold War ushered in an era of prosperity, increasing leisure time and disposable income for many Americans. People often flocked to the suburbs with their newly acquired wealth, patronizing the shopping centers that began to proliferate there. It seems more than coincidental that Disneyland and the first enclosed malls were built in the mid-1950s. Mall scale and design then often recalled a Main Street like

Disney's, where people are friendly, businesses prosper, and the environs are pristine.[92] In 1956 the first fully enclosed, air-conditioned mall, Southdale Shopping Center, designed by Victor Gruen, opened outside of Minneapolis in Edina, Minnesota. Southdale featured a children's zoo and the "Garden Court of Perpetual Spring," providing seasonless respite from the harsh midwestern winters.[93] (In chapter 5 we will see how Gruen became profoundly influential for Walt's Florida plans.) By the early 1980s there were already over 28,500 malls in North America.[94] Since then the shopping mall and theme park have increasingly dovetailed. The best-known example of such is the massive Mall of America in Bloomington, Minnesota (1992). Designed by the Jerde Partnership Architects, it covers 4.2 million square feet and has a seven-acre indoor amusement park at its center.[95] Such epic malls heralded the rise of "shoppertainment," "eatertainment," and "edutainment," in which shopping, dining, entertainment, commerce, technology, and education dynamically overlap. In order to compete with Internet retail, mail order, cable shopping networks, and discount stores, malls have transformed shopping into "a non-utilitarian, visual experience, a quasi-cinematic spectacle, and adventure" in which the shopper becomes a contemporary flaneur akin to a nineteenth-century pedestrian leisurely roaming city streets.[96] Having grown up in a town reputed to have more of its square footage devoted to retail space than anywhere else in the United States, I am intimately acquainted with malls. Their spaces make sense to me. I have been a flaneur as often as I have shopped with determined purpose. In general, I like these places. But, of course, the mall does have its critics. Some lament that it has supplanted Main Street, while others complain that its "cocoon" protects us from "assorted discomforts and also diversity."[97] Margaret Crawford disparagingly likens the mall to a theme park, noting how each creates a realm separated from the outside world with a coherence of vision not found in daily life. Like television, such sites radically compress themes remote in space and time, making for abrupt shifts between fantasy and fact that imply their "controlled fiction" is more interesting than "messy reality."[98]

Both Mark Taylor and Peter Gibian attribute the contemporary mall's form to a combination of nineteenth-century shopping arcades (particularly those of Paris) and department stores. These self-contained environments effectively split the spaces of production and consumption, though notions of what constituted outside and inside—and by extension, public and private—became more complex. Today's malls are monumental, introverted places, providing varied activities and diversions within their larger unifying frameworks. Much like Disney World and Las Vegas, they also function to distract us from social tensions and everyday problems with their dazzling goods and displays.[99] Such environments challenge our spatial sensibilities: it is easy to enter a casino or mall, but their massive and winding interiors can become disconcerting, ensnaring us in their consumer spectacles of accumulation and profusion. Disney World is similarly a vast stage set enlivened by our movement through its spaces, though these are often more easily navigated.[100] Many casinos have no windows or clocks to gauge the passing hours: here time is lost, or at least confused, lowering our resistance to the consumption opportunities offered within. Walt also wished to erase temporal markers at his parks, claiming, "clocks and watches will lose all meaning, for there is no present. There is only yesterday, tomorrow and the timeless land of fantasy."[101] At the beginning of the twentieth century, entrepreneur Fred Harvey's string of themed hotels in the American Southwest offered "pseudo-southwestern" architecture, food, and souvenirs "to create an all-encompassing atmosphere of authenticity" that guaranteed safety, quality, and "civilized" amenities. Karal Ann Marling suggests that the Harvey Houses were sources for Disney's parks. The eclectic and fantasy architecture of Los Angeles offered him inspiration, too: Olvera Street, a mission-styled pedestrian mall (1929); the Farmer's Market (1934), with themed elements like a midwestern farmscape and a windmill, was a favorite of Walt's; and Crossroads of the World, a shopping center on Sunset Boulevard (1936), which included mock Shakespearean cottages and a simulated lighthouse. It is easy to imagine why such places were attractive to Walt—they made history and time into malleable entities.[102]

Both Disney World and Las Vegas seem to transcend space and time, most especially at their retail outposts. Caesars Forum Shops (1992) set the trend for themed shopping in Vegas, with stores and eateries set in the guise of a Roman town among ancient ruins. The Forum Shops are immense (250,000 square feet) and feature an illusionistic ceiling painted to look like the sky, which changes from dawn to dusk and back again every half hour. This effect does not really make us feel as if we are outside; rather, it impresses us with technological wizardry and the knowledge that we are protected from the desert climate.[103] Terry Dougall, a designer who worked on the Forum Shops, exclaims: "This isn't great architecture, its great theater."[104] The Forum Shops have remained a successful retail site, outperforming many other U.S. shopping centers. Despite the residual effects of an American economic downturn, as of 2011 the Forum Shops were adding stores and continuing to do brisk business. Discrepancies between ancient Roman "architecture" and contemporary goods are not offensive to most shoppers' senses: these serve as pleasant juxtapositions of fantasy and function, which visitors recognize and appreciate.[105] The Forum Shops' popularity inspired similar shopping venues in Vegas, such as The Grand Canal Shoppes at The Venetian, also sporting a faux sky, though here the setting "sun" is accompanied by the theme from *The Godfather.*

As described in chapter 2, Main Street, U.S.A., is the first "visual node" Guests encounter when entering the Magic Kingdom and also the park's major retail center. Here, names on shop windows pay tribute to the Imagineers and Walt's family, and antiques are integrated with contemporary props and products. "Period décor," Marling observes, has "legitimated consumption by equating . . . business . . . with the historical fiber of the nation."[106] Thus Main Street encourages the consumption of goods and spectacles (it is the optimum viewing post for both parades and fireworks) as well as idealized visions of an American past. Although it has the trappings of public space, evoking municipal functions as a civic center, it is a private place requiring an admission fee. And as the only entrance and exit to the Magic Kingdom, Main Street inscribes shopping as the first and last activity in the park. In fact, its structure is like other malls, in which seemingly separate buildings are interconnected for easy access as smaller shops feed into large department stores.[107] Critics contend that Guests are constrained by, yet remain unaware of, Main Street's restrictive layout, attributing its success to a conflation of adult reality (purchasing things) with playful fantasy (the Victorian setting) that enhances our desire to buy.[108] Certainly, visual forms of manipulation occur on Main Street: downscaled buildings (appearing to be three stories but are only two) conjure romanticized intimacy through forced perspective, subtly recalling the mastery we may have felt as children playing with toys.[109] And the arrangement of space is also meant to incite consumption: for example, stores with the more expensive merchandise are on the right as you enter (studies show that groups of Americans are inclined to walk in this direction).[110] I do not believe that our desire to buy here is less genuine than at other places, or that Guests cannot control impulse purchases. Perhaps the greater issue is the subtext that Disney's paternalistic judgment always triumphs. Main Street is a lovely place to shop—carefully designed, vibrantly active, and blissfully free of cars. It reimagines America not as it was but with Disney's optimistic improvements, implying "that a big corporation could make a better Main Street than a bunch of rubes in a real small town."[111]

As Marita Sturken points out, we can never recapture our original experiences of a time or place: these remain known to us only through images, texts, objects, and stories. She does not view commodities as "empty artifacts" but rather argues that these tell us much about our culture's aspirations and worries. Ultimately, she asserts, "memory is a narrative rather than a replica of an experience that can be retrieved and relived."[112] It is essential to acknowledge that neither Disney World's nor Las Vegas's designers aim for "realism at the molecular level" in their historical recreations.[113] Rather, they seek to stage novel experiences for audiences witting of their contrivances. Geremie Barmé describes this approach to the replica as "archaeo-tainment," which does not carry the burden of preservation and accuracy or beg the same reverent awe, and thus can play with history quite loosely.[114] For example, Caesars Palace (designed by Melvin Grossman in 1966) takes up an ancient Roman theme, yet its street-front entrance recalls Gian Lorenzo Bernini's Baroque colonnade for St. Peter's.[115] But such historically lax juxtapositions are nothing new, as many so-called original sources had bastardized pasts as well. Neuschwanstein, an overwrought architectural confection built for King Ludwig of Bavaria, served as a model for both the medieval-themed Excalibur in Las Vegas and Disney World's Cinderella Castle. Neither of these structures literally mimics Neuschwanstein, nor was intended to: rather, it is a point of departure for their own immersive fantasies. Furthermore, Neuschwanstein was a revivalist building, only "Gothic as Gothic was understood in the later nineteenth century," as Eco noted. Its own creative borrowing from the past preceded the appropriations at Vegas and Disney World, making Neuschwanstein the "original fake" here.[116] Another historical source that playfully combines different eras and cultures is Hadrian's Villa in Tivoli, where ancient Roman classicism meets a curious eclecticism evoking Greece and Egypt. Its diverse and fanciful array of structures (fig. 8) invites comparison to Disney World, despite protestations that any such association confuses "illusion with allusion" by regarding "the Villa as a bizarre place built solely for Hadrian's gratification and thus lacking serious intellectual or cultural content."[117] Both sites were constructed to exacting standards on massive "featureless" plots, blank slates for the grand and odd amalgams envisioned by Hadrian and Walt. Hadrian's potent recollections of travel and conquest inspired the mix of architectural styles found at his Villa (Maureen Carroll described the place as "a microcosm of universal rule"),[118] much as Walt's selectively filtered memories provide much of the content for Disney World's themed lands.[119]

Figure 8. Hadrian's Villa, Maritime Theater, South of Tivoli, Italy. AD 125–134. From the Moreen O'Brien Maser Memorial Collection (Skidmore College), Maser i.d. No. 1960.666.

Some critics argue that the United States lacks the deep historical trajectory of other countries and that this compels us to manufacture a history in which replicas reconstitute the past as a commodity of the present.[120] At their worst, it is feared that such simulations will kill off our "built record," blending the "new and old, real and fake, original and copy" in ways that defy analysis. The redevelopment of Colonial Williamsburg (funded by John D. Rockefeller Jr. in 1934) is a well-known example of a place where history has been themed, edited, and marketed. Ada Louise Huxtable finds little more at Williamsburg than a "studious fudging of facts," yet she is more troubled by subsequent "regentrification" projects that deftly recontextualize a place's original commodity functions, such as James Rouse's South Street Seaport.[121] Barbara Kirshenblatt-Gimblett has related concerns about historical tourism, wondering if simulations are so popular because sites seem mute or ineffectual on their own. She contends there is a conflation of "historical actuality" with "heritage production," though she wisely maintains that "by production I do not mean that the result is not 'authentic' or that it is wholly invented. Rather . . . heritage is not lost and found, stolen and reclaimed." Thus "heritage production" is "always a *double* experience . . . of then and now."[122] Admittedly, things get particularly tricky at Disney World, where historical accounts are overtly skewed and sentimentalized.[123] Yet Disney's view of history maintains some meaningful educational value. Although Michael Wallace warned that the "past is too important to be left to the private sector," he also argued that "one might fairly say that Walt Disney has taught people more history, in a more memorable way, than they ever learned in school, to say nothing of history museums."[124] Furthermore, the symbols and simulations of our past can provide a "sense of stability and coherence" in times of "dislocation and uncertainty."[125]

The popularity of replicas relies upon an ability to make the past feel more "palpable and potent." For centuries, copies were valued as important study aids and examples of "good taste." But increasingly, critics worry that replicas will overshadow or generalize the history of the sites they are supposed to represent and illuminate. David Lowenthal wonders if visitors remain unaware of "the alterations of the past that interpretation" via simulation implies, yet he acknowledges that a replica can reawaken interest in a previously ignored site and "afford an historical experience as 'true' as the original, but it is a *different* experience." He concludes that our need to "tamper with history"—to amend and even transform it—springs from a desire "to become part of it as well as to make it our own."[126] Likewise, Sturken identifies a phenomenon she calls "tourists of history," in which "the American public is encouraged to experience itself as the subject of history through consumerism, media images, souvenirs, popular culture, and museum and architectural reenactments." For such tourists "history is an experience once or twice removed"; however, she reminds us it is "an experience nonetheless," reaffirming the validity of these kinds of touristic encounters.[127] And of course, if it were not for commercial interests, many historical sites would be crumbling ruins.[128]

Certainly, not all simulations and replicas are well conceived or received, as Disney's thwarted attempt to build a Civil War theme park reveals. In the autumn of 1993 Disney announced plans to construct a park approximately six miles from the Manassas battle site (then receiving as many visitors in a year as Disney expected in four days), which drew great public outcry. After scouting more than two dozen regional sites, Disney chose the town of Haymarket, Virginia, about thirty-five miles outside Washington, D.C. Though Disney's America (the name slated for the park) had Governor George Allen's support, it met harsh opposition from both Virginia and District of Columbia political officials. Furthermore, history professionals and groups such as Protect Historic America waged a national campaign against the proposed park, arguing it would commercialize and vulgarize

U.S. history. Disney was apparently taken aback by these reactions, given the park's anticipated benefits to the local economy (even despite the taxpayer-funded highway, water, and sewage improvements it would require). The company employed well-respected historians to consult on the project, which included a replicated Native American village, a country fair, and mock Civil War battles. (Other proposed features were attractions based on the Industrial Revolution and Ellis Island, a Lewis and Clark raft ride, and a controversial exhibition to "make you feel what it was like to be a slave.")[129] Ironically, just outside Disney's tentative site were real Native American trails, county fairgrounds, and even towns that had been sacked and burned by Union troops. As Benjamin Barber observed, in spite of Disney's "exacting standards," it seemed a moot point to insist on "scholastic certification for a virtual reality being raised up right next to the Civil War actuality it was reproducing."[130] Though Eisner, Disney CEO at the time, maintained the company would not give up on the site it did precisely that by September 1994, likely influenced by a softening real estate market.[131] Michael Wines, who tracked the evolution and subsequent demise of Disney's America for the *New York Times*, admitted the park may not have inspired visitors to go see the actual battlefield nearby, yet he recognized that preservationists had "drawn a line in the sand that they themselves occasionally ignore."[132]

I am glad that Disney's America was not built, for it was an ill-conceived concept. But I am happy for the complications, rather than simplifications, Disney brings to history. For example, Splash Mountain, a popular flume ride based on Disney's *Song of the South*, downplays the racist, sexist, and classist overtones of the original film to present a "sanitized commercial venture ready for popular consumption."[133] Perhaps the company thinks many visitors have not seen the movie, but knowing the backstory can change one's experience with the ride, as it has mine: despite enjoying the cool water and Audio-Animatronics, I often recall the more-than-problematic social views espoused in *Song of the South* and remain conscious of how these have been banished on the ride. Clearly, there is danger in perpetuating a sterilized, retrograde view of history that does not account for its setbacks. But Walt's desire to construct a perfect world free of conflict was never fully realized, and history's struggles still lurk throughout Disney World if we are willing to look carefully. Walt was not the only person who took liberties in the retelling of history, and as the receivers of Disney's tales we must exercise discretion rather than give blind allegiance. As defined by Sturken, cultural memory "integrates fantasy, invention, and reenactment" as "a process engaging with the past rather than a means to call it up." She insists that the value of such memory lies in its ability to reveal not only "how the past affects the present" but also our differences as divergent and even contradictory stories jockey for their places in history.[134]

As touristic spaces or "staged authenticities" set up to reassure and divert us (see chapters 2 and 3), both Disney World and Las Vegas actually offer the potential for more control than we have in our daily lives.[135] Though cynics argue that such environments kill enchantment because they lack spontaneity, since their simulations are known to and often anticipated by us, we can test ourselves and boost our confidence with minimal risk.[136] Julie Brinkerhof, landscape architect for Treasure Island, suggests that people "want to experience exciting things without the fear of being hurt. They like to get lost safely."[137] Hal Rothman makes a related point: the goal of tourism has shifted from visitor experience to visitor fulfillment. Stumbling upon "the little out-of-the-way inn in rural Ireland no more invents a unique experience than does taking a bus tour of Las Vegas . . . it offers a wrapper that promises a self-affirming authentic experience in the viewer's terms."[138] Today, authenticity might be assessed more accurately by the level to which ones' expectations are fulfilled than by the material quality of the given site.

Fredric Jameson proposed that the postmodern world was defined spatially, not temporally. He described the rise of hyperspace, which confounds the human body's ability to cognitively chart its position in a mappable world.[139] The concept of hyperspace becomes easier to grasp as applied to contemporary technologies (such as the instant replay), which compress time and place.[140] Disney design is rooted in the sensibilities of this hyperspace, its buildings and attractions conceived to create "a sense of time, place and mood" that can, "in a single instant, transport you to a distant land."[141] Imagineer Bob Sewall explicates: "It's a *concentrated* form of nature . . . we string together all the experiences you might see in a lifetime into one thing."[142] Yet Michael Sorkin is unconvinced of Disney's magic, complaining the Imagineers' propensity for "propelling visitors to an unvisitable past or future, or to some (inconvenient) geography," makes a theme park seem "like the world, only better."[143] But Sorkin ignores the fact that Disney's simulations are not just illusions—they are physical environments that we can enter, touch, and move around in, designed to be as fully interactive as possible. The tradition of "experiential entertainment" that can be traced back to ancient cultures (as seen at Hadrian's Villa) is enhanced today with computer-generated media that produce "mixed and augmented reality." The result is not a substitute for "reality" but "a live event" in which visceral sensory experiences and enveloping frameworks—environments, not objects—fully engage the participants. (Imagineer John Hench was mindful to point out that Guests' experiences occur "in *real* [my emphasis] space and time.")[144] Rather than "presentational" forms of entertainment, which perceptibly demarcate the audience's space from the presented one, Disney's audience members are increasingly immersed in "a shared, imagined reality" made palpable through the unified theming of story line, character, and setting. But these elements alone cannot bring the constructed reality to life: without the Guest's imagination, the experience would be dormant. Beyond engagement with the site, Disney's adventures are also designed to enhance "social interactivity" among the participants.[145] This is the lure of spectacle: not only is it larger than life and induces heightened states of awareness, but it can meld an "instant community" among strangers, attesting to the "power of shared experience."[146] At Disney World, the spectacle's appeal is enhanced because it seems that Guests are guaranteed the adventures for which they have come.[147]

Anna Klingmann commends the design and well-defined theming of Disney's parks, admiring the focus on visitor expectations. But ultimately she finds Disney's experiences to be too tightly scripted and overdetermined, leaving little room for personal agency.[148] It is true that Disney World's Guests are initiated into its culture beforehand, primed by mass media and merchandising so that their encounters there are largely a series of "unexpected" expected events. But while Disney can lead us toward particular interpretations, it can never demand them from us: we continue to claim our agency and negotiate our experiences one person at a time. The Imagineers describe their work as "an extreme example of immersive entertainment" blending virtual fantasy and reality, though I would argue not as seamlessly as they claim, which is to the better. As active participants we make individual choices to suspend disbelief, even when we can perceive how dazzling effects are achieved and can readily identify when simulations are being used in Disney World's "content-filled, created space."[149] Today, Cast Members have greater consciousness of the "ideological dimensions" of themed space, and Guests have increased access to insider knowledge (especially via television and the Internet) than patrons of the past.[150] In short, both workers and visitors are savvy consumers of Disney's experiences. Even children, who enjoy creating and participating in fantasy worlds, are often technologically sophisticated enough to discover how Disney makes its magic without its being diminished for them. During a visit to Disney's Hollywood Studios when my daughter was eight years old, she figured out how Muppet Vision 3D's mock explosion was staged. She was not disappointed, however, but delighted, and proud of her ability to grasp how things work.[151]

Since Disney skillfully combines the "real *spatial* movement" of its attractions with a "simulated *temporal* trajectory," motion and narrative are bound together and seem comprehensible to us. We feel as though we have mastery over our experiences, while being prepared for the future via a friendly conception of "technology with a Mouse's face."[152] Yet Disney offers not only technological fantasy but also "a different measure of awareness" in which the Imagineers "wink at us," prompting us to acknowledge our complicity with their simulations. J. P. Telotte concludes that much of the "appeal here is that strange sense of being both bound up in and yet fully aware of the illusion being fashioned."[153] Writing about Vegas, Huxtable similarly observed that there is no longer "real versus phony, but the rela- (*means*) tive merits of the imitation. . . . The outrageously fake fake has developed its own indigenous style and lifestyle to become a real place."[154] Neither Las Vegas nor Disney World is an anomaly any longer; instead, they serve as "potent urban models."[155] At Disney World an overriding commitment to preserving the company's history and traditions is the guiding force. Attractions may be added, renovated, or updated, but they are less frequently destroyed, as it is assumed that Guests want to relive favorite experiences. Conversely, Vegas displays little sentimentality—even for its own past. The city's culture is one of obsolescence, where it is assumed only change will keep visitors engaged.[156]

The Imagineers' dictum—"not to duplicate the real but to fabricate the ideal"[157]—translates well to Vegas, where "the artificiality exhibited . . . isn't phony anything; it has its own resounding, relentless identity."[158] Surely, the proliferation of themed environments can backfire and explode into a vast landscape of placelessness, but Disney World and Las Vegas represent the most lavish and complex examples of the type.[159] In the end, both persist and prosper because they satisfy some of our most basic human desires and can move us in profound ways. At each place I feel more alive and optimistic, and connected to others through shared experiences. As a person who worries too much, who is too often weighed down by "What if?" regrets, I relish the uplifting experiences I have had at Vegas and Disney World, which prompt me to ask "What *is* possible?"

five

Fair Game

Sampling Technology and World Cultures at Epcot

But if we can bring together the technical know-how of American industry and the creative imagination of the Disney organization—I'm confident we can create right here in Disney World a showcase to the world of the American free enterprise system.

—Walt Disney, *Project Florida* (aka the "EPCOT Film")

. . . believe in the future, the world is getting better; there is still plenty of opportunity.

Always, as you travel, assimilate the sounds and sights of the world.

—Walt Disney, *Walt Disney: Famous Quotes*

Walt Disney dreamed his Experimental Prototype Community of Tomorrow (first called EPCOT, then Epcot Center, and since 1994 simply Epcot) would be a living testament to progress and communal life, complementing the Magic Kingdom's fantasy.[1] After proclaiming that the most important challenge of his day was "finding solutions to the problems of our cities," he asserted with bold-faced sincerity, "we must start . . . from scratch on virgin land and [build] a special kind of new community."[2] Walt intended Epcot to be a working model for the future that would demonstrate American industry's prowess. But like the Magic Kingdom, his concept for Epcot still bore Disney's distinctive hallmarks: unquestioning faith in the future and in the United States' leadership role; belief that the conditions of the outside world could be improved upon within controlled borders; and a tendency to oversimplify complex cultural relationships with multicultural platitudes.

As noted in chapter 4, Celebration pays homage to Epcot's initial concept but looks wholly different from the gleaming towers and lush greenbelt

Walt had envisioned. His dream of a future city was molded by science fiction and the World's Fairs, having more in common with Buck Rogers than Ozzie and Harriet. Walt's Epcot raced "toward the next frontier," recalling modernist schemes for vast and sleek urban spaces like Le Corbusier's *Plan Voisin* for La Cité Radieuse (The Radiant City) of 1925 (fig. 9). In contrast, Celebration's candy-colored houses and picket fences seem to yearn only "for lost horizons."[3] Walt succumbed to cancer in 1966 and did not see either the Magic Kingdom or Epcot completed. The Magic Kingdom debuted five years after his death, but he had been alive for much of its planning, site development, and design. Epcot did not open until 1982, and though the Imagineers tried to honor the spirit of Walt's original plans, the final product is nothing like a real community. As built, Epcot is a pleasantly sanitized nod to the heyday of the universal expositions.[4] Joe Flower halfjokingly suggests that if Walt was cryogenically frozen as is rumored, it was done "so that he could come back to correct the mess that he was sure his brother Roy, and his other successors, would make out of EPCOT."[5] Surely Walt would have been greatly disappointed that his city of the future was never realized, yet I think he would have appreciated Epcot if he took it on its present terms as a theme park rather than an urban model.

We have already found many prototypes for Disney World in the built environment, but here we turn our attention to a very direct source: the World's Fair. Like a pilgrimage center, ideal city, or the other examples encountered in previous chapters, the fair satisfied the human desire for community (even if only temporarily) and intensified personal experiences to transcend those had in daily life. That Epcot, in both its form and content, is based upon the World's Fair would have delighted Walt. His father, Elias, worked as a carpenter at the 1893 Columbian Exposition, and Walt was a fair enthusiast who attended the 1948 Chicago Railroad Fair and the joint New York/San Francisco World's Fair of 1939–40, each of which influenced him greatly. Walt also provided attractions for the 1958 and 1964–65 World's Fairs. On more general terms, the fairs were different from the shabby amusement places that Walt so disliked (see chapters 1 and 3), and instead combined entertainment and education in a manner to which Disney aspired.[6] Walt envisioned his Guests much like fairgoers: disciplined crowds proceeding in an orderly fashion through the novel, larger-thanlife, meticulously groomed, carefully zoned settings arranged for them. The successive generations of Imagineers who designed Epcot emulated the fair's function as a testing ground for technology (exemplified by the park's Future World) and as a place where world cultures were made palatable for

Figure 9. Le Corbusier, *Plan Voisin* for La Cité Radieuse (The Radiant City). 1925. © 2013 Artists Rights Society (ARS), New York/ADAGP, Paris/F.L.C. Photo credit: Banque d'Images, ADAGP/Art Resource, NY.

mainstream consumption (as evidenced at Epcot's World Showcase). This chapter begins with a foundational discussion of U.S. fairs and then turns to in-depth examinations of Future World and World Showcase. My intention is to highlight the specific ways in which Epcot is descended from the World's Fair, as acknowledged in the official program for the park's Grand Opening and Dedication Ceremony:

> We believe that in a world where cynicism and negativism abound, there is another story, and we have chosen, with forethought and conviction, to tell it, and to be that voice of optimism. . . . Now we have a way to bring real focus on the import of creative and futuristic processes and the value of friendship among nations. EPCOT Center is a permanent World's Fair of imagination, discovery, education, and exploration built with the help of leading American and international industries and with the cooperation of a number of governments.[7]

The World's Fair showcased the new and exotic within familiar and safe contexts. It planners tried to predict what would come next, promising a higher quality of life in the future. The fair was also used to shape expectations and values as a sort of "camp meeting" for the "dominating middle class."[8] Its celebratory, self-congratulatory nature was tinged with nostalgia for the event, even as it was happening. A "show-me" mentality presided over the fair, implying the world was an oyster opened up to present its pearl to eager visitors. New technologies were touted and capitalist fortunes flaunted. Prevailing racial, ethnic, and gender prejudices were made evident in visitors' interactions with "performers." Thus the fair not only gauged cultural achievements and economic prosperity but also acted as a social barometer attesting to the hopes, habits, and biases of its organizers and audiences. As both a commercial and cultural venture, the fair helps us better understand Disney World, especially Epcot. The World's Fair was more than a curious resource for Walt—it was a beloved model his Imagineers openly imitated, lifting its themes and echoing its forms.

Fair Trade in the U.S.A.?

The Fair was what America was: a synthesis of civicism and commerce,
culture and ballyhoo, high ideals and down-to-earth pragmatism.

—Robert A. M. Stern, *Pride of Place*

In 1851 the first World's Fair was held in London. It was a spectacular and popular event, spurring a flurry of universal expositions into the twentieth century. Many fairs were subsequently held in the United States, but two of them proved to have the longest-reaching aftereffects: the 1893 Columbian Exposition in Chicago and the 1904 Louisiana Purchase Exposition in St. Louis.[9] These fairs allowed Americans to close one century with a sense of optimistic cultural preeminence and to open the next with demonstrations of supposed superiority and leadership. Despite the United States' economic prosperity and expansive landmass, many Americans remained envious of Europe and its Old World traditions so rich in history and culture.[10] The World's Fair allowed them to forge a cohesive national identity and show it off while still under construction. Yet a colonial imperialist spirit clearly informed the fair, in the United States and elsewhere: exhibitors edited and embellished history as suited their needs, while disenfranchised or violated peoples were often ignored or further exploited. Even when fair organizers had reformist intentions, they frequently put pretty faces on ugly realities in the name of "progress." In hindsight, the fair's technological promise does not shine as brightly when viewed alongside the lingering legacies of colonial imperialism.

Chicago's World Columbian Exposition ran from 1 May to 31 October 1893 and was supposedly attended by 27,529,400 people at a time when the country's population was only 70 million.[11] Fifty nations and 50,000 individual exhibitors participated in the Exposition,[12] which Scott Lukas characterizes as "the world's first proto-theme park . . . an all encompassing, enclosed amusement space." Filled with fanciful architecture and thrilling spectacles, the fair fused memories of the past and hopes for the future in a lived present.[13] Its theme—four centuries of progress—celebrated the discovery of the "New World" by endorsing expansionist growth through the colonization of land and people and by hyping the achievements of white male Euro-Americans. The fair's site in Jackson Park on a marshy edge of Lake Michigan required extensive cultivation, as did Walt's Florida swampland (see chapter 3). Spread out over 686 acres, the Chicago fairgrounds inspired the City Beautiful movement with their large-scale planning and classical architectural vocabulary. The Exposition's wide diagonal boulevards, centralized building clusters (often grouped by theme or function), enclosed public spaces, and artificial waterways were later featured in city plans throughout the country and at the Disney parks. In the wake of industrialism, the fair seemed to prove that cities could be rehabilitated through good design, spotless maintenance, and tight security. Daniel H. Burnham, director of works, supervised the official architecture, the formality of which was offset by an irregularly contoured lagoon and Frederick Law Olmsted's Wooded Island park, conceived as a meditative respite from the excited rush of the fair.[14] Much attention was paid to the Great Basin (influenced by Venice's canals) and to the Court of Honor (modeled on Rome), where the so-called White City was located, its electric lights transforming it into a fairy-tale land at night. Margaretta Lovell contends that the fourteen official buildings found here, each wrapped in its own neoclassical casing, were not just visual markers but also containers for socially redeeming values: order, sobriety, knowledge, evolutionary design, cultural and aesthetic sophistication, political and economic well-being, and technical facility—in short, the culmination of human accomplishment. But she also notes that these visual demonstrations of nationalistic power were made possible by a nearly invisible infrastructure and labor force, evoking "a cultural fantasy of effortless achievement and benign cooperation, clarity, order, and unity," a description that reminds me of Disney World.[15]

Taken as a whole, the Chicago fairgrounds were a potent symbol of national pride that situated European architectural history as "chronologically and evolutionarily prior," so that the United States emerged as the next great "empire."[16] (Ironically, the fair's classical revival occurred just as "sky-scrapers of the most advanced design were mushrooming in Chicago.")[17] As the largest exposition to date and the "most complete urban-scale project realized since the planning of Paris and Vienna in the 1860s," Chicago's fair became the standard by which to measure other expositions, and cities, too.[18] Fairs are frozen in time (between opening and closing dates) and controlled in size (by the physical sites) so that they can offer diversity and excitement without forsaking coherence. But limited by such factors of their making and existence, fairs were never cities in the truest sense: they were elaborate stage sets recalling places and eras long vanished or anticipating those yet to be. Fairgoers were not residents but rather tourists taking in the novel sights. And while the fairs encouraged regentrification and bequeathed cultural institutions to their host cities, they rarely addressed pressing urban problems such as poverty and housing.[19]

The unofficial sector of Chicago's fair also captured the public's imagination—and money, grossing more than $4 million.[20] Although the White City offered refined education in an elegant setting, the Midway Plaisance was the fair's sideshow and primary source of entertainment and mirth. At past fairs, midway concessions had been considered unpleasant infringements on an exposition's rarified terrain, but here fair organizers utilized the amusement zone for their own purposes. Chicago's Midway was a mile long and nearly six hundred feet wide, extending west from the official Women's Building. Its irregular plan suggested "deliberately constructed chaos," a place where spectacular things happened too quickly to be analyzed by passing viewers, "window shopping in the department store of exotic cultures."[21] Like Disney World, the Midway bristled with strange juxtapositions: a model of St. Peter's in Rome, mock Yucatán ruins, a New England cabin, an Old Vienna biergarten, an immense panorama of the Bernese Alps, Old Jerusalem, a California ostrich farm, and a Brazilian concert hall. Within the walls of Cairo Street was a bustling cityscape, including a replicated mosque and the "Temple of Luxor" (where the infamous belly dancers performed). Materials were shipped directly from Egypt to ensure "authenticity," and Egyptian people staffed the shops and cafés.[22] Other popular attractions on the Midway, though not official national displays, were the Javanese, Samoan, and Dahomeyan villages. According to official fair literature, the Midway was "a place of good nature and gaiety, and, after returning from a day spent in investigations of its wonders, one feels indeed that he has returned from making a trip around the world."[23]

The Midway's anthropological displays, which exhibited people living in settings constructed especially for the fair, were descended from the colonial villages of the 1889 Exposition in Paris. The Chicago fair was the first truly international exposition, soliciting extensive foreign participation that clearly benefited some nations and peoples more than others. Organizers used ethnographic displays to generate profits while also serving as scientific and anthropological "evidence" of the supposed superiority of white Westerners, thereby supporting their own hegemonic and "utopic" social vision. The fair's Committee on Ways and Means placed the Midway under the Department of Ethnology's jurisdiction, which employed an overarching scheme of cultural compartmentalization drawn along "evolutionary" lines. As fair historian Robert Rydell asserts: "Alternating between specimens and toys in the eyes of observers, the nonwhite people living in villages along the Midway not only were seen through the lens of America's material and presumed racial progress . . . but were neatly categorized into the niches of a racial hierarchy."[24] At its worst, the Midway acted as a peep or freak show.[25] Yet it was also everything the White City was not—spontaneous, heterogeneous, multinational, grossly commercial. Taken together, the White City and Midway implied that the whole of modern experience could be had in a day at the fair.[26]

The 1904 (30 April–1 December) Louisiana Purchase Exposition celebrated the 1803 signing of the Purchase agreement between the United States and France and remains one of the best-remembered fairs. Held in St. Louis's Forest Park, it was America's first full-scale exposition since 1893, the largest World's Fair to date (nearly doubling the Chicago fair's acreage), and attended by over 19 million visitors during its operation. The 1904 fair largely ignored social issues, including the class and ethnic tensions in St. Louis, and focused instead on the latest technology promising a better life, exemplified by the Intramural Railway providing transportation throughout the fairgrounds.[27] (It also hosted the first Olympic Games held in the Western Hemisphere.) As had happened in Chicago, hordes of visitors thronged the midway amusements, but these were now incorporated into the fair's overall scheme.[28] Ultimately, the grand and stately official buildings did not prove as seductive as the Pike—the largest, most expensive ($10 million) amusement district to date—which, for many visitors, was the pinnacle of the fair experience.[29]

Taking its cue from Chicago's Midway, the Pike dovetailed anthropology and capitalism. It was jammed with 540 different concessions and exhibits, the most popular being representations of foreign lands. Both the Midway and the Pike anticipated Epcot's World Showcase, not just as samplers of world cultures—visual proof of an emerging global village—but also as they exoticized otherness and made it safe within their commercial precincts.

Among the Pike's featured exhibits was the Streets of Seville, which offered Bolero and Fandango dancers, marionette bullfights, and replicas of Madrid's Plaza de Toros and the Moorish Alhambra. The Tyrolean Alps attraction included the Tony Faust biergarten (which hosted thousands of daily diners) and a tram ride from which visitors could glimpse re-created Alpine scenes complete with the Schloss Charlottenberg. The Irish Village offered replicas of Blarney Castle, Lake Killarney, and the Irish House of Parliament. In Mysterious Asia, Indian, Hinostan, Burmese, Persian, and Ceylon architectural traditions conflated into a profusion of onion domes and minarets, complemented by a ceramic facade mimicking the Taj Mahal. Visitors here could ride an elephant, sip tea, or shop on a Calcutta-styled street. The Pike also included a Wild West show that reenacted the Louisiana Territory transfer and an Old St. Louis sector where famous homes and government buildings were reproduced. (Old St. Louis was prominently sited on the Pike, much as the U.S. pavilion is at Epcot, taking center stage to impart emphatic American history lessons.) The largest national exhibit on the Pike, Jerusalem, re-created the Holy Land and its sites. Built by the Jerusalem Exhibition Company for $700,000, it made many official structures look paltry by comparison. Within its walls were replicas of the Church of the Holy Sepulchre, the Wailing Wall, and the Dome of the Rock, as well as a cyclorama of Solomon's Temple. Statistics emphasize the magnitude of its production: Jerusalem covered eleven acres, had twenty-two streets, three hundred different buildings, and a thousand inhabitants brought by chartered steamer from Jaffa. John Davis suggests that here, "possibilities for spatial and social interaction were almost limitless; viewers moved into roles that were much more complex than the passive observer status common to most of the other ethnic sideshows."[30]

St. Louis inherited and further promoted Chicago's legacy of social "progress," built on a "scientific" foundation of racial and ethnic prejudice. The famous Geronimo, brought from an Oklahoma prison as a symbol of "savagery" conquered and domesticated, lived in an Indian village during the 1904 fair, selling miniature bows and arrows and autographed photos.[31] The American government also brought nearly twelve hundred Filipinos to live in a forty-seven-acre reservation—the largest living anthropological display of its time—for the duration of the fair, just two years after the United States claimed victory in the American-Philippine War. Instead of goods, human beings were exhibited as living proof of the moral benefits and modernizing effects of "benevolent assimilation" (i.e., pacification), enhancing the United States' imperialist clout. (The Philippine Reservation was wildly popular: ninety-nine out of every one hundred fairgoers reportedly visited it.) Other displays presented indigenous peoples as curiosities or even freaks, such as those of Ainu aborigines from Japan, Patagonian giants from Argentina, and Pygmies from the African Congo. W. J. McGee, chief organizer of exhibitions and head of the fair's massive Department of Anthropology, promoted the classification of people on a hierarchical scale: "enlightened," "civilized," "barbarous," or "savage."[32] While the fair's anthropological exhibitions may have sparked a greater awareness of other cultures, they also strengthened Western, specifically American, ethnocentric jingoism. Even the fair's theme, commemorating the centenary acquisition of the Louisiana Territory, asserted colonial desire for land and power.[33]

The U.S. World's Fairs upheld the assumed sanctity of Manifest Destiny while simultaneously undermining the spirit of some cultures (which had flourished for centuries) through dehumanizing displays. Such displays were organized at the expense of nameless "racial types" exhibited for the amusement of voyeuristic viewers. Many fair photographers, both professionals and amateurs, staged pictures of "the native" in "his element," a bitter reminder that otherness was being performed within prescribed boundaries.[34] In many ways the anthropological displays were human zoos, where people lived and worked, ate and slept, were born and died. The popularity of such exhibitions ensured that successive generations would grow up to become "professional natives," perpetuating the performance of otherness.[35] Clearly, the cultural terrain of the fair was a rocky layering of commercial venture, colonial spirit, faith, and contemporary aesthetics.[36] While national and regional displays were intended to clarify cultural meanings, they actually yielded sociologically complex relationships. Fair organizers were focused on celebrating technological, material, and evolutionary notions of progress, not nuances of cultural diversity or the winds of social change. Claims of democratic freedom and community interest rang hollow when, for example, women and minority groups found themselves disenfranchised at the fair even when included in it, perhaps because their civil struggles complicated the American family portrait.[37]

Ultimately, a World's Fair is a form of "event tourism." The cachet is in its temporality: one must experience the exposition before it is soon over. A fair exists less to celebrate Columbus's "discovery" of the New World or the Louisiana Purchase than its organizers and audiences. As showcases of self-conscious sociopolitical propaganda, the fairs stimulated urban development, boosted material growth, and tried to crystallize identity—regional, national, cultural, and otherwise.[38] Importing seemingly authentic (though often stereotypical) local color reinforced conceptions of the world as "a marketplace in which Americans could play at will." The fair also promoted the belief that international world peace would come through commercial exchange.[39] Only those nations or peoples deemed viable business partners were brought into the emerging global network. (Ariel Dorfman suggests that Walt Disney adopted a similar "existence as marketplace" ethos, which equated civilization with the ability to do business, and education with the exchange of goods and services.)[40] Thus the fair fed and legitimized our need to consume—information, technology, entertainment, diversion, even other cultures.[41] Not surprisingly, souvenirs like guidebooks, postcards, and collectors' items emblazoned with iconic fair imagery were plentiful. Such souvenirs documented the specific time and place of a transitory event, commemorating its existence and consecrating its legacy, much as sacred traces functioned for pilgrims (see chapter 2).[42] The souvenir reserved a memory for the future while the fair experience was still being lived. The fairs effectively compressed and commercialized space and time—practically the entire world was on display at one place, in one moment.[43] It is no wonder Walt was drawn to them. But the World's Fair offered an alluring microcosm that was only temporary: Disney would build a permanent one.

The Future Was Now

Epcot Center opened on October 1, 1982. Hundreds of costumed Disney employees stood in ranks along the walkways and on the pavilion roofs, moving and turning to instructions shouted through a loudspeaker. Columns of costumed men and women carrying American flags and standards with the Epcot insignia streamed into the plaza. Musicians in silver space suits climbed onto the stage and struck up a brassy rock tune. Teams of sequined dancers jumped and twirled. Twenty thousand balloons and a thousand pigeons were released.

—John Taylor, *Storming the Magic Kingdom*

The revelry described above stretched on for an entire month, as the Disney Company churned out self-congratulatory spectacles to mark the opening of Epcot. Each Future World and World Showcase pavilion had its own dedication and ribbon cutting ceremony; representatives from twenty-three countries participated in the International Ceremony of the Waters, pouring water from their homelands into the Communicore Plaza fountain; and *EPCOT Center: The Opening Celebration* was televised on 23 October, with Danny Kaye as its host.[44] But the pageantry that heralded Epcot's debut reminds us of how far the completed park had come from

Walt's original plans for a viable community that would be a model for future living. In the last years of his life Disney was less interested in film and theme park production (things he had already mastered) and, despite his lack of formal training in urban planning, became increasingly engaged with creating an ideal city. Disheartened by urban blight and inept bureaucracy, Walt wondered: "When I see things I don't like, I start thinking why do they have to be like this, and how can I improve them?"[45] He envisioned Epcot as a place where crime, slums, pollution, and poverty would be banished and where problems would be solved by technological ingenuity. The Magic Kingdom was always part of Project Florida and the first thing built, as Walt knew the theme park could generate needed revenue for Epcot. But in his mind, the model city would be the "heart" of Disney World.[46] Initially Disney conceived of two metropolitan centers, the "traditional" City of Yesterday and the "futuristic" City of Tomorrow, but his scheme was eventually whittled down to one place representing the "optimal patterns of urban living 25 years into the future."[47]

Planning for Walt's concept city began in earnest in 1964. He envisioned a place that combined entertainment principles with motifs of social control, as influenced by urban planner Victor Gruen (Gruen's Southdale Mall is discussed in chapter 4). Walt and his staff were familiar with Gruen's *The Heart of Our Cities* (1964), which praised pedestrianism and proposed "cells" of clustered mixed-use development to revitalize dying city centers. Gruen cited Disneyland as a successful example of cellular organization, though he lamented the overdevelopment of the land surrounding it (a point with which we know Walt agreed). He also recommended that utilities be hidden as much as possible, recalling Disney's enforced separation of "onstage" and "backstage" to maintain thematic integrity. Gruen's diagrams of the "Cellular Metropolis for Tomorrow" were likely used as models for Epcot's initial plan of clustered residential and industrial sectors. Gruen and Disney both admired Ebenezer Howard's Garden City, which (as we saw in chapter 3) was an important source for Walt. Disney wished to emulate the Garden City's radial plan and generous greenspace, intended to promote civility and public order. Among the books inventoried in Walt's office after his death were Howard's *Garden Cities of To-Morrow* (1902, reissued in 1965), *The Heart of Our Cities,* and another text by Gruen, *Out of a Fair, a City,* based upon an innovative plan for a World's Fair in Washington, D.C. Although the 1964–65 World's Fair went to New York instead of Washington, Gruen's unrealized scheme to create a "post-fair" city with infrastructure and buildings inherited from the temporary event was profoundly influential upon Walt. Disney understood that if Gruen's plan had been adopted, Washington's fairgoers would have previewed an actual city of the very near future, not just a model.[48]

Walt surrounded himself with a team of experienced experts for his concept city project, including community planner Ray Watson and "Joe" Potter, a retired U.S. Army major general and Robert Moses's chief engineer during the 1964–65 World's Fair (Potter oversaw the first phase of Disney World's construction, too). This inner circle began scouting "classified" corporate research departments, such as those at General Motors and General Electric (Disney worked with both on the 1964–65 fair), for new technologies to test and demonstrate at Epcot. Walt zealously protected his ideas as they percolated, becoming obsessed with the ideal community at the end of his life. He finally premiered its plans in a twenty-four-minute film, *Project Florida* (sometimes called *Walt Disney's EPCOT*, but most commonly referred to as the "EPCOT film"), made on 27 October 1966, less than two months before his death. The film was shot on a set re-creating the secret "war room" (also called the "Florida room") at WED Headquarters in Glendale, California, where Epcot had been planned, and featured a massive aerial map of the Florida property. Despite Disney's ailing health (he was administered oxygen during the filming), he was palpably enthusiastic about the project. The maps and blueprints Walt presented seemed so detailed and finite; in reality these were little more than a concept and numerous reports, studies, sketches, and statistics, though Disney assured the film's viewers that the philosophy for the city would remain the same even if the plans changed. The film was made with two endings, each targeted to a different audience: the Florida legislature, which Disney courted to establish the Reedy Creek Improvement District, a governing body formed "by some spectacular political acrobatics" (see the conclusion);[49] and potential corporate and industrial partners.[50] The film was screened in February 1967; in May the proposed legislation to approve the District's creation passed.

Perhaps the best way to describe Walt's approach to urban planning is "evolutionary" rather than "revolutionary," in that he drew upon preexisting forms, theories, and techniques in hopes of improving infrastructure, reducing traffic, and using the land more resourcefully. Walt and his team conceived Epcot as a radially planned metropolis for twenty thousand people, with a series of three concentric rings around a city core. The outermost ring would contain low-density housing composed of futuristic homes, constantly remodeled to showcase the latest technology (although

Walt appreciated Gruen's clustered plans, in his own city he provided large single-family plots where he imagined his friends would want to live).[51] Next was a greenbelt with churches, schools, and playgrounds. The inner ring consisted of high-density apartments for "modest" rental fees, which offered direct access to the central core. The intention was to encourage economic diversity by offering various housing options. The city center was a climate-controlled business hub enclosed by a fifty-acre glass dome, reminiscent of R. Buckminster Fuller's fanciful Manhattan project circa 1950 (fig. 10), through which a thirty-story hotel and convention center would rise. Public transportation spokes would bring Epcot citizens and visitors to outlying residential and industrial complexes, providing safe, clean, fast, quiet, energy-efficient transit with electric vehicles. He was not "against the automobile," Walt maintained, but wanted to combat its having "moved into communities too much."[52] The design for Epcot was much like that of Le Corbusier's for his Radiant City (see fig. 9), which functionally segregated pedestrians and vehicles.[53] Disney's plan featured a five-layer transportation system: PeopleMovers (a mode of transit developed by WED Enterprises) on elevated tracks; surface streets for pedestrians; underground monorails and more PeopleMovers; further underground were the cars; and deepest below ground were "unsightly" trucks. A monorail would connect to a thousand-acre industrial park, an airport, and the Disney World resort. Walt's city scheme also included International Shopping and Dining Arcades (originally conceived for Disneyland as International Street), recalling World Showcase as actually built. Robert Moses boldly predicted that Epcot would be the "first accident free, noise free, pollution free city in America."[54]

Epcot represented the confluence of Walt's visionary and business-minded aspirations. According to Disney's celebratory biographers, Katherine and Richard Greene, the plans for Epcot "demonstrated his faith in the basic goodness of mankind. He believed that if you gave people a good place to live and the proper information and choices to make it better, they would do so."[55] A pronounced strain of idealism is evident in the Epcot plans, tempered by a narrow-minded reformism. Walt claimed that Epcot would offer a lifestyle not found anywhere else in the world, but an overriding entrepreneurial spirit tarnished the appeal of Disney-concept living. Although Walt wanted Epcot to be a real community, he intended to tightly regulate its residents' lives and to open the city to *paying* visitors. No representative local government, permanent inhabitants with voting rights and/or property ownership (see the conclusion), retirees, or pets would be

Figure 10. R. Buckminster Fuller, *Dome Covering Midtown Manhattan Island*. ca. 1960. Courtesy, The Estate of R. Buckminster Fuller.

permitted. Churches were included in his plan, but other places of worship were not. Dress, grooming, and conduct codes would be strict, and residents could be expelled for unfit behaviors such as drunkenness or unmarried cohabitation. Paul Goldberger observed that Disney's concept privileged technology and physical design but lacked necessary social planning.[56] Steven Watts agreed, noting that despite Walt's "blueprint for engineering happiness, with the best of intentions . . . The ghost of authoritarianism . . . hovered in the background. In jettisoning democracy for technocratic engineering and exchanging the pleasures of citizenship for the rewards of material comfort, EPCOT charted a dangerous course."[57] With paying customers and a projected population consisting mostly of Disney workers living there temporarily, Epcot would have been an awkward combination of a tourist attraction and transient company town. Although Walt seemed unable to see the impracticality of his scheme, Ray Watson quickly identified it and told him that the only way people would live under such scrutiny was if they were paid to do so.[58] Perhaps Walt's vision for Epcot is most valuable to us in its role as an experimental showcase rather than an urban prototype. Disney and his cohorts wanted to counter suburban sprawl and reinvigorate cities, though the ideas they spurred were prohibitively expensive. Epcot was the last project Walt undertook during his lifetime, and many of its details were not worked out, social dynamics being chief among these. The plan to distribute people by housing type would have created an economically segregated population of mostly renters, and the conflicting needs of residents and visitors remained unresolved. Ultimately, it was neither feasible nor desirable to build a real community that put humans on display with the technology.[59]

Walt had worried that if he died before Epcot could be constructed it would never exist as he imagined it. He was right. After his death, Disney Imagineers and executives were left with a dilemma: Walt had promised the public—and Florida legislators—an Epcot, and it was agreed they must provide one, but exactly how that promise should be delivered upon was less clear. A multitude of voices bickered over Walt's concept, and by 1975 it was decided that the company would not build a residential city.[60] Instead, a revised plan for Epcot, one motivated by the company's financial situation at the time, was pursued. Though Disney films were lagging at the box office by the mid-1970s, the Magic Kingdom continued to prosper after welcoming nearly 11 million visitors in just its first year of operation.[61] Shrewdly, Card Walker, then Disney chairman and CEO, dedicated his energies to reviving the Epcot project. In 1976 he outlined the basic goals for Epcot in an address to the Urban Land Institute, characterizing it as a testing ground for emerging technologies as well as an ongoing forum on the future through which industry, government, and academia could collaboratively problem-solve. Walker also claimed that Epcot would further understanding among different nations.[62] Although these descriptions echo Walt's own, and Epcot was built on the site he had personally selected (more than double the size of the Magic Kingdom), Disney's original vision gave way, as David Koenig observes, "to a theme park, entertaining, innovative and educational, but still a theme park. . . . Another amusement park just made more cents."[63]

Some of the "futuristic" technologies Walt endorsed are used at the Disney parks today (monorails, vacuum-based sanitation systems, underground utility tunnels, and a central computer system to manage it all), but these seem dated. Despite his image of a city always "in a state of becoming . . . a *living blueprint of the future*, where people actually live a life they can't find anywhere else in the world," the park leaves the distinct impression of a World's Fair frozen in time.[64] Working cities are subject to constant change as competing social agendas and economic and political forces vie to shape them. By contrast, a World's Fair was a temporary city, achieving the orderliness and harmony that most urban centers lacked because it was "finished." Rather than undergoing revision and renewal, the fair was fixed in time and place, its high maintenance standards financed through admission fees. Purposeful zoning carefully organized fair structures by function, ensuring efficient movement and communication between them. Significantly, as Lovell asserts, the fair was the "result of united, centralized, almost uncontested decision-making."[65] Such autocratic control surely appealed to Walt as a means to create and maintain a structured, perfectible environment. Disney must have also appreciated the fair's use of facadism. Fair visitors suspended disbelief as they wandered through a glorious super-city of faux classical buildings, pasteboard regional architecture, and replicated villages. Caught in the fair's frenzy, one was playfully challenged to distinguish between "what was real, what was simulated, and what was total fantasy."[66]

The 1939–40 World's Fair at New York (30 April 1939–31 October 1940) was attended by nearly 45 million people and had thirty-three participating nations.[67] Although Disney animator Ward Kimball recalled that Walt attended this fair, there is no definitive proof to support that claim. Regardless, information about and images of the 1939–40 fair were widely circulated, and it is apparent that the event informed the development of Walt's theme parks.[68] The fair was held at Flushing Meadows (formerly the Corona Dumps) in the borough of Queens and was directed by Grover Whalen (president of the fair corporation) and city parks commissioner Robert Moses, with whom Disney would become well acquainted during the 1964–65 World's Fair. In the wake of the Depression, the 1939–40 fair attempted to bolster American consumer culture and faith in the future with demonstrations of material abundance and governmental leadership. Foreign countries also showcased their modern architecture, industrial design, and technology. Corporate sponsors were more visible than ever before, hawking new products like Lucite, fluorescent lighting, and television. Although the fair's theme, "Building the World of Tomorrow," was decidedly futuristic, an aura of history permeated there, as evidenced by a colossal statue of George Washington presiding over the grounds in commemoration of the 150th anniversary of his inauguration. By bridging technology and history, the fair catered to its prime audience: "the commercially shaped, nationalized, media-driven middle-class culture that was coming to dominate America."[69] Jeffrey Pepper believes that, as built, Epcot most closely resembles the 1939–40 fair in its layout, design, and ideological program (touting themes such as communication, transportation, and community). Corporate pavilions were organized in thematic bands separating amusement from industry, which radiated out from the fair's architectural centerpieces: Harrison and Fouilhoux's seven-hundred-foot-tall Trylon and the eighteen-story, two-hundred-foot-in-diameter Perisphere, inspired, respectively, by the Eiffel Tower and the Celestial Globe of the 1889 Paris Exposition (fig. 11). (Together the Trylon and Perisphere were called a "Theme Center," precisely the language used in the initial plan for Epcot's Future World.) With their distinctive forms, the Trylon and Perisphere became iconic logos for the fair: the soaring Trylon, a symbol of progress; the globular Perisphere (a source for the Epcot park's Spaceship Earth), a symbol of the universe. They were joined by an elevated ramp called the Helicline, which gave magnificent views of the fairgrounds and Manhattan skyline.[70]

Figure 11. Harrison and Fouilhoux, *Trylon and Perisphere at night,* New York World's Fair, 1939–40, Flushing Meadows–Corona Park, Queens, New York. Photograph: Samuel H. (Samuel Herman) Gottscho, 26 May 1939. From the Collections of the Museum of the City of New York, image No. 56.323.11.

Given Walt's sensibilities, the featured Theme Exhibition of Democracity would have seemed flawless (fig. 12). Displayed inside the Perisphere and glimpsed from above on revolving balconies (accompanied by music and "inspirational rhetoric"), the highly detailed model of Democracity appeared as the official literature presented it: "a symbol of a perfectly integrated, futurist metropolis."[71] Democracity shares conceptual similarities with ideal city planning in general and Walt's original proposal for Epcot in particular. Industrial designer Henry Dreyfuss planned Democracity as an updated Garden City for one million people (Dreyfuss was also an admirer of Ebenezer Howard). Its population would be housed in five satellite towns connected to the city proper by a series of highways traversing a greenbelt, keeping vehicular and pedestrian traffic segregated. Light industry and commerce were focused in a core of tall, widely spaced buildings, with subsequent rings of housing, park, and farmland. Perhaps most exciting, Democracity's example was immediately manifested in the fairgrounds, which were rationally planned with wide axial boulevards and sporting a color palette to unify the whole yet distinguish subdivisions by function.[72]

Notably, the arrangement of Epcot's World Showcase evokes the organization of international displays at the 1939–40 fair. The fair had a government zone behind the technology and commercial sectors. A body of water, the Lagoon of Nations, was at its center. The U.S. Federal Building anchored twenty other national pavilions (with forty smaller ones inside the Hall of Nations), much as the American Adventure pavilion is centralized at World Showcase. In addition to layout, the attractions of the 1939–40 fair were also sources for Disney. The fair's amusement rides, vernacular stage sets, ultra-modern technology, and ideal urban communities, as well as interactive exhibits that transformed visitors into participants, inspired the Imagineers. Sometimes this inspiration was very specific: for instance, Epcot's World of Motion seems directly descended from Chrysler's World of Motion at the fair. (Epcot's Test Track thrill ride has since replaced World of Motion, though it also has roots in the 1939–40 fair, particularly Ford's The Road of Tomorrow, in which cars traversed a track outside the pavilion.) Likewise, GM's pavilion would have interested Disney. There visitors rode over a massive model of Futurama, a "typical" American city of the 1960s, designed by Norman Bel Geddes. Exiting patrons found themselves in a full-size replica of the street intersection above which they had just hovered. As I try to visualize this, I realize the effect must have been staggering for fairgoers. The scale model helped them imagine what it might be like to inhabit a city of the future, moments before they were walking around a

Figure 12. *Rendering of Perisphere Interior (Theme Exhibit)* of Henry Dreyfuss's *Democracity*, New York World's Fair, 1939–40. Photograph of drawing by Theodore Kautzky, 1937–39. From the Collections of the Museum of the City of New York, image No. 2011.15.105.

human-sized version of it. While the model represented a fantastic dream, an inhabitable replica made that dream appear achievable. According to Helen Harrison, the fair's "enlightened planning and development, seductively packaged in a fantasyland format, self-congratulatory and self-assertive," projected a reassuring image countering Depression-era realities.[73]

The fair's heady display made a shiny future seem not only inevitable but also tangible.

A profound shift occurred from the grand fairs of the late nineteenth and early twentieth centuries, which presented "a backward look at many conquests already achieved," to those of the 1930s and onward as a "world of the future seeking objectification."[74] The earlier expositions were marked by an optimistic, patriotic tone, affirming that a Manifest Destiny of "progress" would be delivered through invention and innovation. Cities lobbied hard for hosting duties: being the site of a World's Fair heightened status and brought urban improvements. Furthermore, the fairs functioned as experimental cities, living labs where the problems of security, cleanliness, order, and navigation could be worked out. By the 1930s, however, the classicism of the early fairs gave way to an ahistorical modernism embracing the machine age, streamlined materials, and corporate sponsorship. The role of host city was no longer so coveted, as mass communications now offered numerous opportunities to experience the new and exotic. As a result, fairgrounds increasingly seemed less like unified urban visions and more like expressions of various interest groups, or feats of engineering without clear purpose. The fair promoted its organizers' agendas of making science and technology accessible, assuring visitors the future would be better, but this rosy promise was based on abundant material goods and not necessarily humanitarianism.[75]

Although the 1939–40 fair was a bicoastal event, scholars have paid considerably less attention to New York's counterpart, San Francisco's Golden Gate International Exposition, which we know Walt did visit in 1939. While not as determinedly futuristic as the fair in New York, San Francisco provided contrasts of overwhelming and diminutive scale that surely influenced Disney. Of particular interest to him must have been Vacationland Palace, in which a model train chugged past tiny replicas of American landmarks. The Thorne Room Miniatures (shown simultaneously on both coasts) were also popular: period room shadowboxes that presented an ideal, untouchable world. Karal Ann Marling contends that such exhibits deeply moved Walt: "Rampant nostalgia at the scale of one inch to the foot . . . Disney came home from San Francisco and began to collect miniatures."[76] Disney also loved trains and had been infatuated with them since childhood. His uncle Mike was a train engineer, and at sixteen Walt took a summer job selling candy on the Santa Fe Railroad's run from Kansas City to Chicago. As an adult he became a model railroad enthusiast, immersed in the possibilities of a miniaturized, perfectible world.

He even built a one-eighth-scale model railroad (large enough for him to ride!), the Carolwood-Pacific, which circled a track in his backyard on Carolwood Drive in Holmby Hills. (A playhouse for his daughters replicating the dwarfs' cottage from *Snow White* accompanied the railroad.) Walt drew comfort from railroading and even made an extended train trip in 1931 after a "full-blown nervous breakdown" the press quietly downplayed.[77] He later visited the 1948 Chicago Railroad Fair, which showcased technology and other cultures, much as Epcot does today in its separate sectors. The fairgrounds, former site of Chicago's 1933–34 Century of Progress Exposition, were ringed by a periphery train track and divided into themed lands. Attractions included a replica of Yellowstone's Old Faithful (erupting every fifteen minutes), a French Quarter, a working dude ranch, and a beach representing Florida's Gulf Coast. Disney's excursion to the Chicago Railroad Fair (made with Kimball, a fellow train buff) reputedly spurred Disneyland's conception, which Walt excitedly talked about the whole way home.[78]

From its inception the Magic Kingdom was conceived as a place for children and their parents, but as Epcot's designers started to think about it as a theme park rather than a living community, they decided to target it toward adults. The format of the World's Fair was adapted and pared down to two primary subdivisions—technology and world cultures. The technology sector was given the ponderous name of Future World. Here it seems the Disney Company had finally come to understand the dilemma of visionary futurism that Walt grasped early on: "The only problem with anything of tomorrow is that at the pace we're going . . . tomorrow would catch up with us before we got it built."[79] Clearly, the future's unwillingness to be predicted, controlled, or even stalled presents a quandary for the Imagineers, since Disney parks are designed to suggest that complete mastery can be had over their microcosmic worlds. As John Findlay observed: "By undermining the messages presented inside the park(s), the future could smuggle contradiction and ambiguity" into them.[80] For example, the much-celebrated Monsanto "House of the Future" erected in Disneyland's Tomorrowland (June 1957) was packed with the latest technology foretelling domestic liberation. By the 1970s, however, its utopian promises were outdated and it was demolished, no easy task since the wrecking ball merely bounced off its resilient plastic surface; the "House of the Future" was not razed in a day as was planned, but instead required two weeks to be dismantled with hacksaws.[81] Intending not to repeat such experiences, the Disney Company worked with industry professionals and academics to develop Future World as a supposedly ever-changing place, providing an entertaining and accessible education on the technology of tomorrow.

Like the fairs, Future World's original scheme called for pavilions sponsored by different corporations. A Theme Center consisting of three pavilions (Science and Technology, Communication and the Arts, and Community) would offer films and displays previewing topics addressed at various satellite locations, each satellite focusing on a different innovative technology or attraction (strangely, World Showcase was to be the first "satellite"). Although access to the Theme Center was free, visits to many of the satellites were to require fees.[82] Yet this earlier plan was subsequently abandoned for a circuit of eight pavilions (now designated as residing in Future World East or Future World West) grouped around a central commons and two plazas, addressing subjects ranging from ocean exploration to communities of the future, all with an eye on technology. Sponsors were more forthcoming with funds for Future World than for World Showcase, which Marling suggests resulted in the placement of "the picturesque cultural stuff in the back, in the metaphorical past, and the corporate future up front, where it counts."[83] Future World features "hyperindividual architecture" like that found at World's Fairs.[84] It is presided over by Spaceship Earth, a 184-foot-high, 165-foot-in-diameter pseudo-geodesic dome, its design and central siting evoking Buckminster Fuller's dome for the 1967 Montreal Expo and the New York Perisphere discussed earlier. When originally sponsored by AT&T, the Spaceship's interior attraction traced the evolution of communications. Revamped several times, it now offers an exhibit on life in the digital age sponsored by Siemens, which the unofficial Walt Disney Imagineering site laments has made what was once "a solid hit" into "a dud."[85] The Innoventions East & West plazas (renamed in 1994, formerly the Communicores) present interactive technology exhibits. Hands-on discovery is also found at the Imagination! pavilion (long sponsored by Kodak, though without sponsorship today), which hosts 3D films and play areas inside its twin mirrored glass pyramids. Environmental issues are emphasized at The Land, a mesa-shaped building, and The Seas with Nemo & Friends pavilion (originally named The Living Seas) evokes the form of a cresting wave. Both of these pavilions have lost their sponsorship too: The Land, once sponsored by Nestlé, and The Seas, formerly presented by United Technologies.[86] The World of Motion pavilion closed in 1996, with the Test Track ride taking its place after a three-year hiatus (both attractions sponsored by General Motors).[87] Horizons' futuristic pavilion debuted on 1 October 1983 (exactly one year after Epcot's opening) but was destroyed after having lost General Electric's sponsorship in 1993. It was eventually replaced in 2003 by Mission: SPACE, an intense simulator ride (sponsored by HP). The Universe of Energy pavilion is much the same since it opened, its most notable change being the addition of Ellen DeGeneres as its host personality.

Future World's pavilions, as well as other Disney attractions, were indebted in spirit and often form to the 1964–65 New York World's Fair (22 April–18 October 1964, 21 April–17 October 1965). This was held on the same site in Queens as the 1939–40 fair and presided over by the Unisphere, a massive globe sculpture built by U.S. Steel, which stood on the same foundations as the Perisphere.[88] The 1964–65 fair received over 51.5 million visitors, even though only twenty-four nations participated. At first, Walt's desire to contribute to this fair by designing attractions for hire perplexed his employees: A man who spent his career making durable entertainment commodities was now interested in projects with limited lifespans, which served the interests of other companies? But Walt cleverly recognized that the fair presented opportunities to experiment with other people's money, developing technology and attractions to use later in his own parks.[89]

Joe Fowler, an ex-U.S. Navy admiral who had overseen the construction of Disneyland, consulted on a number of Disney's 1964–65 fair projects, including Progressland with its Carousel of Progress for General Electric (GE) and Ford Motor's Magic Skyway. The Carousel's theater physically revolved around six vignettes of a "typical"—albeit robotic—family in period costumes and settings ranging from the late 1800s through the 1960s. (Skye Jethani notes the paradox here: "progress assumes linear advancement. . . . A carousel . . . is designed to repeat its course in endless cycles.")[90] As the theme song, "There's a Great Big Beautiful Tomorrow," played, the accompanying narration assured visitors that a bright future powered on electricity lay ahead: "Now most carousels just go round and round without getting anyplace. But on this one we're really going places—and that's progress! . . . Progress is the fulfillment of man's hopes and dreams for a better way of life. It is measured by our ability to harness electric energy for the betterment of mankind . . . And because of man's dreams, tomorrow will find us further than today."[91] The Carousel of Progress went to Disneyland after the fair and was brought to the Magic Kingdom's Tomorrowland in 1975 (it enjoyed GE sponsorship until 1994). Today even its contemporary set looks dilapidated, equipped with outdated appliances, but its message of faith in a better future brought by technology lives on at Epcot. In Steven Watts's opinion, the Carousel, "combining nostalgia with rosy predictions of progress," was the fair project closest to Walt's heart and mind.[92] At the fair, riders exited past a 115-by-60-foot diorama of Progress City, based upon Walt's concept for Epcot. Voices from the Carousel family provided four minutes of commentary on the model's wonders, which were individually spotlighted. The metropolis sported a huge dome-like structure at its core, punctuated by a thirty-story hotel tower. A greenbelt with civic buildings and an amusement park surrounded the city center, with single-family homes and parks lying beyond the greenbelt. In the far distance stood a nuclear power plant. The diorama was incredibly detailed, fitted with working streetlights, moving sidewalks, 22,000 trees and shrubs, 2,450 vehicles including monorails and PeopleMovers, and more than 4,500 lighted buildings. Walt's love of miniatures was manifested in this model, which proved itself a useful tool for visualizing potential strengths and weaknesses in the urban design.[93] Today only a small portion of Progress City is on display at Disney World; the Alamo-sponsored PeopleMover rides past it on a tour of Tomorrowland as a recorded voice announces, "The City of Tomorrow is a great electric machine working for you."

The Magic Skyway, a feature attraction in Ford's Wonder Rotunda, has multiple descendants at Epcot, including Spaceship Earth, the Universe of

Figure 13. Magic Skyway, Ford's Wonder Rotunda, New York World's Fair, 1964–65, Flushing Meadows–Corona Park, Queens, New York. Photograph: Bill Cotter (www.worldsfairphotos.com).

Energy (which culled its prehistoric imagery directly from the Skyway's), and the former Horizons and World of Motion pavilions, all of which featured rides through vignettes quickly recapping history and predicting high hopes for the future. (Such attractions can be traced back to nineteenth-century tableaux vivants, dioramas, and waxworks.) The Skyway transported visitors from the age of dinosaurs to the city of the tomorrow. Guests rode along in mechanically controlled convertibles on a track that took them outside the pavilion (like Ford's earlier The Road of Tomorrow) for a panoramic view of the fairgrounds (fig. 13).[94] Another Disney attraction for the 1964–65 fair was It's A Small World, conceived for Pepsi Cola's collaboration with UNICEF. Here, in a salute to "all the world's children," Imagineers took Walt's vague idea for "a little boat ride" and expanded it into a nine-minute trip around the world. Animated childlike dolls, whose costumes, coloring, and slightly modified facial features were the only indicators of racial, ethnic, and cultural differences, populated the attraction. In the finale, all nations come together in a bright white setting (each figure dressed in white, too), singing rounds of "It's A Small World (After All)" in different languages. While today the ride may seem like nothing more than an overly sentimental platitude, fair audiences loved it. After the fair closed, It's A Small World was relocated to Disneyland and later adapted for Disney parks in Florida, Tokyo, and France. Furthermore, this attraction and others such as the Carousel allowed the company to develop high-capacity rides that could ably handle the massive crowds flocking to its theme parks.[95]

Yet the attraction from the 1964–65 fair that would have the maximum impact on Disney's parks was Great Moments with Mr. Lincoln, sponsored by the state of Illinois. Since the late 1950s Walt had tinkered with his idea for "One Nation Under God," an exhibition with robotic American presidents. Disney collected mechanical toys, which inspired his company's development of Audio-Animatronics (figures powered with hydraulic fluid and puffs of compressed air). WED Enterprises' design and fabrication division, MAPO (Manufacturing and Production Organization; a name derived from Mary Poppins as a nod to the mechanized robin built for the film), was responsible for animatronics. For the fair, Walt proposed an ambitious idea to create a walking, talking Abraham Lincoln who would "interact" with visitors. Although Disney's other fair attractions utilized the proprietary Audio-Animatronic technology, none was as sophisticated as the Lincoln exhibit. Walt recalled a visit to his studio by fair president Robert Moses: "Lincoln stood up and put his hand out and Moses went over and shook hands with him. Well Moses . . . said 'I've got to have Lincoln in the Fair.' But I said, 'This is five years away anyway.' . . . before I knew it, I had my arm twisted and I said, 'Yes.' We now had to get Mr. Lincoln on the road . . . in about 13 months."[96] In the rush to complete Lincoln, many kinks had to be worked out. A complex series of facial and body movements complemented excerpts from his Gettysburg Address, but the robotic Abe shook and trembled. As Imagineer John Hench remembered: "Every time . . . we had a drop in current, it was exactly like an epileptic fit. My God, he was a terrifying guy."[97] Yet once such problems were corrected, the Lincoln show became one of the most popular at the entire fair. Realizing he could staff his parks with armies of unpaid, untiring, non-union animatronic actors, Walt could not contain his excitement: "Many of the attractions will 'come-to-life' . . . hour after hour and show after show."[98] Yet attempts to render technology as user-friendly and benevolent fell short for fairgoers fearing that relentless "progress" would replace people with machines. In this context, Disney's Lincoln must have seemed disturbing and even threatening. A further complication was the nonpartisan portrayal of Lincoln's politics, as Disney's Abe did not even mention slavery. Only after decades of many complaints—and Walt's death—did the theme parks rectify this glaring omission.[99]

Though the 1964–65 fair ended in insolvency, falling short of its projected attendance of 70 million visitors, it was a great success for Walt. He was praised as its "presiding genius," a "Magician" who beguiled the masses and left "a Disneyesque air" permeating the whole event. Participating in the fair benefited Walt immensely: here he experimented with crowd control, debuted attractions, and market-tested a large East Coast population sample for the viability of a new theme park.[100] Four of the five most popular fair attractions were Disney's. Nearly 91 percent of the total attendees (about 150,000 people daily) saw at least one of the Disney attractions, and judged them to be among the best. Thus East Coast audiences were primed for the Disney experience, as Walt quickly cultivated a group of new rides and shows—at the expense of others—that could be effectively transposed to his parks with little revision. Obviously, Disney's involvement in the fair made good business sense, but the ideological underpinnings of the event also appealed to him. Although international in its scope, with the theme of "Peace Through Understanding," Moses planned the fair as "a showcase for the American way of life, particularly with regard to material and technical progress," a mission that surely resonated with Walt. While detractors attacked the fair as grossly commercial, overtly conservative, and uncritical of technology, it remained unwaveringly cheerful, ignoring the atomic bomb's legacy and current-day sociopolitical turmoil. Watts surmises that this fair, "a self-conscious display of the United States' confidence and might at the high tide of the American century, gave Walt Disney . . . a springboard into the creation of a bold new project in Florida."[101] Indeed, Imagineer and Disney executive Marty Sklar confirmed that the fair "was one of the great stepping stones to Walt Disney World."[102]

At the 1964–65 fair, American industry and Disney ingenuity were cemented in a visionary bond in which showmanship transmitted images of material comfort, improved quality of life, and technological growth—even if in actuality not everyone would reap these benefits. Corporate sponsorship had been part of the Disney formula since the opening of Disneyland in 1955. Today, concessionaires pay considerable sums to ensure the exclusivity of their products at the parks, associating their brand names with an atmosphere of "family fun."[103] At least 50 percent of Epcot's construction was funded by corporate sponsors paying as much as $75 million in licensing rights and building and operating costs per a pavilion for ten years of representation at the park. These corporations must comply with standards determined by Disney, which retains ownership and control of all facilities. Direct product sales to a captive clientele are not the prime motivation for sponsorship; rather, the aim is to capitalize upon Disney's loyal demographic and associate with its "magic." In this way, sponsorship enhances corporate image as the connection to Disney becomes "the Good Fairy Seal of Approval."[104] Furthermore, the undergirding ideology of the parks—that the problems of the past are behind us and the challenges of the future will be skillfully met by industry—is appealing to many companies.[105] Perhaps not so ironically, the design of Future World evokes a 1960s office park situated on a carpet of green lawn, a model that was dated before the theme park was even built. Epcot's atmosphere was meant to be otherworldly, with exotic plantings fronting gleaming pavilions, but it could also seem harsh and unwelcoming. As Joe Flower described it: "Unlike almost every other part of Disney World, Future World held no gingerbread, nothing quaint, no whiff of nostalgia. The hard, curving surfaces and massive, beetling structures, unfriendly and corporate at the street level, the central plan obvious and over-powering in its symmetry . . . all spoke of a 1960s image of a clean and utterly ordered future, George Orwell's *1984* with sunflowers and fountains."[106] In an effort to make Future World seem more inviting, exhibitions were changed, new technology was showcased, brighter colors and bolder graphics were used, and rides were reconfigured or scrapped altogether. By the end of the 1980s the tone of the attractions also changed, as staid presentations of scientific information gave way to a lighter-hearted attitude. Yet despite the revisions, multiple sponsors opted not to renew their Epcot contracts.[107]

Michael Wallace suggests that Future World exemplifies a 1950s approach to history developed by Walt and carried on by his Imagineers. Here the free enterprise system and technological progress are linked to forge positive corporate identities. The Disney methodology puts absolute faith in technology, business know-how, and commodity goods to improve lives and increase leisure. Epcot's underlying messages, which downplay the most serious ecological hazards and sociological ills, reinforce capitalist development as natural and inevitable. "Corporate desire to fudge the past" and "Disney's ability to spruce it up" together fashion an image of the future in which private industry can overcome any obstacle, even if in truth it was the problem's source.[108] By emphasizing the "futuristic" over the "future" itself, Disney tends to overlook its own achievements in trash collection, fiber-optic communications, and environmental conservation, perhaps perceived as unexciting for visitors. J. Tevere MacFadyen claims it is not the "insistent optimism" of Epcot that is "distressing" but that Disney does not capitalize on its qualifications to address social and technological challenges outside of its parks.[109] But according to Marling, Future World's biggest disappointment is the implication that the future already happened, and indeed has passed us by.[110] For me, the biggest problem is that this vision of the future is not particularly compelling. When I am at Epcot, I always tour Future World first. Although I enjoy its thrill rides like Soarin' and Test Track, the rest of it does not really hold my attention. Future World feels like something I must "get through" before I can move on to something better. Like a kid who eats her perfunctory dinner so she can have dessert, Future World is just a precursor to something I find much sweeter—World Showcase.

The World Is Your Oyster

Guest: You sell Swedish fish in Norway?
Cast Member: Yes, and they're made in Canada!

—Conversation overheard at Norway pavilion, Epcot, 2011

As mentioned above, I find the second sector of Epcot, World Showcase, to be infinitely more satisfying than Future World. There are all kinds of food and beverages, charming nooks and crannies of different "regional" architecture to explore, and waterway promenades throughout. With the relative ease of a nineteenth-century flaneur leisurely strolling about Paris, Epcot visitors can partake of many pleasant delights selectively culled from the countries included here. Admittedly, World Showcase is much like a Whitman's Sampler of chocolates, with the sum total of its offerings representing only a small fraction of the world. These depictions are also limited by an emphasis on the consumable products of the given cultures (notably food and souvenirs), while their attendant political, economic, and religious issues are downplayed or ignored.[111] Nagging concerns over the consumption of national cultures are well founded here, yet it would be unfair to dismiss World Showcase so completely. While most of the cultural experiences available are second- or thirdhand, indigenous art and artifacts are on display, and the representations of architecture, dress, and customs accurately reflect cultural heritages though err on the side of quaint nostalgia. Most importantly, each pavilion is staffed by people from its respective country, increasing opportunities for curious visitors to have firsthand exchanges that transcend the ethnographic displays of the past.

Though World Showcase borrowed the format of nationally sponsored pavilions from the great fairs, it was also descended from Disney's 1950s film series "People and Places," which explored the cultures and histories of different countries and was intended for distribution to schools.[112] At a ceremony held in Disney World's Contemporary Resort in July 1975, dignitaries from around the world were invited to see Epcot's plan (then focused on World Showcase instead of Future World) in an attempt to entice countries to sign on for a pavilion, which required a minimum ten-year lease and payment of design, construction, and employee housing costs.[113] World Showcase's initial scheme included a high-rise Observation Tower presiding over the Courtyard of Nations, girdled by two gigantic semicircular structures housing thirty national pavilions. Each pavilion was projected to have a Disney-designed ride and equal street frontage to alleviate visual competition (but could extend as far back as the sponsor wanted), as opposed to the current-day pastiche of individual waterfront exhibitions that vie for our attention. Today, represented nations are immediately recognizable through indigenous architectural forms, but the pavilions do not really blend in a "harmonious" and "seamless" manner; rather, a cacophony of the senses ensues as we can often see, hear, and smell the offerings of one country while still visiting its neighbor. We are not enclosed in a single vast space, but meander outdoors from pavilion to pavilion, which makes for, according to the Imagineers, "a fun and unique way for guests to visit eleven countries in one day."[114]

Securing World Showcase sponsors was challenging; Disney wanted to charge $25 million for a ten-year pavilion license (as opposed to the single-year commitment of most World's Fairs), and the number of participating countries was scaled down.[115] Plans for a television series promoting Epcot, as the *Disneyland* program had promoted the first park, fell through.[116] Yet Epcot was the largest, most expensive private real estate project undertaken anywhere when its construction began in October 1979. Built for $1.2 billion—triple its original estimated cost—the Disney Company accrued substantial debt and spent heavily to construct Epcot.[117] Today eleven countries are represented: Mexico, Norway, China, Germany, Italy, the United States, Japan, Morocco, France, the United Kingdom, and Canada (the order in which they are encountered, proceeding clockwise around the lagoon entering from Future World). Although there were hopes for five new pavilions within the first three years of operation, no new pavilion has been added since Norway's in May 1988 (Morocco was the only other addition to the original lineup, joining World Showcase in September 1984). A Russian pavilion with onion domes and a Switzerland pavilion with a rollercoaster were proposed, but both lacked sufficient sponsorship to be realized. Plans for Denmark, Spain, and Israel to be represented were also aborted. Reportedly, India (1986), Turkey (1988), and South Korea (2002) approached Disney about inclusion in World Showcase, but each was turned away.[118] The company did temporarily expand international representation with Millennium Village, which hosted exhibitions of countries not already in the Showcase (such as Chile and Saudi Arabia) for a fifteen-month period to celebrate the millennium.

In his Disney-sanctioned discussion of World Showcase, Richard Beard describes "a permanent community of nations whose pavilions stand side by side in exemplary amity" as "good neighbors to one another." The supposed result is "an authentic visual experience of each land," after which "you feel that you have really 'been there.'" He maintains that Epcot employees as well as visitors benefit from the park, describing workers as "favored guests" in a fellowship program that is "certain to enrich their outlook." Beard also implies that the landmarks reproduced here are as satisfying as the actual ones, noting that visitors "will be able to photograph many of the world's famous places without leaving Florida."[119] In truth, World Showcase offers just a modest sample of international cultures, as so few countries are represented. It draws upon the traditions of the fair's midway, where the "character" of other cultures was adjusted to bourgeois tastes in "aseptic, cleaned-up versions."[120] While designing Epcot, Imagineers toured participating Showcase countries to study their history and culture, basing their pavilions on recognizable landmarks.

Each pavilion offers "local" architecture, restaurants, and shops; some also include attractions such as boats rides (Mexico and Norway), panoramic films (France), or Circle-Vision 360-degree theaters (China and Canada). The use of film is directly indebted to World's Fairs, where governments and industries promoted their agendas in optimistic movies. Even Walt produced a Circle-Vision film for the U.S. pavilion at the 1958 World's Fair in Brussels.[121] World Showcase also adapts the forms and functions of fair architecture. The mock villages and streets that crowded midways were translated into permanent exhibitions at Epcot. A building can offer an instant and seemingly accurate impression of the nation represented while also fueling cultural myths in a fairytale-like conception of "others." This dichotomy presents an exhibiting dilemma for countries wishing to project a contemporary face without compromising their cultural heritage. More often than not at the fairs, highly stylized adaptations were favored over exact replicas, and building types with specific functions were modified for other uses. As Zeynep Celik observes, "what was considered typical, representative, and, ultimately, timeless" became "frozen in an ambiguous and distant past," implying that certain countries were incapable of evolution, architectural or otherwise.[122] Yet, national pavilions were never about architecture as much as representing cultural differences and providing immersive experiences.[123]

At World Showcase a smattering of regional architectural styles rub shoulders with each other as they never could in the outside world, which makes it especially fun to be there.[124] Mexico's "Aztec-inspired" pyramid (which features a surreal repetition of the same form inside itself) directly abuts Norway's cobbled village square and a castle modeled after Akershus, a fourteenth-century fortress in Oslo's Harbor. On Norway's other side is China's pavilion with its meticulous replica of Beijing's Temple of Heaven. Next there is the brief distraction of an outpost featuring African woodcarvers and their souvenir wares (the site seems to be ever waiting for the proposed African Nations pavilion, unlikely to be constructed given the leading representation of Africa at Animal Kingdom).[125] Guests then encounter Germany's steeples and turrets, based on the medieval Eltz Castle on the Moselle River.[126] Next is Italy, where replicas of Venice's campanile of St. Mark's and the Doge's Palace are "in reverse position," displayed alongside a re-creation of the Trevi Fountain in Rome. Not surprisingly, the U.S. pavilion is at the center of the Showcase's semicircular plan, as was typical for host countries at the World's Fairs. Ironically, the "typical" American architecture used to symbolize the country's progressiveness and independence is Georgian, based on a colonial past strongly derivative of

England.[127] Although this style was chosen to blend with the other pavilions, it is vastly different from the modernist, two-story structure originally designed to represent the United States. At first the inclusion and placement of the American pavilion was questioned, fearing it would be received as "arrogant" and "aloof." "Finally," Jeff Kurtti asserts, "the Imagineers decided to celebrate the very spirit that could produce a project like EPCOT Center." The American Adventure—the longest show in Epcot at thirty-five minutes—combines Audio-Animatronics and film to summarize American history. It is hosted by figures of Mark Twain and Benjamin Franklin, selected, respectively, for their "circumspect outlook and wry humor" and "cheery gifts of insight and invention."[128] Of course, one questions how much and whose history is communicated (both to Americans and foreigners) in Disney's deftly edited presentation. The company has made changes to the attraction for the sake of accuracy and political correctness, reflecting the contemporary shift toward a new social history. Now the American Adventure includes references to the tragic losses of the Civil War and 9/11 and cites the Great Depression and AIDS as struggles past and present. Frederick Douglass reminds us of slavery's legacy, Chief Joseph attests to genocide, and Susan B. Anthony represents women's suffrage efforts.[129] Yet collective social movements, political protests, and the rise of labor unions are neglected. The United States is conceived as a land of individual "dreamers and doers" who overcome great difficulties in the pursuit of progress. The show ends with Twain and Franklin atop the Statue of Liberty, foreseeing a wonderful future in which our most pressing problem will be to avoid the perils of plentitude. Wallace asserts: "Forced to confront a changed American popular historical consciousness and to incorporate the work of radical scholars, [Disney] opts for damage control."[130]

Continuing the world tour, one next finds Japan, marked by a *torri* gate modeled on the Itsukushima Shrine in Hiroshima's bay—a curious choice given the United States' atomic bombing of that city. There is also a pagoda adapted from the seventh-century Horyuji Shrine at Nara, a massive Mitsukoshi department store, and Japanese gardens (a large show or ride was also initially planned but never built).[131] Japan's neighbor, the Morocco pavilion, was scheduled to debut with the others in 1982 but did not open until September 1984. The pavilion is divided, as are Moroccan cities, into "old" and "new" sections. Replicas include the Koutoubia minaret of Marrakesh, the Nejjarine Fountain, the Bab Boujouloud gate in Fez, and the minaret at Chella. Concerned for authenticity, Disney brought in Moroccan *maalems* (artisans) to work on the elaborate mosaics. After Morocco comes France's pavilion, its scaled-down Eiffel Tower and mansard roofs evoking Paris, especially as planned by Baron Georges-Eugene Haussmann. The no longer extant Les Halles market is reconstructed so that it exists "only in memory and at World Showcase." After passing the International Gateway (connecting Epcot resorts with the park), the United Kingdom looms ahead. Here, mock Elizabethan, Tudor, Victorian, Yorkshire, and Regency buildings from the sixteenth through the nineteenth centuries coexist. The tour ends in Canada, where the French Gothic–inspired Hotel du Canada, patterned after Ottawa's Château Laurier, meets the rugged charm of the northwest coast. Like the fairs before it, World Showcase makes other cultures consumable, demonstrating that they "continue to live" while simultaneously relegating them to apolitical positions.[132] As Guests enter each new pavilion they are greeted as if they are in the country itself: "Welcome to China!" or "Welcome to Morocco!" English-speaking employees from the host country, meant to legitimize the respective cultural exhibitions, staff each pavilion.[133] Though architecture may be replicated, food and drink made palatable to American taste buds, and art taken out of context, the people are real, providing a "visible and tangible connection" to the country presented.[134] In essence the employees are on display, too, although I have thankfully never seen visitors imbue their interactions with the ethnological "inquiry" that pervaded the fairs.

Like a World's Fair, the Showcase presents cultural fragments that come to stand for their wholes, which in actuality can never be encapsulated. Surely these cultural representations reach broad audiences that might not have opportunities to visit all of the simulated places, but does World Showcase feed the inclination to experience other cultures, or kill it? Is the Epcot visitor satisfied enough with a mini Grand Tour that a trip to France would be redundant, a journey to Japan passé? Of course, a trip to either of these countries—or any place for that matter—would not be superfluous just because one has been to Disney World. Epcot presents a limited international sampling that highlights notable features, characteristic architecture, and famous sites. The pavilions only hint at the range of pleasures and possibilities available out in the world, offering a summary of potential life experiences compressed into a one-and-a-third-mile jaunt around the lagoon.[135]

Walt was concerned that his visitors not get tired or lost unless they wanted to, so his parks offer manageable scale and selectively edited activities. This approach is distinct from the encyclopedic evolution of World's Fairs—ever larger and more comprehensive.[136] At Epcot the sights, smells, and sounds of otherness are neatly adapted for theme park audiences and mostly frozen in the past, where, conveniently, they cannot become antiquated like the visionary prospects of Future World. Thus Germany is represented as a "rowdy" biergarten tended by lederhosen-wearing staff, and Mexico is a perpetual shopping bazaar. Here visitors remain aware of their existence in present-day Florida, despite—or more accurately, in contrast to—World Showcase's enveloping framework of international clothing, architecture, cuisine, and Cast Members. Ultimately, these elements never fully transcend their realities as costume, replicas, theme park food, and Disney employees. Within Epcot's inscribed borders, the countries represented undergo more cultural change than do their visitors. Here the challenges of diversity are softened so that the global village becomes a less scary and ever more hospitable place. Disney Guests make few adjustments to other cultures: in fact, these are adjusted to our preferences and pocketbooks. There are no language or currency barriers at Epcot, where complex international relationships or any real cultural frictions (between the countries or between visitors and employees) are mollified. But it is unfair to fault Disney alone for potentially deflating the impact of travel, especially if the eleven countries are content to represent themselves through shops and restaurants. If we complain that World Showcase is no more than a global marketplace, then the nations included here must share some of the blame.

Brian Wallis reminds us of "the manufactured nature of national identity and the extent to which that identity is constructed through cultural representations." Fairs and cultural festivals have many functions, including diplomacy and public relations, through which countries present themselves as alluring business partners and tourist destinations. National culture is a social construction, dependent upon not only contemporary circumstances but also the images, rituals, and artforms most consistently used to signify a given country. The challenge is to reconcile static "essence" with a nation's "actual history of dynamic change." This is certainly true at Epcot, where heritage and culture are condensed: countries are represented by allegedly characteristic—and frequently stereotypical—imagery and customs, while politics, factionism, and controversy are neatly pruned out.[137] The remaining sum is then viewed through Disney's filter. At times the national pavilions do address current struggles, such as environmental issues in China's Circle-Vision film, but these presentations always end on a reassuring note, affirming that the nation has its problems under control as it looks toward a bright future. Even the footage of a blatantly and bitterly political site, Tiananmen Square, was only accompanied by an oblique reference to its loaded history as the voice-over proclaims, "To stand here is to stand at the heart of China."

The cultural gawking that takes place at Epcot is rooted in the tradition of the *Kunst-* or *Wunderkammer* (art or wonder cabinet), literally a cabinet of curiosities. Dating back to the sixteenth century and extending into the nineteenth, when these essentially evolved into massive World's Fair exhibits, such cabinets presented strange juxtapositions of odd and beautiful objects, ranging from artworks to scientific items and natural wonders. Although most cabinets began as private collections, some were later made accessible to the public, either on a limited basis or to those willing to pay to gaze at such marvels. The grander and more bizarre the collection, the more distinct and even noble became its collector's reputation. World Showcase employs a similar methodology, presenting a piecemeal collage of different objects, places, and people that we pay to see. The more exotic these seem, despite being framed in an Americanized context, the more delight and wonder they can elicit. A form of cultural caricature ensues that meshes with visitors' expectations, implying that we go to places like Epcot "not to test the image by the reality, but to test the reality by the image." Critics still fret that we are unable or unwilling to distinguish between staged and "authentic" cultural practices, but conceptions of the "authentic" are not fixed and actually grow and change through accreted experiences.[138] Although fragmented presentations of world cultures detached from their social, economic, and political contexts are obviously not fully representative, I believe they can offer unique and rich possibilities: the visitor who is awestruck by Disney's wonders is having an authentic encounter, even amid cultural simulations. The use of fragmented display to represent a larger culture or context is neither a new practice nor exclusive to theme parks and fairs. Art and science museums have exhibited items and represented cultures in displaced contexts for centuries. Such displays are based on availability and quality, not exhaustive, encyclopedic quantity. "It was not the specific geographical provenance of the artefact which was important," Peter Mason argues, "but its capacity as a singular object to partake in the world of *exotica* in general."[139]

Epcot's subtle—and not-so-subtle—colonial imperialist messages were preceded by those of the Magic Kingdom, where fragmented representations evoke different historical epochs and geographical regions. At the Magic Kingdom the past is conquered, nature is tamed, other cultures are entertainment, and the future is always promising. Disney's calculated depiction of U.S. history privileges white Euro-American males while neutralizing racial unrest and gender inequities and rendering social conflicts as temporary setbacks. Similarly, World Showcase makes the "other" seem more familiar and the "exotic" palatable to middle American tastes.[140] Such reductive cultural depictions, however, are not exclusive to the United States or Disney, as proved by the many foreign tourists, or even by critics, who perceive Disney World as a shorthand representation of American society. The World's Fairs were products of similar cultural opportunism. The economic growth and political sway they celebrated sprang directly from capitalist and colonial imperialist ideologies. The natural resources and cheap (even slave) labor plentiful in non-Western countries called for their inclusion in a unified, if not equal, emerging global economy. Although the fairs were lionized as showcases for architectural wonders and the newest technology, they were also visible demonstrations of colonial dominance and desire. World's Fairs sought to overwhelm and entertain, smoothing over the rough patches that come with cultural difference. The political prestige and economic clout of a privileged elite (including the fair organizers) was consolidated and perpetuated at the fair. Thus the fair was fettered by paradox: promoted as peaceful display of and between different cultures to promote international cooperation, it often reinforced stratified power relationships. It also seemed to reaffirm colonial ideology: that certain people (i.e., Western and white) were racially, technically, scientifically, physically, intellectually, politically, economically, and morally—thus evolutionarily—superior to others (i.e., non-Western and non-white). In the end, the fair never completely transcended its reality as a social exchange between uneven partners. Cultural anxieties were produced and relieved at the fair, and cultural prejudices were "scientifically" justified there.[141] Yet the fairs also liberated some minds and challenged some preconceptions, too.

Despite the great fanfare with which Epcot opened, it quickly sunk into an attendance slump by 1983 (and as mentioned previously, has lost a considerable amount of corporate sponsorship since the 1990s). Business analyst John Taylor suggests its theme may have been at fault—Epcot was just another fair "at a time when the country was glutted with such expositions," including "the disastrous 1981 fair in Knoxville."[142] Taylor's observation prompts several questions: Is the World's Fair still a valid medium of international expression, especially given the widespread use of media to disseminate information? Have the scientific institutions, cultural museums, and theme parks spawned by the great fairs supplanted the functions of their parentage? Is there a sustained interest in global competition, and if so, is this better satisfied by other entities like the Olympics?[143] The 1893 fair was conceived amid economic panic yet opened as scheduled and was hugely successful. Of course, Chicago's fair was a temporary event, whereas Epcot offers a permanent manifestation of the World's Fair tradition.

Furthermore, the desire for a microcosm of the world has shifted. During the time of the great World's Fairs, travel was still difficult and expensive, making virtual travel a popular and exciting alternative.[144]

Analyzing the 1904 fair, Eric Breitbart proposed that "few visitors went . . . for a serious educational experience . . . and the sensory overload probably diluted many of the messages intended by the organizers." He concluded its lasting effect was to introduce the public to a world of simulated experience, in which objects and even people are offered for consumption.[145] While the educational endeavors of the World's Fairs were at times, no doubt, compromised, these cannot be dismissed altogether. Fairgoers were indeed amazed, amused, and distracted, but as Helen Harrison proposed, many were also deeply affected by the expositions. At the fair lives were changed.[146] Likewise, we should remember that Walt approached Epcot not only as a business venture, but also as a teaching opportunity. For some Guests, Epcot will be their first taste of a new technology or another culture. World Showcase has many ideological weaknesses, but focusing solely on these blinds us to its strengths: a message of respect for cultures other than one's own; the opportunity to meet people from other places, even if in a too-narrow context; and exposure to the customs and heritage of other countries that can nudge us out of comfort zones. A trip to Epcot could stimulate desire to become a technologically savvy citizen of the world, who travels and experiences more firsthand. It would probably be inaccurate to proclaim that most visitors come to Epcot to broaden their intellectual and cultural horizons. But it would also be wrong to assume that none of them have transformative experiences while there: I know this because I have. World Showcase is more than an international diorama, it is a real place where people from around the globe come together and interact, regardless of the limitations implicit in this kind of setting. The inscription of Epcot's dedication plaque reads like a saccharine platitude, but for some Guests it surely rings true: "To all who come to this place of Joy, Hope and Friendship, Welcome. EPCOT is inspired by Walt Disney's creative vision. Here, human achievements are celebrated through imagination, wonders of enterprise and concepts of a future that promises new and exciting benefits for all. May EPCOT Center entertain, inform and inspire, and above all, may it instill a new sense of belief and pride in man's ability to shape a world that offers hope to people everywhere."

conclusion ▶ Manifest Disney?

Like . . . Coca-Cola, Mickey Mouse has achieved total market penetration. When Mickey Mouse wiggles his ears, the world squeaks.

—Mark Derr, *Some Kind of Paradise*

It's not like just opening an office and selling a product. We have a castle.

—Don Robinson, managing director of Hong Kong Disneyland, 2005

I think by this time my staff, my young group of executives and everyone else are convinced that Walt is right. The quality will out. And so I think they're going to stay with that policy because it's proved that it's a good business policy. Give the people everything you can give them. Keep the place as clean as you can keep it. Keep it friendly, you know. Make it a real fun place to be. I think they're convinced and I think they'll hang on . . . if . . . as you say . . . well, after [Walt] Disney."

—Walt Disney, *Disneyland: Inside Story*

Throughout history, people have sated their desires for worship, respite, diversion, enlightenment, and social interaction in built environments. Places have been constructed to mark sites of consecration, tweak nature to fit man's designs, and provide temporary centers for gathering and learning or more permanent cities for living. Despite Disney World's connections to the pervasive human needs for community, heightened awareness of life's pleasures, and states of existence enhanced beyond survival and routine, critics continue to attack it as a setting for unreal and inconsequential encounters. Though Disney World certainly offers extraordinary levels of fantasy theming, I hope this book emphasizes how it is part of the well-established traditions of our built environment that nurture social life, or as Douglas Brode describes it, "a distillation of the human condition" to meet "the demands of an enlightened public."[1] Disney World intensifies encounters through its use of simulations, but Guests are cognizant of these, partaking in a hybrid of lived and simulated experiences that is by no means an "unreal" one.

Terence Young notes an increased use of the term "Disneyfication," which has come to broadly define any landscape developed to communicate with multiple audiences, particularly to stimulate consumption.[2] But as we know, Disney World is still a unique place, and Walt worked hard to ensure its preservation before he died. To stabilize the Florida resort's future, his company established the Reedy Creek Improvement District, a self-governing entity functioning like "The Vatican with Mouse Ears."[3] In subsequent decades Disney's territory and power expanded elsewhere, especially via its parks in Japan, France, and China. The company's international impact is unquestionable. Eight of Disney's eleven theme parks are among the ten most visited across the globe. Disney is ranked the number one entertainment corporation in the world, enjoying a massive base of not only regular customers but also devoted fans, supporting the contention that it has "raised our expectations on how the built environment can meet the public need."[4] Yet the company is not an infallible or impenetrable force, and Disney World is not impervious to everyday mishaps or economic decline. What are the effects of the widespread dissemination of Disney's merchandise and philosophy and of their associated benefits and difficulties? Is Disney really omnipotent? Has its worldwide embrace simply spread good cheer and modeled for other businesses ways to sell products and experiences in a competitively unpredictable and dynamic international marketplace?[5] Or is there something more ominous, or at least dubious, in the company's global expansions—a sort of Manifest Disney? To think productively about such questions—although not necessarily answer them definitively—it is helpful to turn to Disney World and see how the place has changed over time. Thus this conclusion considers further the company's development into and current existence as a powerful (though certainly not evil) multinational corporation, and ends by looking at how Disney World has surprisingly evolved, as they say, after Walt.

Can Disney Take Over the World?

> We all remember seeing . . . those slick futuristic drawings saying what the future
> of the American city was going to be—gleaming buildings, fast monorails, people
> in one place, cars in another. Well, this is the future and none of it has happened.
> Nobody has done it but Disney.
>
> —David Brinkley, 1972 news broadcast

Before his death, Walt Disney campaigned for the designation of his Florida property, straddling Orange and Osceola Counties, as its own improvement district (including the creation of two municipalities, Bay Lake and Lake Buena Vista). In 1965, Governor Haydon Burns shepherded a bill establishing this as the Reedy Creek Improvement District (RCID, named for a creek running through the property), signed into law on 12 May 1967 by the Florida State Legislature, then led by Governor Claude Kirk Jr. These politicians were enticed to act on Disney's behalf by $6.5 billion of economic benefits Florida was projected to reap in Disney World's first ten years alone. Despite assertions that Reedy Creek is independent from Disney, the company is its major landowner and power base. The district's voting public is a narrow sector of Disney employees who in turn elect its supervisory board. Reedy Creek is, in effect, Florida's sixty-eighth county: it levies its own taxes, funds its utilities, provides stand-by power plants for its property, organizes its security, and develops and enforces its building, zoning, and environmental codes (often stricter than most municipalities). The District even has permission to build its own airport and a nuclear reactor (both yet unrealized). Disney manages RCID's planning, local variances, sewage systems, waste collection, flood and pest control, roads, public transportation, and fire and security forces, though it pays taxes to Orange and Osceola Counties for police, education, and welfare services. As Governor Kirk later admitted, Reedy Creek "was in truth, a fiefdom."[6] The RCID has, quite literally, "more powers than most elected governments in the United States," and Disney holds them in perpetuity.[7] Eisner biographer Joe Flower concludes: "It was, to say the least, an unusual arrangement."[8]

Disney did benefit Florida: it created a thriving tourist industry, provides employment, and is the largest taxpayer in the state ($46 million annually), paying property taxes and bringing in the highest sales-tax revenues.[9] Reedy Creek allowed Disney to enact high-concept planning without the approval of state agencies; in return, Florida taxpayers did not directly contribute to its construction (nor were federal tax dollars spent here). But the subsequent growth and population boom brought by Disney World has strained Floridian highways, drainage and sewage facilities, and the infrastructures and services of surrounding counties, which usually pay for such improvements while Disney remains exempt from impact fees. The tourist economy Disney fostered brings jobs but often keeps wages low or stagnant. The state's credit on tax-free development bonds allowed a private company to build its own infrastructure and create an autonomous municipality, insulated physically and administratively from the outside world—designed, constructed, and maintained entirely by Disney. According to Richard Foglesong, the people of Florida do not hate Disney World: it is "more like a simmering resentment."[10] In retrospect, Orange and Osceola County public officials often lament Reedy Creek's creation and the limitations it placed on their ability to manage further growth. As onetime Orange County commissioner Paul Pickett proclaimed: "You don't make Cinderella do anything. Down here you are talking about a deity."[11]

Unlike other companies seeking tax incentives to lure them to particular locations, Disney asked for less (road and infrastructure enhancements leading to its property) but took much more (rebuffing Florida's government in favor of its own). Disney's detractors rightly contend that Florida officials approved the RCID because Disney proposed to build a city with permanent residents rather than a resort with transients (Cast Members and Guests), which needed flexible planning. The company assured Florida legislators it would maintain high standards but needed the liberty to experiment, explaining that its "model city required a model government, free of the bureaucratic red tape that normally strangled innovation." Today critics would argue that Disney World remains an ambiguous, "autonomous political settlement" without the settlers; as Jeremiah Sullivan summarizes it, "strictly speaking Disney World shouldn't exist." The persistent question is: To what extent did Walt knowingly deceive Florida's legislature? Those who believe he blatantly did so emphasize the many press conferences and hearings about Reedy Creek's creation, at which Walt and his cohorts repeatedly verified that Epcot would have permanent residents. Yet the "Helliwell memo," drafted by Paul Helliwell (a Florida lawyer hired by Disney), indicates otherwise. Throughout the memo, found in Walt's desk after he died, Disney had crossed out all mentions of "permanent residents" and replaced these with "temporary residents/tourists." At one point the document stated that Disney's private government would need popularly elected officials in order to plan and zone in the district, to which Walt simply replied, in large red letters, "NO."[12] As discussed in chapter 5, Walt initially wanted people to really live at Epcot. But his need to determine practically everything that would go on there eventually led to altering his scheme for permanent residency to temporary extended stays (no more than nine months).[13] Perhaps Walt's biggest fault here was being an unrelenting control freak, willing to compromise too much of his original vision for a "utopian monarchy."[14] We may never know the full extent to which Walt purposely engaged in deception, but at the very least, he bent the truth in his negotiations with Florida officials. We should remember, however, that the legislation approving the RICD was passed after Walt's death, an event marked by Governor Kirk's witty remark to Roy: "Mr. Disney, I've studied the Reedy Creek Improvement District. It's very comprehensive. I noticed only one omission. You made no provision for the crown."[15] Yet this kingdom in Florida was not enough—the Disney Company wanted more.

Numerous analysts have studied how exported Disney culture functions as a form of globalization. John Rennie Short defines "globalization" as "the increasing tendency for the world to be a single network of flows of money, ideas, people and things," enabled by international distribution practices.[16] To this we can add Alan Bryman's definition of "Disneyization" as "the process by which *the principles* of the Disney theme parks are coming to dominate more and more sectors of American society as well as the rest of the world." According to Bryman, these principles are theming; de-differentiated or hybrid consumption, as a breakdown of distinctions between different types of consuming; mass merchandizing; and emotional or performative labor consisting of scripted interactions. Disney certainly did not invent all of these tactics, though the company's high profile has helped popularize and propagate them.[17] While a product of American sensibilities, the Disney park formula has been successfully adapted in other countries. Perhaps the best example is Tokyo Disneyland, begun in 1978 when the Keisei Electric Railway Company approached Disney to develop less than five hundred acres of Tokyo's suburbs as a theme park. Disney executives had their doubts: the climate could be cold and rainy; there was a language barrier, as well as significant cultural differences; and Disney's finances were overextended by Epcot. But eventually it was agreed that the Oriental Land Company would build (at a cost of 150 billion yen), own, and operate the park, while Disney would design and license it, receiving a percentage of admission revenues and concessions sales.[18] It seems Disney underestimated the phenomenal success of Tokyo Disneyland, which opened on 15 April 1983 and has received 10 million visitors annually since then. (The Urayasu suburb also experienced the most rapid appreciation of land values in Japan, in which Disney had no share.) Contrary to prevailing arguments, several critics assert that the park does not represent the one-way imposition of Western consumer culture on a subordinate Eastern receptor. The Japanese are also cultural imperialists here, playing upon Disney's "metanarrative" and re-encoding it for their own purposes. Aviad Raz notes how the park was "carefully edited and modified to cater to Japanese consumerist and cultural predilections," contending that Disney's culture was actively appropriated by the Japanese.[19] Mary Yoko Brannen concurs, maintaining that "it is the Japanese, not the Americans, who have defined Tokyo Disneyland. That is to say, it is the *importation* of the artifact rather than its *exportation* that begs to be analyzed." From the beginning, developers rejected Disney's proposed Japan-themed attractions, demanding a close "copy" of Disneyland. Such a copy offers a firsthand comparison of the two cultures, in which Japan's identity is not subsumed, but its sense of "cultural uniqueness and superiority" is preserved.[20]

The planning of Disneyland Paris (originally named Euro Disney) was more complex than the situation in Tokyo. The site of Marne-la-Vallée (about twenty miles east of Paris) appears a baffling choice for Disney's European park given the differing cultural attitudes of France and the United States and the fact that several other countries (Spain, Portugal, Italy, and England) wished to host it. But Disney did learn from its mistake of underestimating profitability and escalating land values as it had in Japan. In France the theme park was built first, and then nearly eight square miles of land, all designed and controlled by Disney, were carefully developed. A fifth the size of Paris, the project was budgeted at over $4 billion for the construction of several theme parks, commercial and office space, thousands of hotel rooms, and even houses, condominiums, and time-share apartments. Trains drop visitors right across the street from the park's entrance. The French made several substantial concessions to get the park, which probably motivated Disney to build there, a decision that might seem ill advised in retrospect.[21] Euro Disney opened on 12 April 1992; a small band of protestors and two bombings the night before foretold of coming tensions. Although the park has rebounded, it had been as much as $3.57 billion in debt, and a $2 billion restructuring plan had to be implemented to save it.[22] From its initial stages European adaptations were built into the scheme, including designing Sleeping Beauty's Castle to recall a French château. But many Europeans worried the park was a "cultural Chernobyl," the harbinger of a homogenizing invasion of American fantasy that threatened their precious traditions. Having visited the park just a few months after it opened and then again in 2012, I can attest to the changes there over the past twenty years. On the first visit the park felt unfinished, as if there was not enough to do. It was also confusing to orient oneself in its space, probably because things seemed incomplete, making passage from one themed land to the next unclear. The earliest Guests were openly disgruntled by the parameters the company had set for their experiences at Euro Disney. They complained about so many things: having to stand in such long lines, the high prices of the merchandise, the lack of wine to have with their meals. Unlike the Japanese, who wished for their Disneyland to replicate the American models as closely as possible, the French evidently wanted Disney to accommodate them in a more robust manner. And Disney has, as I witnessed during my most recent visit. Disneyland Paris is now home to two theme parks, Disneyland (the first park) and Walt Disney Studios (similar to Disney's Hollywood Studios in Florida). Although neither is as expansive in its offerings as those at Disney World, there is certainly more to do. I also found it easier to navigate the plan of the French Disneyland, although this still has more twists and turns and the attractions are spread further apart than at the Magic Kingdom (a comparison of the maps for each place confirms these impressions). The French Guests were still not happy about the queues, but they seemed to enjoy the wine that was now abundantly available. George Ritzer once commented, "for a while it seemed unlikely that Euro Disney would survive the French."[23] While a few frictions may persist, Disneyland Paris and the French have figured out how to cohabit better.

Obviously, the company's colonial sweep is not imminent, despite what detractors claim. The construction of additional theme parks, however, suggests that Disney's expansionist desire is not easily subdued. On 8 February 2001, Disney's California Adventure was added to the Anaheim site, at a cost of $1.4 billion, in the hopes of encouraging Guests to make longer visits (trips to Disney World averaged seven days, while those to Disneyland were only two days, with Guests there also spending less on lodging and meals).[24] DisneySea, next to Tokyo Disneyland, opened on 4 September 2001. In 2002 Walt Disney Studios (see above) joined the Disneyland Paris Resort. Hong Kong Disneyland, contained in just 311 acres, premiered on 12 September 2005. Given that Shanghai Disney Resort is slated to open next, in late 2015, it is instructive to consider how Hong Kong Disneyland has combined Chinese and Western cultures. The Hong Kong park was built to capitalize on a market primed for Disney products but largely untapped, and tainted by media piracy. Though much of it looks like its

American counterparts, Hong Kong Disneyland features Chinese architectural prototypes ranging from a tea shop to a temple. The restaurants cater to Chinese palates, and a feng shui master consulted on the placement of elements—including cash registers—throughout the park. A desire to take part in global culture (and that of the United States in particular) is expected to lure Chinese visitors. As one of its chief Imagineers, Tom Morris, describes the park, "It's turn of the century America, with a Disney overlay, with a Chinese overlay."[25] But instead of being upset by this pastiche, Guests usually embrace its eclectic richness. Some supporters contend that Hong Kong Disneyland (unintentionally) supplies "an alternative, creative counterforce" to the Chinese government's repressive control, presenting a freer view of culture than the nationalist agenda usually allows.[26] Andrew Lainsbury, a former Disneyland Paris employee, is especially optimistic about the company's foreign ventures. He appreciates how the "permeability of national borders" becomes "delightfully complex" at the parks and is hopeful that Disney will promote internationally sensitive "cultural globalism" rather than mere "cultural homogenization."[27]

Sharon Zukin suggests that Walt's American parks succeeded because he was able to capitalize upon changes wrought in postwar culture: the advent of television, the increase in domestic consumption, and the baby boom.[28] Certainly, the Cold War period must have been a heady time for Walt. His vision of a strong, virtuous America seemed collectively shared and consecrated. The theme parks were products of this postwar state of mind: celebrations of American ingenuity, productivity, private industry, optimism, and prosperity. Yet while this noble image of the United States was being galvanized, a global culture was simultaneously emerging. The Cold War era's advanced electronic communications diffused geopolitical and intellectual borders as well as the parameters of time and space. Many believed a global village, in which electronic media could create a sense of empathetic wholeness, would safeguard cultural difference and individual determinism.[29] While this is true, we also know that capitalism's free marketplace can give rise to concentrated entrenchments of power, compromising diversity while shaping "choice" to serve corporate needs. Rather than advancing collective interests, transnational corporations might be tempted to ensure their own livelihoods, enabled by media promotion of their products.[30] In the bleakest picture of capitalism, private corporations like Disney become totalizing forces employing "corporate paternalism and technocratic solutions to social problems" that unburden citizens of their rights.[31]

The West, especially the United States, is a ready target for critics predicting an economically and culturally homogenized world.[32] Surely this concern gains credence from Westerners' long history of imperialist politics and colonial expansion. As a major multinational conglomerate, the Disney Company is a highly influential player—though not the sole one—in an increasingly globalized consumer culture. But many cultural imperialist arguments against Disney tend to exaggerate the company's power and simplify its functions, fearing the entire planet is in danger of becoming "Disneyfied." The most egregious of these attacks make sweeping proclamations with little concern for historical accuracy or critical responsibility (such as Edward Ball's indiscriminate linking of Nazism with Disney: "To be in the crowds at Disneyland is to have a sense of what Joseph Goebbels meant when he said that 'the finest art is sculpting with the masses.'")[33] Although globalization can endanger local cultures' particularities, the threat of total homogenization is implausible. The survival instincts of local cultures—along with the impulse toward individualized decision making—cannot be underestimated. As more cultures are brought into the global fold, each has the opportunity to change the others with which it comes in contact. At its worst, globalization oppressively neutralizes diversity, but at its best it can increase interconnectivity, reveal contradictions, give rise to new cultures, or even allow people to "live between . . . and across cultures."[34] Cultural globalization can link people, places, and events around the world, allowing ideas, information, and values to be shared. And even when the same images and commodities are circulated internationally, they are interpreted and consumed differently. As posited by Short, "cultural globalization is not making us more alike, but both more alike and different at the same time."[35]

Furthermore, as Jonathan Weber points out, the "image of Disney—and of America in general—as an unstoppable cultural juggernaut is misleading. The truth is that selling American culture overseas is a tricky business" (case in point, Disneyland Paris). Disney and other U.S. corporations expanding business abroad are more invested in making money than in spreading American values. And despite its considerable efforts, only 20 percent of Disney's revenues come from foreign markets, indicating that fears of a "global monoculture" are exaggerated.[36] Yet skeptics still insist that the company wields too much cultural influence, complaining about its lack of sensitivity to multiculturalism, its ability to monopolize media, and its blurring of "the boundaries between public culture and commercial interests."[37] For example, the documentary film *Mickey Mouse Monopoly* charges that Disney's corporate agenda is hidden behind a "spectacle of in-nocence" as it perpetuates gender, racial, ethnic, and classist stereotypes.[38] Thankfully, some scholars offer compelling counterpoints to these standard criticisms, such as Douglas Brode, who proposes that Disney actually lam-poons and condemns bigotry and sexism in its works. He also advanced another unexpected argument: that Walt was not a conservative "sentimen-tal rightist" but laid the foundations for 1960s counterculture by promoting youthful rebellion against unjust authority and addressing environmental concerns before it was popular to do so.[39] Even Eric Avila, who remains wary of Disney's endeavors, acknowledges a broadening of the company's cultural content as audiences outgrew the themes and stereotypes of a post-war "culture of suburban whiteness." Moreover, Avila surmises that Walt's "business acumen and sensitivity to the changing moral climate . . . seem to imply his willingness to make such modifications in the midst of a rapidly changing world," reflected now in the company's openness to and inclusive-ness of formerly marginalized perspectives.[40]

Since Disney has worked hard to gain our trust and make us feel like we can relate to its values, it is less likely to escape social critique than "faceless" media conglomerates such as Viacom. That Disney's reputation is a good one, "relatively consistent and widely understood," makes it the perfect foil for naysayers who know they can attract attention by attack-ing the high-profile corporation. Detractors—ranging from the religious right railing against the immorality of Disney products to cultural critics complaining about Disney's "inauthentic" experiences—blame all kinds of problems on the company.[41] Carl Hiassen marvels at, but is unnerved by, Disney's ability to sustain customer fidelity and confidence: the company "is so good at being good that it manifests an evil; so uniformly efficient and courteous, so dependably clean and conscientious, so unfailingly *enter-taining* that it's unreal, and therefore an agent of pure wickedness." It seems the Southern Baptists, the largest Protestant denomination in the United States, agreed (though without Hiassen's sense of irony) and launched an unsuccessful boycott of Disney's businesses, including the ABC network, beginning in the mid-1990s. The embargo was spurred by same-sex partner benefits for Disney employees, "Gay Days" at the parks, and ABC programs such as *Ellen* (in which the star's lesbianism became a focus of the series). The Southern Baptists perceived these actions as attacks upon conserva-tive Christians and "family values," even suggesting that Disney had be-come a pagan, alternative religion competing for worshippers.[42] Pondering the boycott, Hiaasen reconsiders his position on Disney and determines:

"Given a choice between intolerant moralizers and unflinchingly ruthless profiteers, I'll have to stand with the Mouse every time."[43] He is right in that the company exists to make profits, and it would be senseless to ignore this fact. But I do not believe financial motivations negate Walt's more philanthropic ambitions: to teach us about history, human culture, technology, and the environment, even if these lessons are limited by Disney's restrictive view. Walt always asserted that his parks were more than business ventures: "We didn't go into it with just the idea of making money."[44]

Despite the company's seemingly untouchable status, Disney is actually vulnerable to economic downturns and ambitious competitors. In March 1984 corporate raider Saul Steinberg (with his Reliance Group) attempted a hostile takeover of Disney, buying up over 12 percent of its outstanding stock and intending to sell off the company piecemeal while retaining the U.S. theme parks. Although Disney executives and shareholders viewed Steinberg's overtures as nearly blasphemous, the company bought back the shares for a premium over-market price and paid an additional amount to cease the takeover. Steinberg walked away with $31 million in proceeds, while Disney spent almost $900 million and found its stock values dipping nearly a third.[45] Lacking the savvy to assuage Steinberg's attack, Disney's old guard was largely replaced in October 1984 by the team of Frank Wells (president and chief operating officer), Jeffrey Katzenberg (chairman of the film division), and Michael Eisner (chairman of the board and chief executive officer).[46] Walt's successor, Card Walker, was dedicated to high-quality entertainment, but his unwillingness to raise ticket prices, build additional hotels, or advertise the parks (for fear of overcrowding) left profits sagging. Eisner's team changed all that, successfully capitalizing on Disney's real estate holdings, marketable characters, and popular parks. Admission fees were raised, classic films re-released to cultivate new generations of consumers (and insulate the company if current offerings underperformed), and business ventures expanded. In 1986 the name was changed from Walt Disney Productions (which connoted film and television) to the Walt Disney Company (alluding to the full range of Disney's enterprises). Not everyone at Disney was an Eisner fan, but under his direction the company was revitalized and became a truly international business.[47] Yet Disney was to face tough economic times again. After 9/11 the Disney parks were deemed possible terrorist targets, which hurt visitorship and incited cost-cutting measures like reduced park hours and shuttered attractions. In 2004 another attempt at a hostile takeover occurred, this time from Comcast Corporation. Although this was fended off, Eisner found himself ousted by stockholders whom Roy E. Disney (who ironically lobbied for Eisner in 1984) had rallied.[48] Robert (Bob) Iger, already president of Disney by 2000, succeeded Eisner as its CEO in 2005 and is credited with having "recovered the 'pixie dust.'"[49] (He is both chairman and CEO as of this writing.) Iger's "pixie dust," however, has been generated by some less-than-magical practices: price hikes, outsourcing of jobs, and selling off real estate holdings.[50] In fact, Disney World itself is shrinking, that is, in land mass. Under Iger, plots of "excess" property on Disney World's fringes have been sold to residential developers, while additional "borderline acreage" is leased to outside hospitality and retail businesses,[51] reducing the company's landholdings in Florida to about twenty-five thousand acres.

In the end, the anxiety over Disneyfication engulfing our culture is both oversimplified and overstated. Consider New York's formerly seedy Times Square jammed with tourists and families after being "restored"—or as Hiaasen describes it, "deloused and revitalized"—by Disney. Although politicians vowed to clean up Times Square for years they seemed unable to do so, but Disney swiftly banished the XXX theaters and prostitutes. In 1994 Disney announced it would stage theatrical productions in the New Amsterdam Theatre it was renovating for approximately $38 million, about 75 percent of which was covered by low-interest loans from the city and state. While New York–based competitors regarded the "outsider" with "a combination of jealousy and fear," Disney hired Robert Stern to work on Times Square's renewal plan and consulted with city officials on which family-oriented businesses should be allowed to follow them into the area. Along with its theater, the company opened the World of Disney Store on Fifth Avenue (closed in 2009 and subsequently replaced by a flagship Disney Store on Broadway), offering a test market for Disney's urban audiences.[52] Such development certainly raises concerns about public space being privatized for profit, particularly as entertainment conglomerates increasingly involve themselves with urban planning.[53] Yet it would be unfair to say that Disney overtook Manhattan, especially given all of the high-profile companies that have also made themselves at home there. Manhattan does seem more homogeneous now than it did in years past, but the Starbucks chain, with an outpost on nearly every corner, feels more to blame than does the Mouse. Furthermore, despite its success at cleaning up Times Square, Disney remains cautious about the influence it can have in preexisting cities. As noted by Peter Rummell (a central figure in Celebration's development, see chapter 4), "the question in these urban environments really becomes, Is there a way you can have enough control? Because we are control freaks."[54] The company's first proposal for an entirely non-Disney urban project to restore Seattle Center (1985–89), which included charging admission fees, was turned down.[55] Architect Charles Moore swooned over the efficiency and participatory communality of Disney's parks, insisting that "the experience of being in" them "is a real one, and an immensely exciting one." But he also noted that to enjoy Disney's amenities "you have to pay for the public life."[56]

There are valuable lessons in urbanism to glean from Disney World. Richard Foglesong acknowledges that the establishment of the Reedy Creek Improvement District relied on the abuse of governmental powers but also Disney's creative genius. Although the model city of Epcot was never built, Disney World is, in effect, a working city with a comprehensive plan, massive workforce, facilities for shopping, dining, and entertainment, and a nightly population of more than one hundred thousand. The existence of the RCID prompts questions about the future of city planning and about the power balance between elected officials and private industry when deciding matters of public interest. Foglesong suggests that one way to interpret Reedy Creek is as a reformist approach to city governance. As capitalism (property and voting rights via individual ownership) and democracy (decision making by elected public officials) were both deemed "problematic" in their "fragmentation of effort," Disney proposed its own "solution . . . centralized administration—benign, paternalistic, based on expertise."[57] To my mind, RCID was business as usual for Disney: the company managed the situation—in this case, the creation and governance of a municipality—believing it could do so better than anyone else. The issue remains as to how comfortable individuals are with Disney's "solution." Disney World also offers lessons on coping with and in an increasingly complicated, globalized world. Aside from providing opportunities for people to interact with emergent technologies, it also nudges us to examine technology's role in our lives. J. P. Telotte describes Disney World as a "great technological marvel, massive machine," with attractions that can make technology "transparent" and even "suspect," reminding us of its potential for human benefit and liberation but also for exploitation and manipulation. Telotte proposes that Disney actually empowers us to tackle technology from points of greater awareness, noting that "technology is simply *technology's* everywhere" in the Disney parks, "and its signature . . . is not, as we might expect, erased to aid the fantasy, but writ surprisingly large."[58]

I find Telotte's analysis of technology at Disney heartening. While remaining mindful of globalization's pitfalls, I still have faith in people to recognize when our decisions are being constrained, our senses dulled, and our beliefs undermined—and to react accordingly. I do not concur with Mike Budd's assertion that "brand synergy" subsumes individual experience, or to clarify, that it has to.[59] Complicity with world markets is not a foregone conclusion, and we all share the responsibility to examine our own consumption patterns. We do not have to be passive receptors in the global village: we can be active participants, recontexualizing media's messages on individual bases. Public reception can never be fully controlled, especially in the case of Disney, when the numerous places where we buy and consume its products are often outside the company's reach. Transnational corporations like Disney cannot prosper without customers, and we decide who gets our business. Susan Davis has argued that in the first half of the twentieth century, entertainment conglomerates created "a nearly all-penetrating national and international mass culture" disseminated through products like film and music. In the second half of the century, this mass culture was brought into our homes via new technologies such as television. In the twenty-first century, she claims, the challenge is to weave together these collective and private spheres.[60] It is a challenge, I believe, that Disney is well positioned to take on, given its proven track record of sustaining worldwide appeal by pleasing Guests one at a time.

As the (Disney) World Turns

This will not be a sequel.

—Walt Disney, *Walt and the Promise of Progress City*

As emphasized throughout this book, the differences between Disneyland and Disney World extend beyond their respective home states, as indicated by Walt's retort above when asked about the future of Disney World. Disney*land* was just that: a relatively modest parcel of land devoted to Walt's first foray into the theme park business. By the time he embarked on Disney *World*, his sights were set on larger goals, and he needed a lot more property to pursue them. Building a park was no longer enough for Walt: he envisioned a city that would be a model for communities around the globe. After considering the names Disneyland East and Disneyland Florida, Walt decided to call his new resort Disney World. But his brother Roy insisted on clarifying the name: "Everybody knows the Ford car, but not everybody knows it was Henry Ford who started it all. It's going to be *Walt* Disney World, so people will always know that this was Walt's dream."[61]

Of course, that dream is not frozen in time (as Walt's body reputedly was upon his death): it continues to change, morph, and grow. Many Disney World modifications are made in response to shifts in visitor preferences and spending habits. For example, Pleasure Island is currently undergoing a conceptual reimagining: Disney has closed its clubs and bars, which attracted a mix of Guests, locals, and off-duty Cast Members, to incorporate the site into its larger plan for Disney Springs (see chapter 1). There have been other noticeable changes in Downtown Disney: the twenty-four-screen AMC cinema was revamped as AMC Dine-in Theatres, where restaurant and bar services accompany the movies; the massive Virgin Megastore was not so lucky and was shuttered by 2009. These alterations reflect larger trends in the entertainment industry as consumers embraced home theater and digital download technologies. Disney is clearly aware of the trends brought by digital culture and is willing to respond to them as patrons become more like curators, customizing our own experiences. Ever more we expect to personalize our travels the way we do our iTunes playlists and Netflix queues, and the company understands this. In 2013 it premiered MyMagic+, encompassing a variety of Guest services, most notably a set of vacation-planning tools for the Walt Disney World Resort called MyDisneyExperience.com. Website users can create custom profiles, make resort reservations, compile must-do lists, and personalize MagicBands for their wrists that act as passes to Disney World facilities (even allowing them to make purchases and check in for reservations). MyDisneyExperience also offers a free mobile app featuring GPS-enabled maps of Disney World as well as the ability to check character greeting and attraction wait times and make dining reservations from anywhere. Disney plans to add a revolutionary feature in the near future, FastPass+, expanding the current FastPass service of picking up timed tickets for popular rides while in the parks to now include making advance and on-the-go reservations for attractions, character greetings, and even parade and firework viewing areas. Yet it remains to be seen if Disney World's new and expanded offerings—both in the physical and virtual worlds—will be able to refresh the place and reinvigorate business as the company hopes.

Though affected by the aftereffects of 9/11 and the U.S. recession, Disney World persists.[62] Queues seem a bit shorter and staffing looks a little lighter, but the parks still teem with Guests. Theme parks make up the $11.5 billion "backbone" of the Disney Company's annual business and function as its "consumer confidence bellwether," especially in tough economic times. (Magic Kingdom remains the best performer among the Florida parks, still drawing crowds in excess of 15 million visitors a year, even without the addition of new attractions.)[63] Key to the parks' sustained viability is the commitment to theming as an effective means of storytelling. Themes reign at Disney World, from the most obvious (Mickey-shaped sprinkles on your complimentary birthday cupcake) to the most elaborately developed and crafted (The Twilight Zone Tower of Terror ride, in which every element inside and out evokes a once-glamorous-now-decrepit hotel with a faulty and fast elevator). Though rides are sometimes retired, Disney often opts to retool beloved attractions such as the classic Pirates of the Caribbean, which now features Jack Sparrow as an Audio-Animatronic figure modeled after and voiced by Johnny Depp (who plays Sparrow in the popular movie series). Yet the Imagineers acknowledge the difficulty of "keeping a dream alive in a world of concrete and steel, exit signs, politics, gravity, and physics."[64] Perhaps as a result of such challenges, Disney World has become less focused on insulating itself and more willing to let in real-world concerns, albeit in carefully selected bits and pieces. For example, the Animal Kingdom has increasingly articulated ecological issues and conservation measures throughout the park. Yet it is difficult to escape the irony of being informed about the dangers of deforestation while careening down the Kali River Rapids if one considers the wetlands animals and vegetation that were displaced to bring Animal Kingdom into being, no matter how many trees were airlifted into the park afterward.

It is easy to forget that prior to Disney World, Florida's tourist economy was based on visits to the beach and more modest attractions, but today the company contends with many themed competitors.[65] It must keep up with the latest technology and trends to lure customers, but it has done so in a manner consistent with the brand and style it has established, always with a concern for immersive experience. During the Eisner era Disney responded to a decline in intergenerational play and began focusing on age-segmented thrill entertainment like that proffered by Universal Studios' Islands of Adventure (1999). (Disney may not have to worry too much; attendance at Islands was only half of what was projected, and Universal has not stolen away too many of Disney's visitors, even with "The Wizarding World of Harry Potter.")[66] Disney World now offers wilder rides (Epcot's Soarin' and Test Track, Expedition Everest in Animal Kingdom, and Rock 'n' Roller Coaster and Tower of Terror—both in Disney's Hollywood Studios) and attractions emphasizing interactivity (e.g., Monsters, Inc. Laugh Floor in the Magic Kingdom, Epcot's Turtle Talk With Crush, and The American Idol Experience at Hollywood Studios).[67] The interactive attractions allow for greater spontaneity: though the basic outlines are predetermined, various methods (texting jokes, asking questions of computer-animated characters in real time, being a contestant) are used to invite audiences to participate, thus changing the shows each time they are performed. In the Magic Kingdom, Fantasyland is being nearly doubled in size with exciting additions still to come, although Guests can already mingle with Princesses Belle and Ariel in several new attractions. Bruce Vaughn, chief creative executive for Walt Disney Parks and Resorts, asserts that these "immersive" experiences will make "the guests more active rather than passive," no longer "voyeurs."[68] No doubt this is true, but Disney World was never as passive as critics claimed it to be: there were always choices to make, opinions to challenge, lessons to question.

To safeguard its livelihood, the Disney Company has diversified its business beyond the theme parks. Under Eisner (head at Paramount Pictures before coming to Disney), the company rallied with a string of popular, critically acclaimed films: *Little Mermaid* (1989), *Beauty and the Beast* (1991), *Aladdin* (1992), *The Lion King* (1994), and *Toy Story* (1995, made with Pixar Animations Studios). In the 1990s Disney expanded its reach into a wider film market inclusive of independent and foreign features, then collaborating with Merchant Ivory Productions, and purchasing Miramax Films in 1993 (since sold to Filmyard Holdings in 2010). Disney also maintains a profitable distribution company, Buena Vista Home Entertainment. The company has intensified its publishing activities, too, often with books that promote its other products. In particular, there has been an uptick of fictional literature (both Disney-sponsored and otherwise) that takes Disney World as its setting.[69] The best known of this genre is Ridley Pearson's series *The Kingdom Keepers* (currently six massive volumes, all published by Hyperion-Disney Editions, 2005–13), detail-packed thrillers aimed at kids nine and up. The series brings readers into each of the four Disney World theme parks and onto the Disney Cruise Line, as its teen protagonists (and their holographic projections) fight the "Overtakers" (mostly Disney villains come to life) who threaten Disney World and life beyond it. The seventh installment is slated for a 2014 release. Pearson is supposedly contracted for ten books, perhaps trying to emulate the *Harry Potter* dynasty of juvenile literature. The books were accompanied for a time by a popular multiplayer computer game, *VMK* (*Virtual Magic Kingdom*, 2005–8), offered without charge through Walt Disney Parks and Resorts Online. Since then the *Kingdom Keepers*, another free online game, was introduced in 2010: single players work collaboratively to combat the Overtakers, who have commandeered the Internet. Obviously, Disney recognizes the market share today's kids represent, as well as their comfort with digital culture.

As evidenced by *The Kingdom Keepers* series, Disney is expert at target marketing, which the company has practiced since after World War II to connect with previously untapped consumer bases. Disney perceives the need to reach diverse audiences, and it even employs different advertising campaigns for the same product (i.e., ads for Disney World aimed at families versus those geared toward couples). Disney's willingness to cultivate multiple markets and respond to social shifts (though sometimes slowly or grudgingly) has forged an audience that is more widely constituted than customarily acknowledged. For example, as early as 1978 members of the gay community started organizing events at Disney parks for "overt cultural confrontation." In the 1980s the parks were being rented out for AIDS charity fund-raisers, though Disney warned its other Guests about the queer visitors with signs (a practice that was rightly seen as "propagating homophobia" and was halted). By the early 1990s these events became known as "Gay Days" (though Disney did not advertise them as such), which eventually evolved into lavish annual "Gay Weekends." Gatherings such as these allow gay people to share communal experiences and articulate their presence in society. The company also permits gay couples to purchase wedding packages at its parks or on its cruise ships, and by 2007 it gave them access to official Disney wedding planners. Jesse Walker observes: "If Mickey is cool with gay marriage, the rest of the country can't be that far behind."[70] Disney also did not buckle under pressure from the Southern Baptist Convention, which boycotted the company from the mid-1990s to 2005, claiming that it promoted homosexuality (e.g., by providing benefits to same-sex partners of employees). Dann Hazel and Josh Fippen, a couple and coauthors of *A Walt Disney World Resort Outing*, commend "Disney's inclusive stance" and affirm that they are afforded "the same degree of respect and civility that heterosexual guests receive." They believe Disney acknowledges that families come in all forms. All that is required to be part of Disney's family is "the price of admission," which Hazel and Fippen find a welcome relief from the "stress and frustration from living in a world that cares too much who we are. The Mouse doesn't."[71] While Disney is careful not to offend straight Guests, its acceptance of gay culture is significant. Including gay audiences is a savvy business strategy, but it also reflects the considerable number of gay employees throughout Disney's enterprises and, hopefully, increasing tolerance in the world at large. Although Sean Griffin maintains that the company upholds "the discourse of heterosexual primacy," he also thinks it has helped some people define their identities as part of the gay community.[72] Here Disney demonstrates its ability to evolve corporate philosophy and practices, and even display deeper social conscience, too. The Disney animated films support such notions of progressivism, portraying alternative families (without blood relations or even being of the same species) whose members have great affection for and loyalty to each other. Susan Brockus argues that while Disney is often blamed for squashing diversity, its films are reassuring for families working their way "through dysfunction and difficulty to achieve a comfortable sort of camaraderie." Thus, Disney is "both accepting of family differences and representative of idealist American culture."[73]

Over the years, critics have focused on Walt's conservative politics, though it should be noted he was a Democrat in his youth. Walt's conservatism flourished as he got older: he backed Republican candidates and was an official informant for the Federal Bureau of Investigation, testifying in front of the House Un-American Activities Committee (which blacklisted Hollywood figures) after a bitter animators' strike. Disney also served as vice president of the highly conservative Motion Picture Alliance for the Preservation of American Ideals.[74] Biographer Steven Watts believes Walt's shift from Democratic populism to conservative Republicanism resulted from a suspicion of regulatory government, furthered by his trust in private industry to solve social problems with creative technologies and minimal bureaucratic interference.[75] (It might be possible that he was also in some way rebelling against his socialist father, Elias.)[76] Yet I think Walt would have had misgivings about his company's recent alignment of forces with the Ronald Reagan Presidential Foundation. Although Reagan served as one of the hosts for Disneyland's televised opening, he and Walt "were never particularly close." The foundation hosted a temporary exhibition (July 2012–April 2013) of memorabilia from the massive, and usually inaccessible, Disney Archives at its Presidential Library (Simi Valley, California). Though Walt would have certainly appreciated that Reagan's foundation picked up the tab for the show, promoted Disney's official fan club (D23), and sold Disney merchandise in its gift shop, he always understood the importance of appealing to a mass audience. Thus Disney would have probably balked at such overtly public political affiliation, even though his company had full jurisdiction to choose the five hundred items on display (including an accurate replica of Walt's office) and determine how these were presented.[77]

Recently, more scholars are acknowledging that theming can facilitate social practices of great meaning for both visitors to and workers at themed places. Behavior within a themed space "is as culturally significant" as that outside it, especially when considering personal interpretations of and varying responses to it. Scott Lukas notes that while theming is snubbed as a too tightly proscribed form of culture, often its "promised order . . . is thwarted by the realities of everyday life." Even when corporations attempt to use themed environments to manage the actions of patrons and employees, "unexpected circumstances prevail" and theming falls short of the "desired forms of spatial and social control." Lukas concludes this makes theming "a frustrated undertaking" for organizations seeking predictability.[78] Such ruptures in order present opportunities for resistance. I believe Disney World will live a long life, not just because of Walt's vision but also in spite of it. While the appeal of Disney World owes much to Walt's dreams, its longevity is ensured only with some defiance to the levels of regulation he established. Alan Bryman cautions us to "not generate unduly deterministic" accounts of Disney's control and surveillance, arguing that Cast Members and Guests "can hit back if they choose, perhaps sometimes unconsciously."[79] I agree. Employees and visitors do not always carry out the Disney code of conduct dutifully—consciously and otherwise—and in doing so they reinvent Disney World for themselves.

A quiet revolution has been taking place at Disney World ever since it opened, gaining steam over the last couple of decades. Workers of the past seemed to abide more fully to Disney's official party line. Today's employees are often less content to be hemmed in by the strictures of Disneyism, echoed in training handbooks professing: "We hope that you enjoy thinking our way." As David Koenig keenly retorts, "this Fantasyland was built and is operated by and for real people."[80] Thus, while they perform their jobs, wear their uniforms, and recite their scripts, more and more of Disney's employees have reclaimed varying degrees of personal individuality, an evolution that was endorsed—at least in part—by the company. Former president of its theme parks and resorts, Judson Green, urged Cast Members to improvise and express themselves more, although still within "an agreed-upon framework."[81] Some employees stray from this framework more than others, including lampooning the company and volunteering off-the-record opinions on the cost and value of visiting Disney World. I have encountered such candor and spontaneity from many Cast Members throughout the years: whether it is a bus driver playing music to suit herself instead of setting the "Disney mood," or an attraction host making hand shadows against a wall during a mechanical malfunction, the monolithic behavioral codes are increasingly broken.[82] The company is also more willing to allow jokes and satire at its expense. For example, the Magic

Kingdom's dated Jungle Cruise was revived with clever patter from "tour guides" poking fun at Disney. On a cruise I took in 2011, I laughed heartily with the other Guests as our guide wondered aloud what we would find inside a tunnel: "Danger? . . . Adventure? . . . Who am I kidding? This is Disney, it'll be a gift shop." As the ride ended the humor continued with the guide asking us to "magically please leave."

In the 1990s Green also supported a shift in Disney's corporate culture toward enhanced power sharing. Instead of the top-down management style that had reigned so long at the company, Green vested employees at all levels with decision-making capacities. Meanwhile, higher-level executives were asked to take a turn working the parks' rides and restaurants. Lee Cockerell, former executive vice president of operations at Disney World, described this transition as "bumpy" at first, but ultimately the new philosophy thrived: trust, motivation, and teamwork increased since workers felt their ideas were valued. Disney has endeavored to fill 75 to 80 percent of its jobs by hiring from within, and employee turnover is under 20 percent (less than half the industry average).[83] Going forward, the ability to continually revisit and revise its business practices will be essential to the company's sustainability.

Like many other critics, Adelaide Villmoare and Peter Stillman claim that Disney proffers a "clean, organized, commercial lack of freedom," which suppresses individual rights and public dialogue to avoid the "plain messiness of democracy." They characterize—by default—Disney's Guests as inattentive and uninformed, jettisoning our intellectual faculties and civic responsibilities to have "a particular kind of fun—not to indulge in vices, read Shakespeare, or discuss politics; and once they have set their course on fun at WDW, they have limited their possibilities to what WDW offers and on WDW's terms." While it is true that Disney World supplies a restricted range of experiences, any sphere of interaction—public or private, commercial or otherwise—will have its limitations, too, often predetermined to prompt desired outcomes. It is neither fair nor accurate to assume Disney World's visitors are unthinking or socially disengaged if we choose to vacation there. And surely, we have more than "complete freedom of choice within a completely controlled environment," as Villmoare and Stillman purport.[84] No such complete control exists at Disney World, and I doubt could elsewhere. For Disney Guests, an act as simple as chewing gum becomes a form of defiance when a store clerk reminds you of Walt's insistence that gum not be sold at the parks, as happened to me. Likewise, the Kodak PictureSpots found throughout Disney World underscore notions of corporate control but are potential sites of resistance. The PictureSpots girdle Disney World views with picturesque purposefulness, ensuring aesthetic soundness while simultaneously packaging its landscape as a consumer product, crystallizing experience and time as the "Disney perfect" moment.[85] But, of course, Guests take pictures constantly, not usually at the PictureSpots but when the impulse strikes. Often visitors ignore the PictureSpots altogether, relying on their own judgment instead of Disney's or Kodak's.

Some forms of rebellion are bolder, such as ignoring rules on the rides, or sadly hostile, as when visitors attack the costumed characters as has happened on multiple occasions.[86] But one of the most amusing chronicles of insubordination I have read came from Jeremiah Sullivan, writing in the *New York Times Magazine* about his family vacation to Disney World. Although Sullivan was not very excited about the trip, his young daughter, wife, and family friends were looking forward to it. Among the friends who joined Sullivan on the vacation was another father, a heavy marijuana user, who had diligently researched places that gave relatively safe haven to smoke in the parks. As a means of coping with the rigors of carting their two families around the World, and in willful resistance to the constraining morality and rules of Disney, Sullivan and his friend slipped away numerous times to smoke, reveling in how pot's hallucinatory effects mingled with those of the parks. Sullivan proclaims that his euphoria inside Disney's fantasy is precisely the kind of thing Walt wanted to cultivate.[87] (I assume he meant Walt would appreciate the immersive experience, if not the drug-induced high.) Sullivan and his friend negotiated an alternative relationship with Disney World, surely not one sanctioned by the company, but nonetheless one that allowed them to engage the place on their own terms. Far less amusing and benign than Sullivan's "trip" is the scandal of wealthy families hiring disabled people as Disney World tour guides, which broke in May 2013. Offered rates of over one thousand dollars a day, these guides can jump to the front of lines due to Disney's accommodations for them with the accompanying families in tow. While some defended the practice as providing employment for the disabled, most others, including myself, bristled at the exploitative implications and sense of entitlement as an anonymous "Park Ave mom" decreed, "this is how the 1% does Disney."[88]

Leonard Kinsey recently published *The Dark Side of Disney*, conceived as the "Anarchist Cookbook of Disney Travel Guides," which is "absolutely, unequivocally, NOT authorized by Disney." The book (accompanied by a blog at darksideofdisney.com) presents unexpected anecdotes and advice, though the author insists that the mostly illegal behaviors it chronicles are not endorsed by him: how to sneak into the parks and enter restricted areas; where to drink and use drugs while there; how to scam Guest Assistance Cards (for those with disabilities) and FastPasses; suggesting you lie about your birthday to receive free perks; and scouting locations on Disney property to have sex. Kinsey also describes monorail bar crawls, flashers on the rides, and hook-ups with Cast Members. The author proclaims his admiration of Disney World throughout, but after visiting there countless times he became restless and wanted to "push the limits." Thus Kinsey's book is a sort of manifesto, articulating a desire to explore Disney World on terms other than those endorsed by the company and providing explanations of how to do so. His approach is akin to that of "urban explorers" who make risky investigations of "off-limits" locales (often abandoned industrial sites). Such explorers are not thieves or vandals but rather curious individuals in search of "the sense of wonder and beauty . . . from witnessing firsthand the crumbling and decaying architecture and technology of years past." Kinsey interviews two of Disney World's urban explorers: Shane Perez, who visited the defunct but still extant Discovery Island (see shaneperez.blogspot.com for a narrative and pictures posted after the statute of limitations had passed); and "Hoot" Gibson, a former Disney employee who repeatedly left ride vehicles to make infiltrations of Epcot's Horizons pavilion with his partner "Chief" before it was demolished (mesaverdetimes.blogspot.com provides extensive video, audio, and photographic documentation). Kinsey also details his own unsanctioned tours of the Magic Kingdom's utilidors and provides tips for other would-be explorers (with hints on how to pass oneself off as a Cast Member, images of unmarked access doors, and the latitudinal and longitudinal coordinates for the entrances via Google Earth). Reveling in his unauthorized exploits, Kinsey exclaims that "Walt Disney World had become fun again." Yet he is wary that the "alternative" activities outlined in his book might ruin more conventional vacations. Kinsey asks his readers to follow a "do no harm policy," as Disney World is "vast enough in scope and imagination to accommodate" all kinds of people harmoniously: "regardless of how much we fly outside the realm of conventional theme-park morality, we still have to respect the fact that a lot of other people have saved up a long time to experience their idea of utopia."[89]

In sympathy with Kinsey's insurrectionary spirit is writer-director Randy Moore's first film, *Escape from Tomorrow*. The low-budget movie, which premiered at the 2013 Sundance Film Festival, was shot mostly on location at Disney World and Disneyland without the company's prior knowledge or approval. Described as a "fantasy-horror" film, *Escape from Tomorrow* follows a man who finds out he has lost his job on the last day of his family vacation at Disney World. He loses his grip on sanity and has disturbing visions involving the Disney settings and characters, while inappropriately becoming fixated on two teenage girls. Eventually he is seized by security and brainwashed in a secret facility under Epcot's Spaceship Earth, and subsequently released only to die of "cat flu" in the Contemporary Resort. Critical assessments of the movie vary: while most praise the "audacity" of the filmmaking, there is disagreement about its artistic, technical, and narrative merits. Since Moore's cast and crew did not have Disney's permission, they had to employ guerrilla filmmaking tactics, including shooting on handheld video cameras and reading their scripts on mobile devices, to blend in with the tourists. The limited control over lighting accounts for the movie being in black and white, which reputedly enhances its surrealism. According to Moore, the film explores "our cultural obsession with these fake, manufactured worlds of so-called fantasy."[90] Obviously, he knew Disney would not embrace *Escape from Tomorrow*, and he even edited it in South Korea (removing the company's proprietary content such as song lyrics) to keep his secret for as long as he could. While the movie made the rounds of a few film festivals, and was slated for wider release in October 2013, distributors are still likely wary of tangling with Disney. Although the company is aware of the film, as of this writing it has not taken any legal action against it, contrary to what many bystanders expected. Legal analysts have indicated that while Disney would have a clearer case against the cast and crew for breaking the terms of entry to its parks, the film is a separate issue. The company does not have general intellectual property rights over all of Disney World, and as a work of art the movie could be considered within fair use as a social parody or commentary, and therefore under the protection of the First Amendment. Furthermore, it is obvious to viewers that Disney did not sponsor or endorse the film. But even if the company could win a legal suit, it seems smart to let the movie slide and to hope the hype settles down. If Disney's full legal might was levied against the film, it would bring more attention and probably cult status; by ignoring the movie it is more likely to become another soon-forgotten indie flick. I have not seen it—*Escape from Tomorrow* remains in my Netflix queue with a notation that the date of availability is "unknown."[91]

While Kinsey's approach to Disney World is decidedly fond if rebellious, Moore portrays the place as potentially hostile and even sinister. Similarly, there are wide-ranging responses to Disney among the broader public. No one is surprised to find out about the existence of Disney fan groups and online communities such as Disneyana Fan Club, which put a positive spin on the company and its products. Even urban planner and author Sam Gennawey has his own blog about Disney (samlanddisney.blogspot.com). But ironically other fan sites (including LaughingPlace.com, MousePlanet. com, and MiceAge.com) are often conduits for information that Disney would doubtfully share, including crimes on property and firings at the company. Disney Haters clubs have also popped up on social media sites such as Facebook. Hank Stuever suggests that railing "against all things Disney is nearly as American as a trip to Orlando" and that Walt spread a kind of "dark joy" for those who love hating him: "The Disney experience would probably not be what it is today without the grouchy, cynical input of those who cannot abide it."[92] Furthermore, such opposition in reality helps ensure the company's survival: the right to despise Disney—and publicly espouse that hatred—keeps it culturally relevant, discussed, and debated by those with passionate opinions. Acts of resistance such as those described here have transformed Disney World into a truer microcosm of our time and culture. Walt's dream has given way to a less perfect but more human place that is rougher around its edges. And in truth, Disney World was never "perfect" anyway.

Kathy Merlock Jackson contends that Walt was "only an average artist and writer," yet he "excelled as an oral storyteller, motivator, persuader." Disney's gift was an ability to express his vision so that it resonated widely. Walt felt a sense of responsibility to his company's legacy,[93] realizing it would live beyond him, and quite frankly, needed to: "It is my belief that if this is to be a strong, self-sufficient organization, it cannot be run by one man. . . . This organization must perpetuate itself; it must be able to carry on if anything should ever happen to me."[94] Though it was proposed that had Walt lived longer he would have kept his company smaller and begged off mass media, evidence points elsewhere.[95] When still alive, Walt worked to build the company up and out, diversifying its interests and products. Disney had already built one theme park, was working on another and a model city, too, all while continuing to produce films and television shows. Walt's impetus toward synergy, cross-pollination, and brand identification was apparent from the start. Yet while the company's influence continues to be pervasive, Walt does not loom as large as he once did in our cultural psyche. Kids continue to love his parks, but fewer today recognize Walt's likeness or know much about him: the company's own research revealed that many Guests under age fifteen did not even know he was a real person.[96] Steuer quips that Walt has "become like a face on currency—vaguely important, possibly historical, some old dude."[97] When he was still alive not even the trademark "Walt Disney" signature was his own; Walt could only reproduce it with great difficulty. Although the signature establishes him as the origin of the entire Disney enterprise, there is an inherent irony here.[98] As the work of others was absorbed under "Walt Disney," that name no longer stood for the individual, and this shift was not lost on Walt: "I'm not 'Walt Disney' anymore. Disney is a thing, an attitude, an image in the eyes of the public. I've spent my whole career creating that image, and I'm a great believer in what Disney is. But it's not me, the person, anymore."[99] Disney World has already outlived its progenitor, and Walt knew this would happen.

For a long time, Disney had preserved its secrets and hidden much labor, believing experiences of the parks would be less magical if Guests knew how things were actually done. But over the years the company softened on this position, and now it offers its most curious Guests a variety of "backstage" tours for a fee. In recent years more theme parks have increased such behind-the-scenes activities, revealing their modes of production to visitors. This tactic not only challenges "the passivity of the consumer by resurrecting consumption as an act of invention and discovery"[100] but also gives us a sense of mastery as we get to inspect and understand how things work.[101] I got to play the role of "visitor-as-participant" in January 2011, when I took the Keys to the Kingdom Tour at Magic Kingdom, available since the mid-1990s and restricted to Guests sixteen and older for fear of spoiling the magic for younger children.[102] (The company has an array of other tours, including family excursions, treks of eight or more hours in multiple parks, customized VIP jaunts, and visits for businesspeople looking to emulate Disney's success.) For nearly five hours we explored the park's nooks and crannies, including backstage areas and the famed utility corridors called "utilidors." I imagine Walt would have hated sharing these "offstage" spaces with Guests, but over the years so much has been written and revealed about these places that Disney presumably figured it would tell its own version of the story, with the visual proof to match, and charge a price for the privilege. The tours are designed to present the "history and heritage of the Walt Disney Resorts and Walt Disney himself." Tour guides are dressed in equestrian garb (though oddly the women wear heels for a multi-hour walking tour), including crops to lead us rather than having us follow a "nasty orange flag." (The equestrian motif conceives guides as "land jockeys" who can go from themed land to themed land without "breaking the show.") Our guide, "Elaine," had been working at Disney World for about five years and seemed sincere in her wish to "share my knowledge and passion" for the place. She described the Magic Kingdom as "Walt's movie . . . in fact . . . a show, and we allow you to walk around the show." The tour provided a chance to see how the show's props and scenery worked. But in order to go backstage, "Elaine" had to make us "honorary Cast Members" for the day after we introduced ourselves and declared our favorite characters (mine has always been Goofy). We were also informed of the "backstage rules": while onstage we could take as many pictures as we wanted, but no photography (including via cell phones) is permitted in any backstage area to "preserve the magic for others." And we had to respect Cast Members' offstage privacy, when "it's their time to escape the fantasy and be themselves."

The Keys to the Kingdom Tour focuses on the "cornerstones" of Disney's business, in order of their priority: (1) Safety; (2) Courtesy; (3) Show; and (4) Efficiency. "Elaine" explicated Cast Member training at Disney University, particularly the "Traditions" mantras such as "I go above and beyond" and "I stay in character in the show." Interestingly, when onstage "Elaine" was a more formal version of her informative self: offstage she was nicely conspiratorial, willing to reveal juicier secrets about the park. As one would expect, the tour was well planned and service-oriented. During lunch we ate in our own roped-off area of the restaurant, where attendants even held the garbage can flaps open for us. And we did not have to wait in long lines for the tour's featured attractions, the Haunted Mansion and Jungle Cruise. Distances between attractions are much closer offstage than they appear onstage. For example, the Crystal Palace restaurant on Main Street is actually just steps away from Adventureland's Jungle Cruise. "Elaine" acted as our Cruise captain, but instead of the kitschy jokes Cruise guides now dispense she told us about the ride's history, pointing out camouflaged blast heaters warming the plants, and the shallow water dyed to disguise the animatronic animals' mechanics and the tracks on which the "boats" are driven. Elsewhere in the park we learned that Liberty Square and Frontierland were conceived to symbolize "America in totality": Liberty Square represents the East Coast, but as we move into Frontierland the topography shifts and architectural styles gradually change to suggest the passage of time along with the acquisition of the western territories. It was a good reminder about Disney's desire to develop coherent themes, even when their subtleties would escape the notice of many Guests.

Throughout the tour "Elaine" highlighted details that might otherwise be overlooked. Above the Crystal Arts shop on Main Street appears the name "M. T. Lott"—a reference, she told us, to the massive swath of land Walt was able to acquire in Florida after he realized that too much "reality [was] seeping into his fantasy" at Disneyland. "Elaine" indicated that most backstage areas have "transition points," which let lost Guests know they have wandered into the "wrong place." Yellow marks on the backstage pavement indicate sight lines behind which one cannot be seen, especially helpful for a character who does not want to be caught with his head in his hands, literally. Posts for character heads are just beyond sight lines, though performers have a special signal—cover one eye and raise a hand—if they need a handler to get them offstage right away. The pavement along parade routes is studded with small filled holes that are actually RFID (radio-frequency identification) tags to help guide floats. Many backstage facilities are painted "go-away green" to blend in with the foliage. We visited a shed storing vehicles for the revived crowd favorite, the Main Street Electrical Parade. Nearby, partially costumed dancers practiced their routine against the backdrop of Splash Mountain's bare metal skeleton (only portions visible from onstage look like a mountain). Back onstage "Elaine" told us about the Cinderella Dream Suite (third floor of the castle), designed though not used as a residence for Walt's family, which hosts winners of promotions and sweepstakes today.

Much of what "Elaine" said was not new information but rather things I had read many times in different sources. Yet there was also fresh material, some much less optimistic than one might assume to hear on the tour. I was particularly surprised at how candidly "Elaine" answered so many of our questions and how she detailed some manipulative and even contradictory Disney business practices. She explained that the three o'clock parade is intended to counteract mass exits from the park in the afternoon, sucking "us back in . . . to buy more merchandise, to buy more food, to go on more rides." "Elaine" told us about Disney's expired contract with McDonald's, which meant no more Disney-themed toys and Happy Meals at McDonald's restaurants outside the parks, while restaurants on Disney property were closed. Supposedly Disney wants to provide "healthy food" (indeed, there has been an effort to offer better options, especially for kids), though Coca-Cola and Orville Redenbacher are still prominently featured in the parks. Coke and Redenbacher products are supplied for free in exchange for advertising, with Disney keeping the profits. Similarly, Kodak donates guide maps to the parks and is heavily promoted throughout Disney World. "Elaine" remarked that a lot of "bartering" goes on "to help us with our business." She also revealed that many of the aromas we smelled (such as freshly baked cookies) are replicated and pumped into the park, while others (like popcorn) are circulated with exhaust fans to enhance the immersive experience and increase their consumption. As "Elaine" gestured to Roy's name on the window over Main Street's confectionary, she characterized Walt as "a tremendous failure," saved only by his brother's business savvy: Walt was "the Dreamer," but Roy was "the Doer." A Disney Cast Member, giving an official tour, described Walt as a flawed man rather than an infallible legend. I found it reassuring.

"Intrusions" (when Guests get out of their vehicles and physically enter attractions) are a constant problem, despite the addition of lap bars and other restraints. "Elaine" reported that "intrusions" occur several times a week, and the rule is that once someone has gotten off a ride it is stopped and everyone else must be evacuated, which can take an hour. Sometimes evacuees have to be taken into offstage areas, as was the case with a little girl who had to disembark from Splash Mountain but was worried about leaving the animatronic "critters" behind (paw prints have since been painted on the ground to imply their safe escape, too). "Intrusions" are particularly common in the Haunted Mansion and on the Carousel of Progress: "Elaine" joked that "a lot of people don't want to see progress fully realized." Any "intruders" with "malicious intent" are ejected from the parks, such as two teenage boys who squirted ketchup and mustard inside the Haunted Mansion. It took two days to clean the attraction, and the boys were automatically expulsed from the Magic Kingdom, never to be admitted again. "Elaine" reminded us that cameras are everywhere: "You're constantly being watched on rides and while going around the park." (And counted, too, as Disney continually assesses crowd size in "phases" based upon park capacity.) Other persistent problems include shoplifting and people attempting to spread the ashes of cremated loved ones in favorite attractions. Less frequent but more serious are bomb threats. "Elaine" warned "we have an Orange County Sherriff" and then laughed to lighten the mood, but the message was clear—control yourself or else you will have Disney to deal with, and Disney does not mess around.

As we turned a corner to go offstage, the practicalities of maintenance facilities awash in "go-away green" seemed jarring, reminding me of a recent trip to Las Vegas when we approached the Strip from its back view and the dazzle quickly dissipated. I worried that my chance to go inside Disney's utilidors, designed by Admiral Joe Fowler to emulate a submarine, might have the same effect. Gladly, that was not the case. Though it was not a spectacular setting (this is, truly, a network of purely functional utility corridors), I was entranced by it, probably because being there felt transgressive. Although I was in the utilidors with the Disney Company's sanction, it did not feel like I had Walt's blessing to do so, and that, well, thrilled me. The "utilidors" (a term first used in Canada in 1957) recall other utilitarian places with their information boards, safety protocols, employee lockers, and toilet paper and hot dog buns stacked in the halls. But here there are also upbeat reminders about "Our Disney Heritage" and "Adopt-a-Tunnel" programs. Walls are painted different colors coordinated with the themed lands (except Frontierland, which has no utilidor access), and signs marking onstage entrances implore Cast Members to "Please be Disney Look Compliant When Entering." Some employees acknowledged us, while others just went about their work, carting packages, hauling trash, and scurrying by in every imaginable costume. Pictures of Cast Members with accompanying quotes such as "I stay in character and play the part" decorate the utilidors. We did not visit the wardrobe facility, which processes thirty thousand radio-chipped garments a day, but screened a video of it. And although we cannot visit the "Disney jail," we are assured it exists here, too. The music played in the utilidors used to be the same as that onstage, but "Elaine" disclosed that the employees revolted, needing a "break from the fantasy."

A tunnel map charts the utilidors' one and a quarter miles, covering nine and a half acres. The map reveals a plan akin to the Magic Kingdom's above: roughly circular with a straight alley in the center aligned under the castle. Most fascinating to me was "Heritage Hall" and its satellite photograph of the park, in which could be seen how small the attractions' facades are in comparison to the sheds housing them. Historically, especially in literature and film, subterranean spaces have been metaphors for imagination and play, with access to them representing initiation or a search for hidden knowledge. Though critics complain that Disney World focuses on the past and the future at the expense of the current day, David Pike maintains that the rationally efficient utilidors function as "an eternal present" that helps maintain the mythology of effortlessly produced fun above ground. He concludes that the utilidors look "like a space in constant use, with very little evidence of the seamless control of the Magic Kingdom above." They are "not decrepit" but rather "merely normal, and therein perhaps lies the shock."[103] "Elaine" closed the tour by telling us it once offered greater backstage access—including under the castle—but since 9/11 they have limited such due to security concerns.

Initially I was surprised that despite constant, frenzied scribbling in my notebook for the entire tour, "Elaine" never once asked me what I was writing or why (although several of the other Guests did, to whom I offered vague answers). But then I realized others must have taken the tours for their own research, and in the end, the information is no longer classified if Disney is dispensing it to the public for a price. The tour required a lot from its participants: a chunk of time that could otherwise be spent in the attractions, the endurance to walk for hours, and rapt attention. But it was apparent that I was not the only one who was fascinated: everyone seemed deeply engaged, taking the tour for her or his own personal reasons.

In 1995 the Canadian Centre for Architecture commissioned Catherine Wagner to photograph Disney's parks around the world. Wagner focused on moments before the parks opened and after they closed, producing an arresting series in which most images depicted the parks emptied of Guests and Cast Members. These are startling because they reveal the parks for what they are: masterfully designed and executed places, but ultimately lifeless without the most essential element—people. I think Walt would have been displeased with Wagner's photographs, as the parks' facilities seem oddly beautiful though also rather absurd when not in use. On a 2011 trip I gained early entrance to the Magic Kingdom (my daughter had an appointment at the Bibbidi Bobbidi Boutique for some "princess treatment"). It was exhilarating to walk down Main Street, reach the central hub, and pass through Cinderella Castle in a moment of stillness before the park opened, with no more than a handful of employees milling around. But there was an eerie deadliness, too. As I walked I remembered Wagner's photos—the loneliness of rides without riders, the strangeness of Minnie's open fridge filled with plastic foods—aware that Disney's magic is not generated autonomously. I anticipated the crowds that would soon come rushing through the gates: I guess you could say I even longed for them. After a visit to Disneyland, critic Ada Louise Huxtable claimed she could not bring herself to go to Disney World as her "masochistic impulses" were "limited."[104] She missed out on an opportunity for self-discovery. I go to Disney World not because I am "masochistic" or easily placated, but because it excites and delights, provokes and challenges me. It wakes up my heart, but also my mind. On a visit to Animal Kingdom in 2009, while on the Kilimanjaro Safaris, my daughter turned to me and said, "This is the best day I ever had. I think it's like a whole dream." She was right: Disney's magic resides in the ambition of its immersive vision—it is not a partial fantasy, but an attempt to evoke the fullness of "a whole dream." Over the years I have become a shrewd Guest, one who does not endorse Disney's methods wholesale, though I do embrace its complications. I also better recognize how Disney World contributes to our histories of the built environment and human culture: fostering community, intensifying lived experience, and enhancing existence beyond routine subsistence. After all of these years, the joy still remains, at least for me. I will have to wait for my daughter to grow older to see if it remains for her, too.

Notes

Introduction

1. *Walt Disney Family Museum* website.
2. See Greene and Greene.
3. Malamud; Shortsleeve, 17, 23–24; Bell, Haas, and Sells, 2, note that "Disney" desig-nates a man, a studio, a film canon, a multimedia corporation, and an ideology.
4. Sperb, 924.
5. Malamud.
6. Huxtable, 10.
7. Wasko, "Challenging Disney Myths."
8. Stuever, C.1.
9. Shortsleeve, 1, 4, 8–12, 19–20, 24.
10. For example, *Inside the Mouse: Work and Play at Disney World,* by the academic collective The Project on Disney, questions "whether there is any pleasure in mass cul-ture" at all.
11. Such as "Imagineer" John Hench's *Designing Disney,* which is undeniably informa-tive but lacks critical distance.
12. Corbin, 205.
13. Linkletter qtd. in Green and Green, 177.
14. Mannheim, 68.
15. Sorkin, "See You in Disneyland." Also see Levin for Disney's litigation against the Air Pirates' counterculture comics based on Disney characters.

Chapter 1. Smart Business and Simulations

1. Harris, "Expository Expositions," 22; Ritzer, *Enchanting a Disenchanted World,* 3.
2. Disney qtd. in Thomas, *Walt Disney,* 1st ed., 349. Walt married Lillian Bounds in 1925. Diane, their first daughter, was born in 1933. They adopted a second child, Sharon, in 1936.
3. Allan, 226–27.

4. Telotte; Hench with Van Pelt, 2, 67; Klingmann, 71–73. Storyboards, perspective drawings, and scale models are used to design the parks.

5. Evans qtd. in Green and Green, 155.

6. Gabler, xiii, 497.

7. Pine and Gilmore, 2–3, 12–13, 67–68.

8. A. Williams, 482–83, 485, 488.

9. Thomas, *Walt Disney*, 2nd ed., 243, 250–52; Zukin, 222–23.

10. Findlay, 60–61. ABC gave Walt $5 million in exchange for the series and a 35 percent interest in Disneyland. Ironically, on 31 July 1995 the Disney Company acquired the Capital Cities/ABC network for $18.9 billion.

11. R. Disney, 216–17.

12. Disney qtd. in Smith, *Walt Disney: Famous Quotes*, 68.

13. Apgar. Susman, 197, claims the era was as much of Mickey as it was of FDR.

14. Dorfman, 45; Susman, 197.

15. Disney qtd. in R. Disney, 215.

16. Disney qtd. in Wolters, 29.

17. Kurland, 13; Eliot, 214–15; J. Taylor, 10–11. Retlaw got 5 percent of every Walt Disney Productions merchandising deal, could invest up to 15 percent in all Disney projects, and could purchase up to 25 percent of Walt Disney Productions' stock at any time.

18. A. M. Davis, 140n251, suggests that WED was founded to finance and oversee Disneyland when Walt could not get studio money for it.

19. Disney qtd. in Bennis and Biederman, 43.

20. Birmingham, 276.

21. See Bailey; Childs; Kurtti; and Finch, *Walt Disney's America*, for examples of the type. Books are also "written" by Disney's Imagineers, including a series of *Imagineering Field Guides*.

22. For example, see Flower; J. Taylor; and Grover, *The Disney Touch*.

23. Yee, *Mouse Trap*; C. Mitchell, especially 27–30.

24. The show traveled to the following venues between June 1997 and April 1999: Canadian Centre for Architecture, Montreal; Walker Art Center, Minneapolis; Armand Hammer Museum of Art and Cultural Center, Los Angeles; Cooper-Hewitt National Design Museum, New York; and the Modern Art Museum of Fort Worth.

25. B. J. Coleman, 297–306. *The Mickey Mouse Club* was later successfully exported to other countries, most notably Japan.

26. Allan, 205.

27. Findlay, 59. *Walt Disney Presents* eventually replaced *Disneyland*. Eisner later revived the TV series format with *The Wonderful World of Disney*.

28. Flower, 33–34; Eliot, 231–32. Other misfortunes occurred: Walt was accidentally locked in his Main Street apartment the previous night; some visitors used counterfeit tickets or hopped the fence; a plumbers' strike left the park short on drinking fountains; women's high heels stuck in wet concrete; and studio employees got sick repeatedly riding attractions for the cameras.

29. Sammond, 316–17, 320, 322.

30. Susman, 21–22; Marling, *As Seen on TV*, 88, 123, 286.

31. S. G. Davis, 165.

32. Disney qtd. in "The Greatest Triple Play in Show Business," 72.

33. S. G. Davis, 163–64, 166, 168.

34. Bennis and Biederman, 34, 46.

35. Brockus, 191, 199, 208–9, notes that grouping characters with similar traits, such as princesses or villains, cultivates their collectability.

36. Telotte, 118–21, 138; Trowbridge and Stapleton, 60.

37. Findlay, 54–55, 69–70, 88.

38. Findlay, 74, 77–78; Ritzer, *The McDonaldization of Society*, 92; Shuit, 40. Female employees wear minimal jewelry and makeup, and most males are not permitted to grow facial hair. Exposed tattoos are only allowable as part of a costume.

39. Anonymous park official qtd. in "Tinker Bell, Mary Poppins, Cold Cash," 75.

40. Cockerell, 2; Findlay, 74; Haden-Guest, 232; Raz, 211, 213–14, 219, 223. Students in the Disney World College Program work at the parks and take seminars in exchange for school credit. See W. Jones with Esola for an insider perspective on these internships.

41. Koenig, *Realityland*, 12.

42. Gutierrez qtd. in Stewart, 11. Stewart, 11–15, recounts the training required to play a character, which includes learning to produce its distinctive autograph signature.

43. Cockerell, 4–5, 11.

44. Shuit, 36, 38; Gross. See Bannon, B1, B5; and Ritzer, *The McDonaldization Thesis*, 154–55, on the original Disney Institute.

45. "Recreation: Disneyland East," 82, discusses Walt's disillusionment with Anaheim and plans for Disney World. Today the Disney Company owns about twenty-five thousand acres in Florida.

46. Barrier, 317; Derr, 378; Gabler, 630.

47. By 1970 Disney World was the largest private construction project in the United States, with more than eight thousand workers. Roy, who oversaw the project, died three months after its completion. The opening ceremony, on 23 October 1971, featured conductor Arthur Fiedler.

48. Asian-, Venetian-, and Persian-themed resorts were also planned but not built.

49. Disney Institute, *Be Our Guest*, 15, 17. Employee statistics as of May 2009.

50. Adams, 159–60, notes that the park opened ahead of schedule, upstaging Universal Studios' Florida premiere in 1990.

51. River Country ceased operation in 2001 and was officially shuttered in 2005.

52. "Disney Unveils Vision for Disney Springs."

53. Initially, visitors bought lettered tickets (basic rides were "A" tickets, the most thrilling were "E"). "World Passports" supplanted these and were since replaced by the current "Magic Your Way" tickets, which require extra fees to "park hop" or visit the water parks. Children under three get in for free.

54. Cross and Walton, 196.

55. "50 Things You Didn't Know about Disney World." This 2009 estimate includes all four theme parks and Downtown Disney.

56. Ritz, 1.

57. Sehlinger, 1992 ed., 3, 8.

58. Flower, 21–22.

59. Koenig, *Mouse under Glass*, 257–58; Marling, "Imagineering the Disney Theme Parks," 166.

60. Jencks.

61. Jameson, 6, 17–19, 25.

62. Sorkin, "See You in Disneyland," 207.

63. See Baudrillard: *America*; *Simulations*; *For a Critique of the Political Economy of the Sign*; *The Consumer Society*; *Selected Writings*; and "The Precession of Simulacra."

64. See Barthes: *The Pleasure of the Text*; "Rhetoric of the Image"; "The Death of the Author"; and "From Work to Text."

65. Eco, 4, 6–11, 18–19, 26, 30–31, 38–39, 43–44, 56–58.

66. Goldberger, 40–41, 92–99.

67. Congdon and Blandy, 268, 270–71, 273–74, 276.

68. Derrida, 285.

69. Fjellman, 16.

70. Sammond, 301.

Chapter 2. Keeping the Faith

1. Durkheim, 3.

2. Reader and Walter, 16.

3. Chidester, 18–19, 145–46, 149.

4. Mazur and Koda, 301–2, 308, 310–13; Chidester, 1.

5. C. W. Perry, *The Church Mouse*.

6. Hench with Van Pelt, 1–2.

7. Capodagli and Jackson, *The Disney Way*, 10; Disney Institute, *Be Our Guest*, 18; Shuit, 38.

8. Bhardwaj and Rinschede, 9–14.

9. Fussell.

10. E. Cohen, "Pilgrimage and Tourism" and "A Phenomenology of Tourist Experiences."

11. Van Gennep.

12. S. Coleman and Elsner, 6, 8, 202, 204, 208–9, 212.

13. Ritzer, *The McDonaldization of Society*, 4; Pinsky, 233. M. J. King, "Empires of Popular Culture," 117, argues that Disney constitutes a double pilgrimage: visiting the parks as a child, then returning as an adult with one's own children.

14. Lewis; Kendall, 21; Layton, 191–92.

15. Morinis, 24.

16. See V. Turner, "The Center Out There," 193–95, 200, 205, 220; V. Turner, "Pilgrimage and Communitas," 309, 316–18; V. Turner, *Process, Performance and Pilgrimage*, 154; Coulton; Newcomb, 7.

17. V. Turner and Turner, 31, 37–38.

18. Relph, 56–61, 68, 80, 82–83, 85, 87. Aziz, 247–61, contends that Turner's conception of *communitas* makes groups seem more coherent than they actually are.

19. Sturken, *Tangled Memories*, 2–3, 8, 259. Also see Sturken, *Tourists of History*.

20. A. Williams, 489.

21. *Your Guide to the Magic!* (Lake Buena Vista, Fla.: Walt Disney World, 2010). Guide compliments of Quilted Northern.

22. Brinkoetter qtd. in Shuit, 36.

23. Mann, 61, 63–68.

24. For more on Saint James and Compostela see Starkie; Stone; Dunn and Davidson, *The Pilgrimage to Compostela in the Middle Ages*; and Stokstad, *Santiago de Compostela*.

25. Nolan and Nolan, 276, suggest that this apparition led to the "authentication" of Saint James's relics.

26. Chidester, 10, 54, 145–46, 149.

27. R. Disney, 212–14.

28. Buskirk, 84.

29. Schickel, "Bringing Forth the Mouse," 96.

30. Preston, "Spiritual Magnetism," 32; Zelinsky, "Nationalist Pilgrimages in the United States."

31. Marling, *As Seen on TV*, 119.

32. Updike, 60–65, 98.

33. Preston, "Empiricism and the Phenomenology of Religious Experience," 10–11, 18–19; Preston, "The Rediscovery of America."

34. Reis, "Brazil," 88–101.

35. Coffey, Davidson, and Dunn, xxxv; Dunn and Davidson, "Bibliography of the Pilgrimage," xxv, xxviii–xxix. The *Codex* is named after Pope Calixtus II. Some scholars believe the French priest/pilgrim Aymery Picaud was its author, while others think he was only a scribe. Its five books may have been written at different times, but were likely assembled in their final form between 1140 and 1172.

36. Munro, 198.

37. Rudolph, ix.

38. Boorstin, 77–78, 104; E. Cohen, "Toward a Sociology of International Tourism," 171–72.

39. Burke, x–xii.

40. Brooke and Brooke, 24; Stokstad, *Medieval Art*, 221.

41. Nicholas, 277, notes Alfonso VI's efforts to stimulate pilgrimage by chartering new monasteries and improving roads.

42. These are the French Road, the Northern Route, the Silver Route, and the Portuguese Road.

43. Travelers provide authorities with Pilgrim Records, which are stamped along the way at churches, post offices, bars, etc.

44. Rudolph, 40.

45. The cathedral's current facade is largely an eighteenth-century replacement.

46. Disney's long waits are reduced by the FastPass, introduced in 1999. Guests with timed tickets gain access to expedited lines, staggering visits to the most popular rides.

47. Atiya, 45–46; Leighton, 17–18. Travelers wore pilgrim's garb for protection.

48. The Turks seized the Holy Sepulchre in 1078, subsequently hampering Jerusalem

pilgrimages with safety concerns and prompting a rise in European ones in the eleventh and twelfth centuries. S. Coleman and Elsner, 104.

49. Dwindling pilgrimage in the eighteenth and nineteenth centuries was reinvigorated by the "rediscovery" of Saint James's relics. Fearing British attacks, Archbishop San Clemente hid the relics in 1588; they were later supposedly excavated and then authenticated by Pope Leo III in 1884.

50. V. Turner, "Liminal to Liminoid," 57.

51. A. Moore, 207.

52. Kunstler, 225; Ritzer, *Enchanting a Disenchanted World*, 74.

53. The Walk Around the World, a path paved with dedication stones people pay to have engraved, encircles the lagoon.

54. Spirn, 236. The controlled access allows for multiple security checkpoints, which now includes biometric identification (Guests' index fingers are scanned when entering a park to match their prints to their passes).

55. The other Florida parks have less restrictive plans. For example, Epcot visitors can enter Future World through Spaceship Earth's plaza, or World Showcase via the International Gateway.

56. A. Moore, 214.

57. Walt is depicted at his "perfect man" height of six feet, rather than his actual five feet, seven inches. Keys to the Kingdom Tour, 14 January 2011. The sculpture's plaque bears a quotation attributed to Walt: "We believe in our idea: a family park where parents and children could have fun—together."

58. Thomas, *Walt Disney*, 2nd ed., 251.

59. Yee, *Mouse Trap*, 11–12.

60. A. Moore, 214.

61. Scully, 8–9; M. J. King, "Empires of Popular Culture," 116–18.

62. Stokstad, *Santiago de Compostela*, 41.

63. Gauthier, 19.

64. S. Coleman and Elsner, 106. Rudolph, 40, notes that pre-Christian pilgrims used such shells in their devotion to Venus.

65. Starkie, 71; Sumption, 175. Compostela's archbishop received a percentage from sales of authorized badges.

66. R. Bright, 48; Haden-Guest, 270. During an animation tour I took at Disney World in December 1997, a young animator commended the interchangeability of his cohorts: "Everyone can do the same thing every time and do it pretty much right every time."

67. Barrett, 8, 15–17, 19, 242; Koenig, *Mouse under Glass*, 188–90.

68. Yee, *Walt Disney World Hidden History*, 9, 57, 211. For example, in the Haunted Mansion's graveyard is a tribute to Mr. Toad, whose ride was replaced by Winnie the Pooh's. Also see Werner Weiss's website, Yesterland.com, which tracks defunct attractions and features at the Disney parks.

69. Pahl, 85, 89, 91, 95, 98.

70. See MacCannell, *The Tourist*, for more on "touristic space."

71. E. Cohen, "A Phenomenology of Tourist Experiences," 194.

72. Hench qtd. in R. Bright, 237.

73. Rafferty with Gordon, 167, 189–90.

74. Real, 54–55. To make shopping easier, package service is available from the parks to many Disney resorts.

75. D. E. Wright and Snow, 326–27, 329, 331, 334–36.

76. M. J. King, "Disneyland and Walt Disney World," 133, 136–37.

77. See by Francaviglia: *Main Street Revisited*, 145–84; and "Main Street U.S.A." A 1956 trip to Marceline inspired the idea for a park to be sited there, Walt Disney Boyhood Farm, but planning was cut short by Walt's death. Allan, 8, 245; Korkis, 83, 90.

78. Disney qtd. in Korkis, 81.

79. Brode, *From Walt to Woodstock*, xxii, 106; Pinsky, 2.

80. Walt told animation storyman Ken Anderson: "You can make some paintings like Norman Rockwell's, and I'll build models of them." Disney qtd. in R. Bright, 39.

81. Neuman, 83, 85, 96. Wallace, 161–63, describes this as "selective amnesia," which manufactures a "happy past" corresponding to a "contented present."

82. Philips, 33–34, 36, traces Main Street and Frontierland sources to western imagery in late-nineteenth-century art and periodicals as well as twentieth-century films.

83. Francaviglia, *Main Street Revisited,* 147, 156. Main Street's design was also influenced by Imagineer Harper Goff's hometown of Fort Collins, Colorado.

84. C. Rowe and Koetter, 46.

85. Wallace, 161–63.

86. Rojek, 127.

87. Sturken, *Tangled Memories*, 2, 7–8, 17.

88. Yee, *Walt Disney World Hidden History*, 51.

89. Birmingham, 275.

90. Eliot, 233–34.

91. Schickel, "Walt Disney," 94–95.

92. Disney qtd. in "The Wide World of Walt Disney," 51. Also see Morgenstern, 68.

93. Francaviglia, *Main Street Revisited*, 157.

94. Kurland, 28.

95. Hayden.

96. R. F. Snow, 22, 24.

97. Jackson qtd. in R. Bright, 169.

98. Newcomb, 21, 38–39, 54, 71, 89.

99. Geertz, 79–88.

100. A. Moore, 215.

Chapter 3. Swampland

1. Mesters.

2. Prest, 12.

3. I suggested such prototypes in Knight, "Adam and Eve . . . and Goofy."

4. Mesters, 28.

5. Wasko, *Understanding Disney*, 3.

6. K. Jones and Wills, 8, 171, 174.

7. Chidester, 143.

8. For *Paradise Lost*'s illustrators see Labriola and Sichi; McColley; and Pointon. For other literary examples see Sicher; and Boesky.

9. A. N. Wilson. Milton penned *De Doctrina Christiana*, an unfinished chronicle of his disillusionment with traditional Christianity, contemporaneously with *Paradise Lost*. *De Doctrina* was published posthumously after its rediscovery in 1823.

10. Frye, 220; Knott, 33.

11. Lieb, 131.

12. Frye, 230; Hunt, 174, 186; Brisman, 150.

13. Giamatti, 301–3, 305, 307, suggests Milton's appealing description of Eden emphasizes the trauma of its loss.

14. Monk, 8–9, 96.

15. Bolger and Bennowitz, 106. Cole's *The Garden of Eden* and *Expulsion from the Garden of Eden* are often treated as pendants and were exhibited as such by him, although *The Garden* was conceived prior to *Expulsion*.

16. Thomas Cole to Robert Gilmor, Esq., 21 May 1828, qtd. in Noble, 64. Also see Merritt.

17. Bolger and Bennowitz, 106, note that Cole was trying to secure Wadsworth's patronage. For more on this letter see Parry, 69.

18. Thomas Cole to Daniel Wadsworth, *The Correspondence of Thomas Cole and Daniel Wadsworth*, 46, qtd. in Bolger and Bennowitz, 110; also see 107, 109. The painting was shown at Elam Bliss's New York bookstore in May 1829 and sold to Charles Wilkes for only four hundred dollars. Cole subsequently denounced *Eden* as "a source of mortification and a waste of precious time."

19. Wallach, 82.

20. Beardsley, *Gardens of Revelation*, 16.

21. Sturken, *Tangled Memories*, 2.

22. K. Jones and Wills, 11–12.

23. Schama, 7, 10–12.

24. Schama, 546–47, 551–59. By the mid-1850s Denecourt had identified more than a thousand new sites and had mapped twenty marked trails.

25. Sears, vii–viii, 3–11, 209, 213, 216.

26. Schama, 7–8, 11–12, 15.

27. Sears, 130–31, 149.

28. Schama, 8–10.

29. Schama, 534, 537; Comito, 34; Lazzaro, 132.

30. Tuan with Hoelscher, 191–96.

31. Bartolomeo Ammannati briefly worked on the Gardens after Tribolo died, but his collaborator Buontalenti completed them.

32. D. R. E. Wright, 45, 47–48. Pietro Leopoldo opened the Boboli Gardens to the public in 1776.

33. See Chatfield, 123–29, for details on one of the Boboli's grandest spectacles, the Naumachia.

34. Spirn, 146, 221, 233.

35. Lazzaro, 80; see 190–214 for Boboli's evolution and features.

36. Kostof, *The City Shaped*, 199.

37. Disney qtd. in Thomas, *Walt Disney*, 2nd ed., 13.

38. Disney qtd. in R. Bright, 56. Disney parks feature many resting spots and are paved with resilient asphalt.

39. Hench qtd. in Blake, 433.

40. Hench qtd. in Goldberger, 96. Lipsitz, 139, and Marling, *As Seen on TV*, 125–26, counter that the episodic organization is more like television.

41. Chidester, 142. Carson suggests that Disney World uses music as an index for the "Disney Experience."

42. Finch, *The Art of Walt Disney*, 393; Findlay, 68–69.

43. Schama, 276, 279. Grotto walls of volcanic tufa were often set with shellwork to lighten their shadowy contours.

44. Pahl, 88, 92.

45. Bryman, *Disney and His Worlds*, 86; Bryman, *The Disneyization of Society*, 134.

46. Disney brochure qtd. in Gottdiener, "Disneyland," 151. Also see Joselit.

47. Mukerji, 23.

48. Malins, 54.

49. Shepherd and Jellicoe, 31.

50. Finch gushes in *The Art of Walt Disney*, 392: "Walt Disney had built the Versailles of the twentieth-century—but it was a Versailles built for the pleasure of the people."

51. Negley and Patrick, 2, 4–5, 7–8.

52. Reps, 5–6, 22.

53. Kostof, *The City Shaped*, 163, 199; Kostof, *A History of Architecture*, 681. See Borsi for an illustrated overview of utopian conceptions.

54. Howard qtd. in Galantay, 55; Kostof, *The City Assembled*, 55–56. The first application of Howard's plan was in 1903 at Letchworth, England.

55. Mumford, 82, 156, 515–16, 518–19.

56. Gennawey, *Walt and the Promise of Progress City*, 229–30. The book was first published as *To-Morrow: A Peaceful Path to Real Reform* (1898), then revised and reissued as *Garden Cities of To-Morrow*.

57. Kostof, *The City Shaped*, 203, 207.

58. Corn and Horrigan, 51.

59. Disney qtd. in Smith, *Walt Disney: Famous Quotes*, 42.

60. Gennawey, *Walt and the Promise of Progress City*, 108–9.

61. Nasaw, 3, 254–55. Cross and Walton, 167, emphasize the large number of working-class, minority, and immigrant people who visited Coney Island, reputedly being among the most likely populations Walt tried to edit out of his parks.

62. Avila, 7, 11, 63, 106, 117–19, 125, 137. Avila, 143, notes that for some minorities a visit to Disneyland was a "right of passage into the materially abundant universe of the middle class," even as it upheld a "dominant vision of suburban whiteness."

63. Cross, 641–43, 645–46.

64. Disney qtd. in Smith, *Walt Disney: Famous Quotes*, 30.

65. Disney qtd. in Thomas, *Walt Disney*, 2nd ed., 292; Bryman, *Disney and His Worlds*, 99–122.

66. For more on Florida in literature see A. E. Rowe.

67. Chandler, 4–5, 268; Derr, 14, 387. For example, Henry Flagler (John D. Rockefeller's partner in the Standard Oil Company) founded the Florida East Coast Railway with 764 miles of track and built hotels and cities along its route.

68. See "Rambler," *Guide to Florida* (1875; reproduced with additional images by University of Florida Press, 1904), for an example of the type.

69. Foglesong, 1–3. Walt considered siting his new park on the Mississippi River banks but walked from the project in 1963, after arguing with beer baron August Busch Jr. Disney decided that no alcohol would be sold in his park; Busch replied that it was foolish to open a St. Louis attraction that did not sell beer or liquor.

70. Barrier, 301; Gabler, 604; Gennawey, *Walt and the Promise of Progress City*, 173–75.

71. Gabler, 605; Gennawey, *Walt and the Promise of Progress City*, 172–75, 232–34.

72. Kelvin Bailey qtd. in Green and Green, 178; Disney Institute, *Be Our Guest*, 15. Mickey Mouse One, the plane used to scout the Florida property, is now on the Studio Backlot Tour at Disney's Hollywood Studios. Yee, *Walt Disney World Hidden History*, 165.

73. Gennawey, *Walt and the Promise of Progress City*, 233, 235–36. The dummy companies were named Ayefour Corporation (a reference to nearby Interstate 4), Bay Lake Properties, Latin American Development and Management Corporation, Reedy Creek Ranch, and Tomahawk Properties.

74. Thomas, *Walt Disney*, 2nd ed., 336–37. Disney lawyer Bob Price Foster orchestrated the land acquisition.

75. Disney qtd. in Stern, 211.

76. Emerson, 2.

77. Sullivan.

78. Adams, 139; Derr, 378–80, 383.

79. Ziebart, 12.

80. Disney qtd. in Thomas, *Walt Disney*, 2nd ed., 345.

81. Jenkins, 1–6; Ritchie; Schroeder. The preference for such lawns was inherited from late-eighteenth-century European aristocratic traditions.

82. Keys to the Kingdom Tour, 14 January 2011. Trash is later hand-sorted and compacted.

83. D. Snow, viii; Goldberger, 41, 92–93. The construction of man-made Seven Seas Lagoon and the dredging of Bay Lake provided more than 7 million cubic yards of landfill for the Magic Kingdom's foundation. Blake, 427, 437, maintains that many city planners aspire toward the utilidors' serviceability.

84. Ritzer, *The McDonaldization of Society*, 57, 91–92.

85. Disney qtd. in Spirn, 237; "A Clean Sweep for Disneyland"; "Tinker Bell, Mary Poppins, Cold Cash," 75. Kyriazi, 15–16, reminds us that early American amusement parks were often descended from picnic groves and beer gardens.

86. Kurland, 5. R. F. Snow, 22, claims that as a boy Walt was scolded for taking naps in apartment hallways to warm up and for playing with toys left on porches when delivering morning papers.

87. Wallace, 161–62; A. Williams, 490.

88. Shearer, 5.

89. Fjellman, 403; Bukatman, "There's Always Tomorrowland," 55; Gennawey, *Walt and the Promise of Progress City*, 266n57.

90. Findlay, 83–84, 112–13; Haden-Guest, 267.

91. Bryman, *The Disneyization of Society*, 133.

92. Haden-Guest, 276–78.

93. Eliot, 200–201. Watts, 446–47, believes Walt drank more toward the end of his life to curb pain from excessive health problems.

94. The 1960s drug culture embraced Disney films, especially *Fantasia* and *Alice in Wonderland*. Despite Disney's anti-drug stance, some visitors find the parks perfect places to get high. Real, 71–72; Sullivan; "Tripping on Disney."

95. Findlay, 115; J. Taylor, 26.

96. Chidester, 143.

97. Kinsey, 74. Disney uses a delay to block offending photos from being shown at the public kiosk.

98. Schweizer and Schweizer, 6–9, 11, 275–77.

99. McReynolds, "Disney Plays 'The Glad Game,'" 787–88, 790–92; Marin, "Disneyland: A Degenerate Utopia"; Bettelheim, especially 5–13. Marling, "Disneyland, 1955," 197, views Disney's dichotomies between good and evil as indicative of Cold War politics.

100. Pinsky, xi–xii, 230–31.

101. Findlay, 86–87, 91–92.

102. Izard; "Here's Your First View of Disneyland," 87; Fjellman, 396; "Walt Disney: Great Teacher," 90–95, 152, 154, 156.

103. Van Riper, 2–4. In 1941 the military essentially took over the Disney Studio, which began producing training, propaganda, and educational films for the war effort. Though Walt disliked having projects largely determined for him, this furthered his exploration of educational filmmaking.

104. Sammond, 324, 326–28, observes that the themed lands of Disney parks mimic the separation of subjects in school.

105. Brockus, 210.

106. Funicello qtd. in Wolters, 30.

107. M. J. King, "Disneyland and Walt Disney World," 129–31; Real, 44–89. Rojek, 121–22, 125–26, 128, 130–32, 134, aligns Disney with "rational recreation" programs in the nineteenth and early twentieth centuries, which used leisure activities to educate and foster self-improvement.

108. Hench qtd. in Haas, 15–16, 18.

109. Susman with Griffin, 30–33.

110. Rafferty with Gordon, 186–87. P. Williams with Denney, xiv, cites Art Linkletter's affirmation of Walt's desire to unite people regardless of their racial, ethnic, and national differences.

111. Sperb, 925. Also see Souther, 804–6.

112. Disney qtd. in Kurland, 15.

113. Reddy, 170; Haden-Guest, 280–81.

114. Hiaasen, 45–48.

115. "Castaway Cay: Past and Present."

116. Schama, 530, 562–64.

117. Mrs. Walt Disney (Lillian Bounds), 107; Schama, 537.

118. Kinsey, 135, 141. It was formerly named Blackbeard's Island and Treasure Island before being dubbed Discovery Island.

119. Holmes and Holmes, 139–41, 143, report that Disney spent $800 million on the African and Asian sections and could not afford to build the mythical zone. Yee, *Walt Disney World Hidden History*, 174–75, notes that though Beastlie Kingdomme's cave was sealed, it remains visible from Camp Minnie-Mickey, and dragon images still appear on the benches, trashcans, and ticket booths.

120. Gunther; Hiaasen, 68, 70–78; Pahl, 97. Thirty-one animals died in the first few months, and Disney was investigated by the U.S. Department of Agriculture.

121. Platt, 72–73.

122. K. Jones and Wills, 140.

123. Kurland, 6, 24–25.

124. Marin, "Disneyland"; Marin, *Utopics*, especially chapter 12, "Utopic Degeneration: Disneyland," 239–57.

125. Armytage, 13.

126. Dunlop, 46, 59.

127. Disney qtd. in Flower, 9.

128. Tuan with Hoelscher, 197–98.

129. Michalos, 222.

130. Sevareid qtd. in R. Bright, 88.

Chapter 4. Fantasy for Sale

1. Halevy.

2. Bradbury, 100, 104.

3. J. Bright, 299–303. Marcus, 203–4, notes that Halevy's suspicion was typical of the left-wing *Nation* and suggests that Bright's defense of Disney is not fully convincing.

4. M. J. King, "Empires of Popular Culture," 116, wonders whether "children supply the culturally obligatory alibi for adults to let themselves experience the parks without the embarrassment."

5. Naylor, 21–22, 24, 26; Serwer, 103; Sims, D1, D7; Streisand, 61–63.

6. Dery, "Past Perfect" (21.C), 15; Dery, "Past Perfect" (*The Pyrotechnic Insanitarium*).

7. Flower, 207; Sehlinger, 1992 ed., 8. For an account of Disney World's evolution over its first decade, see Zehnder.

8. Gabriel, 68, 79, 81, 84.

9. Rothman and Davis, 4.

10. Rothman, *Devil's Bargains*, 13–14, 289, 339, 352; Rothman, *Neon Metropolis*, xiii.

11. For a summary of Clark's Vegas plan, see Schultz, 49, 51.

12. "Dynamite Ducks," 22.

13. Venturi, Scott Brown, and Izenour, *Learning from Las Vegas*; "Las Vegas" (*TCI*), 24.

14. Izenour qtd. in Izenour and Dashiell, 47.

15. Neil, 380; Fowler, 426, 429.

16. Norberg-Schultz; Harvey, 21, 51, 82–83, 98, 338.

17. Blake, 426, 432.

18. Gottdiener, *The Theming of America*, 5–6, 108–10, 112, 114–15, 148–49.

19. Neil, 379–81.

20. Robert Venturi qtd. in Goldberger, 41, 92.

21. Ritzer, *The McDonaldization Thesis*, 9–10, 15, 123–25, 129, 131, 135, 147.

22. Wagner, 69; Phillips, 2.

23. Orvell, 35.

24. Bukatman, "The Artificial Infinite," 255–60, 263–67, 269–70, 279–80, 284, 287–89.

25. Morley, 12, 16, 18.

26. Kyriazi, 12–13.

27. Schama, 540.

28. Schama, 541–42.

29. "The Mirage Volcano."

30. Stratton, 29. The Mirage also features a climate-controlled tropical rainforest.

31. Originally Highway 91, the Strip was nicknamed after the Sunset Strip by Guy McAfee, a former Los Angeles police officer who became a Vegas executive in the 1950s.

32. Moehring and Green, 207.

33. Hoberman, 9; Anderton, 14.

34. Stratton, 2; Izenour and Dashiell, 49.

35. Newman, 82, 84.

36. Stratton, 23.

37. Leccese, 96; "Freemont Street Experience," 88. The "Experience" marks Vegas casinos owners' first willing investment in urban renewal; it received a Viva Vision technology upgrade in 2004.

38. Wolkomir, 55. Over an eighteen-month period in 1993–94, more than twenty thousand hotel rooms were added. After New York, New York Hotel and Casino opened in 1997, Vegas became the first American city with more than one hundred thousand hotel rooms. Rothman, *Devil's Bargains*, 334.

39. Betsky, "Pyramid Schemes," 50.

40. Kirshenblatt-Gimblett, 170.

41. P. A. Young, 72. The Luxor flew Egyptian authorities in from Cairo to attend the official opening of its replicated Tut tomb.

42. Silverman qtd. in Weathersby, 27. Wolkomir, 51, explains that an Egyptologist was hired to devise "crypto-Egyptian" hieroglyphics fed into a computer for random sequences. Of the approximately five hundred phrases generated, about forty were eliminated as they "actually said something."

43. Rothman and Davis, 1.

44. Rothman, *Devil's Bargains*, 328. A primetime TV special on NBC (23 January 1994) covered Treasure Island's opening.

45. D. Johnson, "Las Vegas: Buccaneer Bay," 35.

46. Wynn qtd. in Gabriel, 79, 81. To point, Wynn marketed the historic Dunes' demolition as a media event: it succumbed to "canon" fire from Buccaneer Bay the day Treasure Island opened.

47. Wynn qtd. in Labich, 82.

48. The Sands was imploded to make way for Bellagio.

49. Peterson.

50. Kostof, *The City Shaped*, 15, 162–64, 196.

51. Calthorpe, 9–12.

52. Langdon, 180–82.

53. James W. Rouse, Seventh Urban Design Conference, Harvard University Graduate School of Design, Cambridge, 26 April 1963, qtd. in R. Bright, 29; Barrier, 302; Mannheim, 24.

54. Galantay, 72–75.

55. Langdon, 115; see 111–16 for more on Seaside. Seaside was the setting for the 1998 film *The Truman Show*, which parodied small-town life.

56. Ball, 33.

57. Stern, 166–67.

58. Moehring, xi; K. D. Stein, 71, 74.

59. "Lifestyle."

60. "Cinderella's Condos?" 64; Klingmann, 78–79. In 1972 Disney built a community in Lake Buena Vista as a modest test for Epcot, clustering vacation homes around golf courses and waterways.

61. Kurtti, 164; Beardsley, "A Mickey Mouse Utopia," 79. Stern and Robertson developed the master plan and designed "background buildings." "Signature buildings" were designed by other high-profile architects: Robert Venturi's bank, Cesar Pelli's cinema, Michael Graves's post office, Philip Johnson's town hall, and Charles Moore's visitors center/real estate office.

62. Dery, "Past Perfect" (*21.C*), 17.

63. Beardsley, "A Mickey Mouse Utopia," 92–93. An official pattern book provided basic house types and configurations for the entire town. It also mandated "formal" over "random" landscape design; specified percentages, locations, and species of plantings; and regulated fencing height, opacity, and placement.

64. *Architectural Walking Tour* qtd. in Dery, "Past Perfect" (*21.C*), 15; Adams qtd. in Dery, "Past Perfect" (*21.C*), 16.

65. Wolf, 28; Dery, "Past Perfect" (*21.C*), 16; Gennawey, *Walt and the Promise of Progress City*, 349–50.

66. Marton qtd. in B. Davis.

67. Franz, 31.

68. Riddle.

69. B. Davis.

70. Rummell qtd. in Beardsley, "A Mickey Mouse Utopia," 92.

71. Beardsley, "A Mickey Mouse Utopia," 79, 93.

72. Pollan, 78–79.

73. Dery, "Past Perfect" (*21.C*), 15–16.

74. Huxtable, 42, 64–65.

75. Beardsley, "A Mickey Mouse Utopia," 79, 83, 92.

76. Koenig, *Realityland*, 288.

77. Pollan, 56, 58–59, 62–63, 78, 88. This included stipulations that no more than two

people could sleep in a single bedroom; no pickup trucks, mobile homes, or boat trailers could be parked in front of homes; and only one garage sale a year was permitted. Many newer planned communities, such as Seasons at Prince Creek West (Murrells Inlet, South Carolina), have adopted similarly tight regulations for their residents.

78. Rummell qtd. in Beardsley, "A Mickey Mouse Utopia" 93.

79. A. Ross, *The Celebration Chronicles*; A. Ross, "The Mickey House Club," 25, 100.

80. Franz and Collins; Franz, 31.

81. Pollan, 62–63, 76.

82. Ritzer, *Enchanting a Disenchanted World*, 111.

83. Helton.

84. Foglesong, 172.

85. Koenig, *Realityland*, 316.

86. Keys to the Kingdom Tour, 14 January 2011.

87. Goodnough.

88. Goldberger, 99.

89. C. R. Howard, 163.

90. Helton.

91. Baudrillard, *The Consumer Society*, 46, 99. Also see Baudrillard's "Consumer Society" in *Selected Writings*, 34–35.

92. Kowinski, 65, 67, 69–73, 355.

93. Schama, 567.

94. M. C. Taylor, 259–60; Mann, 73–74. K. Jones and Wills, 154, point to the rise in suburbanization, car usage, and middle-class affluence as major factors in the popularization of malls.

95. The Park at MOA (Mall of America) replaced Knott's Camp Snoopy in 2006. By 2008 Nickelodeon Universe opened, which still operates today.

96. Hannigan, 89–91; Gibian, 270.

97. Huxtable, 107; Barber, *Jihad vs. McWorld*, 97, 128, 130–32; Kostof, *The City Assembled*, 185–86.

98. Margaret Crawford.

99. M. C. Taylor, 293–94; Gibian, 261–63, 271–73, 279; Baudrillard, *America*, 127–28. Baudrillard, "Consumer Society," 31, is struck by the arrangement of goods calculated to incite a "frenzy of purchasing and possession."

100. Gibian, 238–39, 258, 282–83.

101. Disney qtd. in "Here's Your First View of Disneyland," 86.

102. Marling, "Disneyland, 1955," 183–84; Marling, *As Seen on TV*, 106–8. Nearly every structure on Hollywood and Sunset Boulevards in Disney's Hollywood Studios was modeled after real Los Angeles architecture. Yee, *Walt Disney World Hidden History*, 132.

103. Gibian, 273.

104. Dougall qtd. in Shillingburg, 84.

105. Betsky, "Theme Wars Rage in Vegas."

106. Marling, *As Seen on TV*, 116.

107. Fjellman, 394; Francaviglia, *Main Street Revisited*, 162, 164–66, 175; Kowinski, 70; Lipsitz, 138; Philips, 30, 32–33.

108. Ritzer, *The McDonaldization Thesis*, 144–45; Marin, "Disneyland: A Degenerate Utopia," 62–63; Eco, 43, 48.

109. Francaviglia, *Main Street Revisited*, 162, explains: Disneyland Main Street's first floor is built to nine-eighths scale, the second to seven-eighths, and the third to five-eighths; Disney World's Main Street has full-sized upper stories.

110. Keys to the Kingdom Tour, 14 January 2011.

111. Kunstler, 219, 221; Haden-Guest, 237. At Vegas, a similar optimism denies harsh realities: in 1951 the U.S. government tested atomic weapons 150 miles away for which visitors, seeking a better view, flocked to the Desert Inn's Sky Room.

112. Sturken, *Tangled Memories*, 7, 9, 11–12.

113. Wolkomir, 58.

114. Barmé, 29, 32–33.

115. Stratton, 29, notes that developer Jay Sarno omitted the apostrophe in the resort's name: rather than the domain of a single ruler (Caesar's), he wanted every guest to feel like a king (Caesars).

116. Eco, 34, 40–41; N. Perry, 45.

117. MacDonald and Pinto, 329.

118. Carroll, 131.

119. W. J. Mitchell, Moore, and Turnbull, 90.

120. Sears, 215–16.

121. Huxtable, 4, 15, 17, 41, 45, 95–97. Also see Schaap, 1, 12. Zelinsky, "Imaginary Landscapes," 48, contends that Williamsburg represents "the past as it could or should have been if the 18th-century inhabitants had the good fortune to be as ingenious and sanitary as we are today." Cross and Walton, 255, observe that since the new millennium, Williamsburg has experienced a deficit in its operating budget, drops in attendance, staff layoffs, programming cuts, and attacks on its authenticity.

122. Kirshenblatt-Gimblett, 7, 9, 69, 72, 132–33, 135, 147, 150, 167, 171, 175, 194, 199.

123. Bryman, *Disney and His Worlds*, 127, 140–42.

124. Wallace, 158, 179.

125. Barmé, 38.

126. Lowenthal, 247, 259, 271, 273, 293, 306, 331, 350, 408.

127. Sturken, *Tourists of History*, 9.

128. Tunnard and Pushkarev, 421.

129. For more on the slavery exhibition see Styron.

130. Barber, *Jihad vs. McWorld*, 135–36. Also see Koenig, *Mouse under Glass*, 234–35.

131. Huxtable, 47; Hiaasen, 24. In addition to the 150-acre park were plans for 3,000 additional acres of development, spurring concern about land use and transportation patterns. For more on the controversy see D. Ayres; Cushman; Hofmeister; Janofsky.

132. See by Wines: "A Disneyland of History Next to the Real Thing"; "Step Up, Folks! Check It Out! Nationhood!" 1, 24; and "Yes Virginia, the Past Can Be Plasticized."

133. Sperb, 929–36.

134. Sturken, *Tangled Memories*, 1–2, 259.

135. See MacCannell, *The Tourist*, for a detailed account of "touristic space." Also see MacCannell, "Staged Authenticity."

136. Ritzer, *Enchanting a Disenchanted World*, 88, 90, 144.

137. Brinkerhof qtd. in Shillingburg, 84.

138. Rothman, *Devil's Bargains*, 13–14.

139. Jameson, 16, 44, 49, 117–18.

140. Eisenman.

141. Rafferty with Gordon, 91.

142. Sewall qtd. in Feifer, 253.

143. Sorkin, "See You in Disneyland," 208, 216.

144. Hench with Van Pelt, 67.

145. Trowbridge and Stapleton, 57–61; Cross and Walton, 5.

146. Rockwell with Mau, 15.

147. Congdon and Blandy, 269.

148. Klingmann, 75–76, 80.

149. Newcomb, 7.

150. Lukas, "A Politics of Reverence and Irreverence," 273.

151. Pike, 54.

152. Bukatman, "There's Always Tomorrowland," 75–78.

153. Telotte, 138–39.

154. Huxtable, 75.

155. Hess, 8, 10–11, 124, praises the Strip for its pragmatism, innovation, culturally rich infrastructure, distinguishing landmarks, and public spaces. Also see Stungo.

156. Venturi, Scott Brown, and Izenour, *Learning from Las Vegas*, 34.

157. Doss, 181.

158. Newman, 82.

159. Relph, 90, 114, 134, 143.

Chapter 5. Fair Game

1. For clarity's sake I use "Epcot": when the term appears elsewhere here, it does so per another person's usage. Kurtti, 116, says Disney rechristened the park "Epcot" in recognition of its acceptance as a concept rather than an acronym. J. Ross, 64, queries: "Why does the company retain that inelegant acronym, Epcot, with its faintly medicinal overtones, evocative of . . . Ex-lax?"

2. Disney qtd. in Smith, *Walt Disney: Famous Quotes*, 53.

3. A. Ross, "The Mickey House Club," 25–26.

4. Kurtti, 88–89. Initially Epcot was geared specifically to adults and had no costumed characters or related merchandise.

5. Flower, 28–29. Watts, 447, maintains Walt was not cryogenically frozen. Oddly his official death announcement was delayed until Disney was already cremated and interred at Forest Lawn Memorial Park, Glendale. Cryogenic myths persist: in 2010, Postmasters Gallery, New York City, hosted *Defrosted: A Life of Walt Disney* (curated by Adam Cvijanovic and David Humphrey).

6. Harris, "Expository Expositions," 19; Findlay, 66.

7. Official program qtd. in Kurtti, 82.

8. Harris, "Expository Expositions," 19.

9. Kyriazi, 47, emphasizes that the earlier fairs in New York and Philadelphia lacked midways.

10. Sears, 215.

11. Gilbert, 5, believes organizers inflated attendance, emphasizing the implausibility of nearly 40 percent of the U.S. population attending the 1893 fair. Rydell, *All the World's a Fair*, 41–43, notes the irony of celebrating the West Indies' "discovery" a thousand miles away from the Atlantic Ocean.

12. Stern, 310; Mattie, 88. For a nineteenth-century treatment of the fair see R. Johnson.

13. Lukas, *Theme Park*, 30–32.

14. Harris, *Cultural Excursions*, 121–22. Also see Stern, 309.

15. Lovell, 53–54, explains that "distasteful" evidence of physical labor and class differences was downplayed as much as possible.

16. Lovell, 40–43, 46–47. Press coverage emphasized the civility, sobriety, and good behavior of fair crowds.

17. Mattie, 96–97. Tselos proposes that the Chicago fair interrupted the development of progressive architecture.

18. Celik, 81.

19. Harris, *Cultural Excursions*, 123–28.

20. Harris, *Cultural Excursions*, 46.

21. Hinsley, 351–55.

22. Celik, 83, 85, 87–88.

23. White and Ingleheart, 595. This source includes chapters by fair organizers such as F. W. Putnam and F. J. V. Skiff.

24. Rydell, *All the World's a Fair*, 64. Frederic Ward Putnam, head of Harvard University's Peabody Museum of American Archaeology and Ethnology, was in charge of the ethnological exhibits. Visitors were measured by physical anthropologists to demonstrate the relative "superiority"/"inferiority" of the races.

25. Lutz and Collins, 25. For more on ethnographic display see Rydell and Gwinn.

26. Lovell, 43–44, 46.

27. See B. Brown, 142. Technology was highlighted from opening day (30 April 1904), when President Theodore Roosevelt turned on fair fountains by pressing a button in Washington, D.C. In 1893 an electric train made a six-mile loop around the Chicago fairgrounds.

28. Instead of decrying the midway, 1904 fair promoters endorsed it as a means to win support for imperialist aspirations. Rydell, *All the World's a Fair*, 235–36.

29. *Twilight Tuesdays*, 10. My description of Pike attractions is indebted to their recounting here, 4–9.

30. J. Davis, 95–96.

31. Breitbart, 15–16.

32. Rydell, *All the World's a Fair*, 159–78. Rydell, promotional literature, *Meet Me at the Fair*. The fair was a last chance to see the "barbarous" and "savage," claimed to soon be extinct.

33. Diaz-Granados, promotional literature, *Meet Me at the Fair*. Rydell, *All the World's a Fair*, 155, 157, points out the irony that the St. Louis fair's $15 million in start-up capital was the same price the United States paid for the Louisiana Territory.

34. Breitbart, 13, 31, 44–45. Over 750 professional photographers were accredited by the fair's press bureau.

35. Benedict, 43–45; Celik, 18–20.

36. J. Davis, 97.

37. Corbett, and Miller, promotional literature, *Meet Me at the Fair*.

38. Hall, 67, 71, 82, 155.

39. Greenwood, 179, 183; Benedict, 2, 5, 24, 41. Mattie, 8, suggests that weakened international trade regulations during the latter half of the nineteenth century linked world trade with world peace. European fairs were largely government financed, but in the United States private corporations provided most of the funding.

40. Hinsley, 362–63; Dorfman, 29, 54.

41. Gibian, 264–66, indicates that fair exhibition halls presaged the form and function of the shopping mall.

42. Rydell, "Souvenirs of Imperialism," 47, 52–55, 58.

43. Harvey, 264, 300–302.

44. O'Day, 36.

45. Disney qtd. in Watts, 441.

46. Barrier, 303; Koenig, *Realityland*, 13; Gennawey, *Walt and the Promise of Progress City*, 228–29.

47. Michael Crawford, 42; Ridgway, 124.

48. Gennawey, "Walt Disney's EPCOT and the Heart of Our Cities," 103, 105; Gennawey, *Walt and the Promise of Progress City*, 213, 216–18, 221, 225, 266, 350; Gabler, 608; Mannheim, 25; Zukin, 224; K. Jones and Wills, 174. Barrier, 308, contends that Howard's book was "probably the strongest single influence on . . . Disney's thinking."

49. Pedersen, 3.

50. Haden-Guest, 306; De George, 48; Barrier, 311–12; Gabler, 621, 624–25; Gennawey, *Walt and the Promise of Progress City*, 238, 262–65. Walt practiced before the filming for an audience that included Art Linkletter and Welton Becket.

51. Gennawey, *Walt and the Promise of Progress City*, 277, 298, 322, 362, 365.

52. Disney qtd. in Greene and Greene, 158–59.

53. Michael Crawford, 43; Galantay, 56.

54. Moses qtd. in Gabler, 610.

55. Greene and Greene, 159.

56. Goldberger, 93. Findlay, 106, 110–11, concurs with Goldberger.

57. Watts, 444. Avila, 131, suggests Disney's suspicions regarding government bureaucracy prompted his belief that "the social order" could be marketed, "not legislated."

58. J. Taylor, 33–34.

59. Mannheim, ix, xvi–xvii, 9, 27, 90, 118, 129.

60. Gabler, 631; Michael Crawford, 47.

61. Flower, 60.

62. Sklar, Introduction, 29. Sklar, Randy Bright, John Hench, Don Edgren, and Carl Borgirno were central to Epcot's development.

63. Koenig, *Mouse Tales*, 217.

64. Disney qtd. in J. Taylor, 33.

65. Lovell, 48.

66. Breitbart, 38.

67. Harrison explains that attendance fell short of the expected 50 million. Running at a deficit, the fair was held over into 1940, though it still closed with a shortfall of $1.9 million.

68. Mannheim, 15; Mattie, 195, 198–99. Celik, 137, believes the visibility of fair architecture was "disproportionate to the short lives of the buildings themselves" due to publications.

69. Harris, "Expository Exhibitions," 26.

70. Pepper, 304–6, 308–9, 319; Lukas, *Theme Park*, 31–32; Mattie 198–99, 220; Rydell, *World of Fairs*, 9.

71. *Official Guidebook, New York World's Fair 1939*, 27.

72. Pepper, 304–6, 308–9, 319; Gennawey, *Walt and the Promise of Progress City*, 359. Nabisco screened a Disney short, *Mickey's Surprise Party*, but it is not known if Walt attended this fair.

73. Harrison; Zukin, 225–28; Pepper, 305–6, 309–12, 315, 323; Gennawey, *Walt and the Promise of Progress City*, 360. For more on the Futurama exhibit see Corn and Horrigan, 46–50.

74. Harris, *Cultural Excursions*, 68, 112, 115, 117–19, 128–30.

75. Rydell, *World of Fairs*, 10; Corn and Horrigan, 11.

76. Marling, "Imagineering the Disney Theme Parks," 36, 38.

77. Marling, "Disneyland, 1955," 177–78, 186–87. Wolters, 71, claims that the train trip helped Walt take "all the jangles out of his system. His worry-wart days were put behind." Walt admitted: "Things had gone wrong. I had trouble with a picture. I worried and worried. I had a nervous breakdown. I kept crying." Disney qtd. in Menen, 106.

78. Marling, *As Seen on TV*, 96, 98–99, 101–6.

79. Disney qtd. in Smith, *Walt Disney: Famous Quotes*, 62.

80. Findlay, 71.

81. Marling, *As Seen on TV*, 6; Corn and Horrigan, 82–83; Gennawey, *Walt and the Promise of Progress City*, 326–27.

82. Michael Crawford, 48–49, 51–52.

83. Marling, "Imagineering the Disney Theme Parks," 164.

84. Mattie, 9.

85. *Unofficial Walt Disney Imagineering Site*.

86. The Land was extensively revamped. Most notably Soarin', a hang glider simulator, was added in May 2005 (debuted at Disneyland).

87. Yee, *Walt Disney World Hidden History*, 97–98. At World of Motion, and now Test Track, disembarking riders find themselves in the midst of a General Motors showroom.

88. Mattie, 218, 220. The Unisphere was designed by Imagineer Harper Goff, although he was not working for Disney at the time.

89. Watts, 414.

90. Jethani, 37.

91. Carousel of Progress narration qtd. in Watts, 415. Negotiations were swift as Walt had approached GE earlier about sponsoring an unrealized Disneyland attraction, Edison Square.

92. Watts, 415–16; Gabler, 577. Walt personally supervised the Carousel details and conceived its grand publicity stunt: the robotic Granny made a hundred-city tour on her way to New York.

93. Gennawey, "Walt Disney's EPCOT and the Heart of Our Cities," 101–2; Gennawey, *Walt and the Promise of Progress City*, 260–62. A 1967 WED Enterprises report confirms that Progress City was derived from Walt's plans for Epcot.

94. D. Cohen, 11.

95. Gennawey, *Walt and the Promise of Progress City*, 199.

96. Disney qtd. in Smith, *Walt Disney: Famous Quotes*, 11. Moses convinced Illinois to be the sponsor, secretly loaning the state $250,000. Watts, 417–18, observes that Moses's actions were controversial given the Fair Corporation's insolvency.

97. Hench qtd. in Greene and Greene, 156.

98. Disney qtd. in Smith, *Walt Disney: Famous Quotes*, 11.

99. Wiener, 605, 620, 622–23.

100. Watts, 418; Gennawey, *Walt and the Promise of Progress City*, 211. Hannigan, 47–48, reports that Walt considered St. Louis, Niagara Falls, and Washington, D.C., as potential locations for a new park, but their climates hampered year-round operation.

101. Watts, 414, 418.

102. Sklar qtd. in Gennawey, *Walt and the Promise of Progress City*, 197.

103. Lipsitz, 138.

104. Haden-Guest, 263, 297.

105. Fjellman, 400.

106. Flower, 196.

107. Kurtti, 92, 94; T. R. King, B1, B8.

108. Wallace, 158, 165, 167–74; Harrington, 42–44, 86.

109. MacFadyen, 26, 29–30, 32.

110. Marling, "Imagineering the Disney Theme Parks," 166, 168.

111. Adams, 150, 153.

112. Doss, 185; Smoodin, *Disney Discourse*, 7. See De Roos for *National Geographic* as another possible source, particularly for costumes and Audio-Animatronic animals.

113. Goldberger, 94; Michael Crawford, 50. The invited countries were Australia, Denmark, Greece, Israel, the former Soviet Union, the Philippines, Romania, Venezuela, Belgium, New Zealand, Iran, Germany, Mexico, Italy, and the United Kingdom. Of these fifteen, only the last four have Epcot pavilions.

114. Rafferty with Gordon, 68–69; Kurtti, 86, 106. The present arrangement of World Showcase is indebted to Harper Goff.

115. Ridgway, 140.

116. The series was part of the original sponsorship agreement, so Disney had to renegotiate contracts and refund a portion of fees.

117. Eisner with Schwartz, 114; Flower, 94; Alcorn and Green, 1–3, recount mass Disney layoffs in 1982–83, after Epcot's opening.

118. Yee, *Walt Disney World Hidden History*, 121. Pedersen, 262, claims Turkey was told another pavilion was not wanted at the time, and South Korea was denied because Disney thought its pavilion would not attract enough visitors to justify cost.

119. Beard, 134–35, 200.

120. M. J. King, "Empires of Popular Culture," 114.

121. This was titled *America the Beautiful*. B. Brown, 142; Rydell, *World of Fairs*, 204.

122. Celik, 1–3, 56, 136, 178.

123. Kaufman, 22–26, 32–33, 36.

124. Harper Goff suggested using individual buildings instead of linked pavilions. My description of World Showcase is indebted to Kurtti, 106–15. Pepper, 323, likens Epcot's IllumiNations to the Lagoon of Nations extravaganzas at the 1939–40 fair.

125. Beard, 220, 223, 225. Pedersen, 260–61, notes that the emphasis would have been on Equatorial Africa. Yee, *Walt Disney World Hidden History*, 121, explains the minimal theming here was used to test how well a new pavilion would work among the others and to lure sponsorship, but such was never secured.

126. Dunlop, 60, indicates that a planned Rhine River attraction was not completed. Yee, *Walt Disney World Hidden History*, 120, points out that a building constructed for the ride remains.

127. A. Wilson, "The Betrayal of the Future," 51, describes it as a "bastardized Georgian" used to connote "history."

128. Kurtti, 110. Randy Bright proposed the present format, which remains much the same as it was in 1982. Yee, *Walt Disney World Hidden History*, 126, reports the original plan called for a third narrator, Will Rogers, but designers decided three was "a crowd."

129. Featured historical figures and popular icons include Jackie Robinson, Marilyn Monroe, Jonas Salk, Albert Einstein, Billie Jean King, Martin Luther King Jr., John F. Kennedy, and Walt Disney. More recent additions include Run-D.M.C. and Frank Gehry.

130. Wallace, 175–78.

131. Yee, *Walt Disney World Hidden History*, 127.

132. Root, 68–70, 81–82, 84–86, 116.

133. Many Epcot employees are college students earning credits. Koenig, *Realityland*, 318–19, recounts the 1990 passing of the Q-1 visa (the "Disney visa"), which allows the company to hire temporary workers to share their cultures rather than do skilled labor.

134. Mason, 2–3.

135. Hinsley, 356, makes an analogous observation about the 1893 fair. Everett chronicles similar experiences at the 1904 fair.

136. Rydell, *All the World's a Fair*, 157–59, notes that doctors warned the 1904 fair would cause physical and mental exhaustion.

137. Wallis, 265–68, 271–72, 274–79.

138. Boorstin, 3–6, 77, 79–80, 99, 106, 116, 145–46, 256.

139. Mason, 5, 7, 11, 15.

140. Rojek, 128–30; Marling, *As Seen on TV*, 116, 118; Real, 60–62, 64–65; E. Cohen, "Toward a Sociology of International Tourism," 164–82; E. Cohen, "Who Is a Tourist?" 527–55.

141. Celik, 3, 190, 194–95, 198; B. Brown, 149; Rydell, *All the World's a Fair*, 2–7, 70, 235, 237; Rydell, *The Books of the Fairs*, 6–7.

142. J. Taylor, 38–40.

143. Benedict, 59–60; "World's Fairs? Who Cares?" 19; Harris, "Expository Expositions," 22.

144. Breitbart, 39.

145. Breitbart, 49–50.

146. Harrison, 1.

Conclusion

1. Brode, *Multiculturalism and the Mouse*, 257, 259.

2. T. Young, 1.

3. Richard Foglesong qtd. in Hiaasen, 26. Hiassen, 27, 57, observes that Celebration's de-annexation from the main property ensures that "sovereign Reedy Creek will remain largely unpopulated, and therefore safe from the uncertainties of democracy."

4. Gennawey, *Walt and the Promise of Progress City*, 349; A. Stein, 3–4.

5. A. Williams, 484.

6. Claude Kirk qtd. in Clay, 76.

7. De George, 48–49; Foglesong, 5; Ziebart, 3; Blake, 446; Gennawey, *Walt and the Promise of Progress City*, 249–51.

8. Flower, 253.

9. Keys to the Kingdom Tour, 14 January 2011.

10. Foglesong qtd. in Stuever, C.1; Kurtti, 27; Foglesong, 12; A. Wilson, *The Culture of Nature*, 177.

11. Pickett qtd. in "Cinderella's Condos?" 64.

12. Sullivan; Foglesong, 5–6, 15, 63, 75, 172.

13. Koenig, *Realityland*, 15, 40–41; Michael Crawford, 45; Sullivan; Gennawey, *Walt and the Promise of Progress City*, 247–48, 336–37.

14. Shortsleeve, 26.

15. Kirk qtd. in Gennawey, *Walt and the Promise of Progress City*, 249.

16. Short, 10.

17. Bryman, *The Disneyization of Society*, vii, 1, 59, 61. Also see Bryman, *Disney and His Worlds*, 122–26, 143–45, 160.

18. Flower, 87–88. Keisei Electric Company and Mitsui Real Estate owned the then newly formed Oriental Land Company.

19. Raz, 210–11.

20. Brannen, 617–20, 623–24, 626–29.

21. Flower, 207–8. Concessions included an artificially low purchase price for the land guaranteed for twenty years; a loan of up to $770 million from the French government at a reduced interest rate; and first refusal on ten thousand abutting acres.

22. Koenig, *Mouse Tales*, 219; "Euro Disney Expects Losses to Continue"; "Euro Disney Reports Loss."

23. Ritzer, *The McDonaldization Thesis*, 74.

24. Grover, "Now Disneyland Won't Seem So Mickey Mouse," 56–58. Anaheim officials, desirous of the tax revenues and thousands of jobs the new park was expected to bring, gave Disney $200 million in tax subsidies and other concessions.

25. Morris qtd. in Schuman and Ressner.

26. Fung and Lee, 206–7.

27. Lainsbury, 2, 12, 174–75.

28. Zukin, 217–50.

29. For example, see McLuhan and Fiore; and McLuhan and Powers.

30. Said, 292, 309; M. C. Taylor, 195.

31. Dery, "Past Perfect" (*21.C*), 16–17.

32. Tomlinson, 119–21, 125–26.

33. Ball, 32.

34. Hearn and Roseneil, 4, 12.

35. Short, 10–12.

36. Weber.

37. Giroux, 4–5, 7–8, 18, 109, 114. B. Ayres offers a similar view.

38. *Mickey Mouse Monopoly*.

39. Brode, *From Walt to Woodstock*, x–xi, xvi, xxii, 220; Brode, *Multiculturalism and the Mouse*, 8–10, 18, 257–58, 262, 270. Pinsky also conceives of Disney as teaching tolerance and empathy, though he is concerned about stereotypes in its films.

40. Avila, 15, 238–39.

41. Best and Lowney, 431, 433, 446.

42. Chidester, 18, 144; Stuever, C.1.

43. Hiaasen, 12–13, 17–18, 20.

44. Disney qtd. in Flower, 142; Mannheim, 89. Findlay, 58–59, explains that initial Disneyland plans included free admission, but escalating construction costs required charging a fee.

45. Adams, 159; Eisner with Schwartz, *Work in Progress*, 118–19; Koenig, *Realityland*, 247–48; J. Taylor, viii. To protect itself, Disney increased its size and acquired Arvida in June 1984.

46. From 1966 to 1971, Roy O. Disney, Card Walker, and Donn B. Tatum ran Disney. Ron Miller (Walt's son-in-law) eventually succeeded Walker in 1983. Wells died in a helicopter crash; Katzenberg left the company in 1994. See Magnet, 56–58, 60, 62, 64.

47. Ridgway, 228; Brockus, 205, 208; Eisner with Schwartz, *Work in Progress*, xi. Schickel, *The Disney Version*, 3rd ed., 4, proposes that before Eisner, Disney management was "cautious and uninspired."

48. Stewart recounts the "war" between Eisner and Roy E. Disney.

49. Capodagli and Jackson, *The Disney Way*, xii–xiii, 216–17, 221–23. In 2006 Iger purchased Pixar for Disney, paying $7.6 billion.

50. Koenig, *Realityland*, 316–20.

51. Koenig, *Realityland*, 320.

52. Hiaasen, 1–4; Pulley; Rowman and Evans, 1, 50, point out that Disney did not have to contribute to subway repairs or other amenities because it was believed the company would have a nearly instant revitalizing effect on the neighborhood. Also planned for the area was a Disney timeshare center/retail complex/hotel to be sited at Forty-Second Street and Eighth Avenue, but this was scrapped. The New Amsterdam opened on 20 May 1997.

53. S. G. Davis, 159–61.

54. Rummell qtd. in Rose, 102. Also see Rose, 94–98, 100, 102, 104; Bosselmann, 107.

55. Hannigan, 8; K. Jones and Wills, 157.

56. C. W. Moore, 59, 65, 83, 97.

57. Foglesong, xi–xii, 10–13.

58. Telotte, 124, 126–29, 131–32, 134–35, 139–40.

59. Budd, 15.

60. S. G. Davis, 160; Smoodin, *Disney Discourse*.

61. Roy O. Disney qtd. in Thomas, *Walt Disney*, 2nd ed., 357. Roy died shortly after Disney World's opening, on 19 December 1971.

62. Keys to the Kingdom Tour, 14 January 2011. Disney offers discounts to counteract attendance dips during off-peak seasons and economic downturns.

63. Barnes and Martin, B3; A. Stein, 8; Koenig, *Realityland*, 321.

64. Imagineers, *The Imagineering Way*, 14.

65. Mohl and Mormino, 437.

66. Holmes and Holmes, 148–50; Cross and Walton, 197–99, 255. After a 1990s layoff, some Imagineers worked for Universal Studios.

67. Koenig, *Realityland*, 322–23. Perhaps some are too thrilling: riders of Mission: SPACE (a flight simulator in Epcot's Future World) suffered medical problems and several deaths occurred, leading Disney to offer the option of a tamer version.

68. Vaughn qtd. in Barnes and Martin, B3.

69. A former Disney marketing executive, Pontius wrote *Waking Walt*, a thriller in which Disney awakens from a cryogenically preserved state to battle corporate raiders. Doctorow, *Down and Out in the Magic Kingdom*, is a science-fiction novel set in the future: its protagonist resides in Disney World.

70. Walker.

71. Hazel and Fippen, xiii–xiv, xx, note that after Southern Baptists announced their boycott, Disney stock shot up 10 percent.

72. See the following by S. Griffin: "Curiouser and Curiouser," 125, 141, 146; *Tinker Belles and Evil Queens*, xi–xv, xvii–xviii, 188, 228–29; "'You've Never Had a Friend Like Me,'" 206–10.

73. Brockus, 200–201.

74. Eliot, 225; Smoodin, *Animating Culture*, 161–62.

75. Watts, 441–42, 449.

76. Harrington, 39.

77. Nagourney and Barnes suggest that the Reagan Foundation wanted to boost admissions and merchandise sales at and increase the relevancy of its library.

78. Lukas, "How the Theme Park Gets Its Power," 195–96; Lukas, "A Politics of Reverence and Irreverence," 273.

79. Bryman, *The Disneyization of Society*, 149.

80. Findlay, 76; Koenig, *Mouse Tales*, 222. Also see Koenig, *More Mouse Tales*.

81. Green qtd. in Gunther, 123.

82. I observed these acts in the parks. Probably most distressing to Walt would have been workers "going robot." See Bryman, *The Disneyization of Society*, 151; Van Maanen, "The Smile Factory."

83. Cockerell, 6–9, 15; Shuit, 38, 40; Kinsey, 28. Loyalty is rewarded with perks such as the "Silver" Main Entrance Pass given to Cast Members with at least fifteen years on the job, which grants free access for three people a day into the parks.

84. Villmoare and Stillman, 81–82, 95.

85. Doris.

86. Bryman, *The Disneyization of Society*, 151.

87. Sullivan.

88. Levs. Disney has vowed to investigate the problematic practice and take action.

89. Kinsey, 1–3, 20, 43, 83, 95, 122–23, 128–31, 135–37, 141, 143, 153. Rather than a utilidor system per se, Epcot has a small set of rooms under Spaceship Earth and an extensive backstage area encircling the entire park.

90. Moore qtd. in Carey.

91. Carey; Lorentz; Wu. Although shorts and small portions of feature-length films have been shot surreptitiously on Disney property, *Escape from Tomorrow* is the first to have done so extensively.

92. Stuever, C.1.

93. K. M. Jackson, *Walt Disney Conversations*, ix, x, xii–xiii.

94. Disney qtd. in K. M. Jackson, *Walt Disney Conversations*, 19.

95. Schickel, *The Disney Version*, 3rd ed., 3–4, 7–8.

96. Zaslow.

97. Stuever, C.1.

98. Byrne and McQuillan, 5–6; Kurland, 11.

99. Disney qtd. in Sklar, "The Artist as Imagineer," 14.

100. Brigham, 212–14.

101. Telotte, 137.

102. My discussion of the tour is based on the one I took, Keys to the Kingdom Tour, 14 January 2011.

103. Pike, 48, 53, 56, 58–59.

104. Huxtable, 49–50, 52, 54–55, 58–63, 69–70, 75, 112–13, 116, 182.

Bibliography

Adams, Judith A. *The American Amusement Park Industry: A History of Technology and Thrills*. Boston: Twayne, 1991.

Alcorn, Steve, and David Green. *Building a Better Mouse: The Story of the Electronic Imagineers who Designed Epcot*. Orlando: Theme Perks, 2007.

Allan, Robin. *Walt Disney and Europe: European Influences on the Animated Feature Films of Walt Disney*. Bloomington: Indiana University Press, 1999.

Anderton, Frances. "Hurry, Hurry to See the Natural Pop Art Icons." *Art Newspaper* intl. ed., Oct. 1995: 12+.

Apgar, Garry. "The Meaning of Mickey Mouse." *Visual Resources: An International Journal of Documentation* 14 (1999): 263–73.

Armytage, W. H. G. *Yesterday's Tomorrows: A Historical Survey of Future Societies*. Toronto: University of Toronto Press, 1968.

Arnal, William. "The Segregation of Social Desire: 'Religion' and Disney World." *Journal of the American Academy of Religion* 69.1 (Mar. 2001): 1–19.

"The Art of Reverend Howard Finster." *American Artist* July 1991: 10.

Atiya, Aziz S. *Crusade, Commerce and Culture*. Bloomington: Indiana University Press, 1962.

Avila, Eric. *Popular Culture in the Age of White Flight: Fear and Fantasy in Suburban Los Angeles*. Berkeley: University of California Press, 2004.

Ayres, Brenna, ed. *The Emperor's Old Groove: Decolonizing Disney's Magic Kingdom*. New York: Peter Lang, 2003.

Ayres, Drummond, Jr. "Disney Drums Its Fingers as Virginia Debates the Worth of a Theme Park." *New York Times* 22 Feb. 1994: A17.

Aziz, Barbara Nimri. "Personal Dimensions of the Sacred Journey: What Pilgrims Say." *Religious Studies* 23 (1987): 247–61.

Bailey, Adrian. *Walt Disney's World of Fantasy*. New York: Everest, 1982.

Ball, Edward. "To Theme or Not to Theme: Disneyfication without Guilt." *The Once and Future Park*. Ed. Deborah Karasov. Princeton: Princeton Architectural Press/Walker Art Center, 1993. 31–37.

Bannon, Lisa. "Disney Decides World Isn't So Small, Creating Education Resort for Boomers." *Wall Street Journal* 1 Mar. 1996: B1+.

Barber, Benjamin R. *Jihad vs. McWorld*. New York: Times-Random, 1995.

———. "The Making of McWorld." *New Perspectives Quarterly* 12.4 (1995): 13–17.

Barmé, Geremie R. "Archaeo-tainment: Fantasy at the Other End of History." *Third Text* 30 (1995): 29–38.

Barnes, Brooks, and Andrew J. Martin. "Disney Plans 'Interactive' Updates in Theme Parks." *New York Times* (Business/Financial Desk, Late Edition East Coast) 14 Sept. 2009: B3. ProQuest. Emerson College Library. Accessed 23 Nov. 2009. ProQuest document ID: 1858425581.

Barrett, Steven M. *Hidden Mickeys: A Field Guide to Walt Disney World's Best Kept Secrets*. 4th ed. Branford, Conn.: Intrepid Traveler, 2009.

Barrier, Michael. *The Animated Man: A Life of Walt Disney*. Berkeley: University of California Press, 2007.

Barthes, Roland. "The Death of the Author" (1968). *Image Music Text*. Trans. Stephen Heath. New York: Hill, 1977. 142–48.

———. "From Work to Text." *Art after Modernism: Rethinking Representation*. Ed. Brian Wallis. 2nd ed. New York: Museum of Contemporary Art; Boston: Godine, 1989. 169–74.

———. *The Pleasure of the Text*. 2nd ed. New York: Hill, 1975.

———. "Rhetoric of the Image" (1964). *The Responsibility of Forms: Critical Essays on Music, Art and Representation*. Trans. Richard Howard. 2nd ed. New York: Hill, 1985. 21–40.

Baudrillard, Jean. *America*. Trans. Chris Turner. 2nd ed. London: Verso, 1988.

———. *The Consumer Society: Myths and Structures*. 2nd ed. London: Sage, 1998.

———. *For a Critique of the Political Economy of the Sign*. Trans. Charles Levin. St. Louis: Telos, 1981.

———. "The Precession of Simulacra." *Art after Modernism: Rethinking Representation*. Ed. Brian Wallis. 2nd ed. New York: Museum of Contemporary Art; Boston: Godine, 1989. 253–81.

———. *Selected Writings*. Ed. Mark Poster. Stanford: Stanford University Press, 1988.

———. *Simulations*. Trans. Paul Foss, Paul Patton, and Philip Beitchman. New York: Semiotext(e), 1983.

Beard, Richard R. *Walt Disney's EPCOT: Creating the New World of Tomorrow*. New York: Abrams, 1982.

Beardsley, John. *Gardens of Revelation: Environments by Visionary Artists*. New York: Abbeville, 1995.

———. "A Mickey Mouse Utopia." *Landscape Architecture* Feb. 1997: 76–79+.

Bell, Elizabeth, Lynda Haas, and Laura Sells, eds. *From Mouse to Mermaid: The Politics of Film, Gender, and Culture*. Bloomington: Indiana University Press, 1995.

Benedict, Burton. *The Anthropology of World's Fairs: San Francisco's Panama Pacific International Exposition of 1915*. London: Scolar/Lowie Museum of Anthropology, 1983.

Bennis, Warren, and Patricia Ward Biederman. *Organizing Genius: The Secrets of Creative Collaboration*. Reading, Mass.: Addison-Wesley, 1997.

Best, Joel, and Kathleen S. Lowney. "The Disadvantage of a Good Reputation: Disney as a Target for Social Problems Claims." *Sociological Quarterly* 50.3 (2009): 431–49.

Betsky, Aaron. "Pyramid Schemes: Veldon Simpson and Douglas Trumbull." *I.D.* Mar.–Apr. 1994: 50.

———. "Theme Wars Rage in Vegas." *Architectural Record* Aug. 1992: 29.

Bettelheim, Bruno. *The Uses of Enchantment: The Meaning and Importance of Fairy Tales.* New York: Knopf, 1976.

Bhardwaj, Surinder Mohan, and Gisbert Rinschede. "Pilgrimage in America: An Anachronism or a Beginning?" *Geographia Religionum: Pilgrimage in the United States.* Ed. Surinder Mohan Bhardwaj and Gisbert Rinschede. Berlin: Reimer, 1990. 9–14.

Birmingham, Stephen. "Walt Disney—Imagination Unlimited." *Reader's Digest* Nov. 1964: 272–73+.

Blake, Peter. "The Lessons of the Parks." *The Art of Walt Disney: From Mickey Mouse to the Magic Kingdoms.* By Christopher Finch. New York: Abrams, 1973. 425–49.

Boesky, Amy. "Milton's Heaven and the Model of English Utopia." *Studies in English Literature 1500–1900* 36 (1996): 91–110.

Bolger, Doreen, and Kathleen Motes Bennowitz. "Thomas Cole's *Garden of Eden.*" *Antiques* July 1990: 104–11.

Boorstin, Daniel. *The Image: A Guide to Pseudo-Events in American Society.* New York: Harper, 1964.

Borsi, Franco. *Architecture and Utopia.* Trans. Deke Dusinberre. Paris: Hazan, 1997.

Bosselmann, Peter. *Representation of Places: Reality and Realism in City Design.* Berkeley: University of California Press, 1998.

Bradbury, Ray. "The Machine-Tooled Happyland." *Holiday* Oct. 1965: 100–102+.

Brannen, Mary Yoko. "'Bwana Mickey': Constructing Cultural Consumption at Tokyo Disneyland." *Cultures of United States Imperialism.* Ed. Amy Kaplan and Donald E. Pease. Durham: Duke University Press, 1993. 617–34.

Braunfels, Wolfgang. *Urban Design in Western Europe: Regime and Architecture, 900–1900.* Trans. Kenneth J. Northcott. Chicago: University of Chicago Press, 1988.

Breitbart, Eric. *A World on Display: Photographs from the St. Louis World's Fair 1904.* Albuquerque: University of New Mexico Press, 1997.

Bremer, Thomas S. *Blessed with Tourists: The Borderlands of Religion and Tourism in San Antonio.* Chapel Hill: University of North Carolina Press, 2004.

Brigham, Ann. "Behind-the-Scenes Spaces: Promoting Production in a Landscape of Consumption." *The Themed Space: Locating Culture, Nation, and Self.* Ed. Scott A. Lukas. Lanham, Md.: Lexington Books, 2007. 207–23.

Bright, John. "California Revolution 6, Disney's Fantasy Empire." *Nation* 6 Mar. 1967: 299–303.

Bright, Randy. *Disneyland: Inside Story.* New York: Abrams, 1987.

Brisman, Leslie. "Edenic Time." *Modern Critical Views: John Milton.* Ed. Harold Bloom. New York: Chelsea, 1986. 149–61.

Brockus, Susan. "Where Magic Lives™: Disney's Cultivation, Co-Creation, and Control of America's Cultural Objects." *Popular Communication* 2.4 (2004): 191–211.

Brode, Douglas. *From Walt to Woodstock: How Disney Created the Counterculture.* Austin: University of Texas Press, 2004.

———. *Multiculturalism and the Mouse: Race and Sex in Disney Entertainment.* Austin: University of Texas Press, 2005.

Brooke, Rosalind, and Christopher Brooke. *Popular Religion in the Middle Ages: Western Europe, 1000–1300.* London: Thames, 1984.

Brown, Bill. "Science Fiction, the World's Fair, and the Prosthetics of Empire, 1910–15." *Cultures of United States Imperialism*. Ed. Amy Kaplan and Donald E. Pease. Durham: Duke University Press, 1993. 129–63.

Brown, Julie K. *Contesting Images: Photography and the World's Columbian Exposition*. Tucson: University of Arizona Press, 1994.

Bryman, Alan. *Disney and His Worlds*. London: Routledge, 1995.

———. *The Disneyization of Society*. London: Sage, 2004.

Budd, Mike. "Introduction: Private Disney, Public Disney." *Rethinking Disney: Private Control, Public Dimensions*. Ed. Mike Budd and Max H. Kirsch. Middletown, Conn.: Wesleyan University Press, 2005. 1–33.

Bukatman, Scott. "The Artificial Infinite: On Special Effects and the Sublime." *Visual Display: Culture beyond Appearances*. Ed. Lynne Cooke and Peter Wollen. Seattle: Bay, 1995. 255–89.

———. "There's Always Tomorrowland: Disney and the Hypercinematic Experience." *October* 57 (1991): 55–78.

Burke, Bill. *Mousejunkies! More Tips, Tales, and Tricks for a Disney Fix: All You Need to Know for a Perfect Vacation*. Palo Alto, Calif.: Travelers' Tales, 2011.

Buskirk, Martha. "Commodification as Censor: Copyrights and Fair Use." *October* 60 (1992): 82–109.

Byrne, Eleanor, and Martin McQuillan. *Deconstructing Disney*. London: Pluto Press, 1999.

Calthorpe, Peter. *The Next American Metropolis: Ecology, Community, and the American Dream*. Princeton: Princeton Architectural Press, 1993.

Capodagli, Bill, and Lynn Jackson. *The Disney Way Field Book: How to Implement Walt Disney's Vision of "Dream, Believe, Dare, Do" in Your Own Company*. New York: McGraw-Hill, 2001.

———. *The Disney Way: Harnessing the Management Secrets of Disney in Your Company*. Rev. ed. New York: McGraw-Hill, 2007.

Carey, Matthew. "Why Disney Might Want to 'Escape from Tomorrow.'" *CNN Entertainment*. 24 Jan. 2013. Accessed 9 June 2013. http://www.cnn.com/2013/01/24/showbiz/movies/escape-tomorrow-sundance-disney.

Caroselli, Henry M. *Cult of the Mouse: Can We Stop Corporate Greed from Killing Innovation in America?* Berkeley: Ten Press, 2004.

Carroll, Maureen. *Earthly Paradises: Ancient Gardens in History and Archaeology*. Los Angeles: J. Paul Getty Museum, 2003.

Carson, Charles. "'Whole New Worlds': Music and the Disney Theme Park Experience." *Ethnomusicology Forum* 13.2 (Nov. 2004): 228–35.

"Castaway Cay: Past and Present." *Disney Cruise Line* website. Accessed 23 Nov. 2010. http://disneycruise.disney.go.com/cruises-destinations/bahamas/ports/castaway-cay/.

Celik, Zeynep. *Displaying the Orient: Architecture of Islam at Nineteenth-Century World's Fairs*. Berkeley: University of California Press, 1992.

Chandler, David Leon. *Henry Flagler: The Astonishing Life and Times of the Visionary Robber Baron Who Founded Florida*. New York: Macmillan, 1986.

Chatfield, Judith. *A Tour of Italian Gardens*. New York: Rizzoli, 1988.

Chidester, David. *Authentic Fakes: Religion in American Popular Culture*. Berkeley: University of California Press, 2005.

Childs, Valerie. *The Magic of Disneyland and Walt Disney World*. New York: Mayflower, 1979.

"Cinderella's Condos?" *Newsweek* 4 Feb. 1985: 64.

Clay, Grady. *Real Places: An Unconventional Guide to America's Generic Landscape*. Chicago: University of Chicago Press, 1994.

"A Clean Sweep for Disneyland." *American City* Feb. 1957: 15.

Cockerell, Lee. *Creating Magic: 10 Common Sense Leadership Strategies from a Life at Disney*. New York: Doubleday, 2008.

Coffey, Thomas F., Linda Kay Davidson, and Maryjane Dunn, eds. *The Miracles of St. James: Translations from the Liber Sancti Jacobi*. New York: Italica, 1996.

Cohen, David. "Preview of Disney's Worlds Fair Shows." *Science Digest* Dec. 1963: 8–15.

Cohen, Erik. "A Phenomenology of Tourist Experiences." *Sociology* Jan. 1979: 179–201.

———. "Pilgrimage and Tourism: Convergence and Divergence." *Sacred Journeys: The Anthropology of Pilgrimage*. Ed. Alan Morinis. Westport, Conn.: Greenwood, 1992. 47–61.

———. "Toward a Sociology of International Tourism." *Social Research* 39 (1972): 164–82.

———. "Who Is a Tourist? A Conceptual Clarification." *Sociological Review* Nov. 1974: 527–55.

Coleman, Barbara J. "Through the Years We'll All Be Friends: The 'Mickey Mouse Club,' Consumerism, and Cultural Consensus." *Visual Resources: An International Journal of Documentation* 14 (1999): 297–306.

Coleman, Simon, and John Elsner. *Pilgrimage: Past and Present in the World Religions*. Cambridge: Harvard University Press, 1995.

Comito, Terry. *The Idea of the Garden in the Renaissance*. New Brunswick: Rutgers University Press, 1978.

"Companionably Yours: Disneyland." *Woman's Home Companion* June 1954: 12.

Congdon, Kristen G., and Doug Blandy. "Approaching the Real and the Fake: Living Life in the Fifth World." *Studies in Art Education* 42.3 (Spring 2001): 266–78.

Connellan, Tom. *Inside the Magic Kingdom: Seven Keys to Disney's Success*. Austin: Bard, 1997.

Constable, Giles. "Opposition to Pilgrimage in the Middle Ages." *Studia Gratiana* 19.1 (1976): 125–46.

Corbin, Carla I. "The Old/New Theme Park: The American Agricultural Fair." *Theme Park Landscapes: Antecedents and Variations*. Ed. Terence Young and Robert Riley. Washington, D.C.: Dumbarton Oaks Research Library and Collection, 2002. 183–212.

Corn, Joseph J., and Brian Horrigan. *Yesterday's Tomorrows: Past Visions of the American Future*. Ed. Katherine Chambers. Baltimore: Johns Hopkins University Press, 1984.

Coulton, George Gordon. *Life in the Middle Ages (Selected, Translated and Annotated by George Gordon Coulton)*. 2nd ed. New York: University Press-Macmillan, 1931.

Crawford, Margaret. "I've Seen the Future and It's Fake." *L.A. Architect* Nov. 1988: 6–7.

Crawford, Michael. "A Brief History of the Future: From EPCOT to EPCOT Center." *Four Decades of Magic: Celebrating the First Forty Years of Disney World.* Ed. Chad Denver Emerson. Pike Road, Ala.: Ayefour, 2011. 41–55.

Cross, Gary. "Crowds and Leisure: Thinking Comparatively Across the 20th Century." *Journal of Social History* 39.3 (2006): 631–50.

Cross, Gary S., and John K. Walton. *The Playful Crowd: Pleasure Places in the Twentieth Century.* New York: Columbia University Press, 2005.

Cushman, John H., Jr. "New Disney Park Raises Environmental Concerns." *New York Times* 3 Apr. 1994, sec. 5: 3.

Davis, Amy M. *Good Girls and Wicked Witches: Women in Disney's Feature Animation.* Eastleigh: John Libbey, 2006.

Davis, Brandy. "New Urbanism: Cause for Celebration?" Accessed 26 May 2011. http://www.impactpress.com/articles/aprmay97/celebrat. htm#otherside.

Davis, John. *The Landscape of Belief: Encountering the Holy Land in Nineteenth-Century American Art and Culture.* Princeton: Princeton University Press, 1996.

Davis, Susan G. "Space Jam: Media Conglomerates Build the Entertainment City." *Gender, Race, and Class in Media: A Text-Reader.* Ed. Gail Dines and Jean M. Humez. 2nd ed. Thousand Oaks, Calif.: Sage, 2003. 159–70.

Debord, Guy. *The Society of the Spectacle.* 1967. Trans. Donald Nicholson-Smith. New York: Zone Books; Cambridge: MIT Press, 1994.

De George, Gail. "A Sweet Deal for Disney Is Souring Its Neighbors." *Business Week* 8 Aug. 1988: 48–49.

De Roos, Robert. "The Magic Worlds of Walt Disney." *National Geographic* Aug. 1963: 158–67+.

Derr, Mark. *Some Kind of Paradise: A Chronicle of Man and the Land in Florida.* New York: William Morrow, 1989.

Derrida, Jacques. "Structure, Sign and Play in the Discourse of the Human Sciences." *Writing and Difference.* Trans. Alan Bass. Chicago: University of Chicago Press, 1978. 278–93.

Dery, Mark. "Past Perfect." *21.C* 24 (1997): 14–17.

———. "Past Perfect: Disney Celebrates Us Home." *The Pyrotechnic Insanitarium: American Culture on the Brink.* New York: Grove, 1999. 171–80.

Disney, Mrs. Walt (Lillian Bounds), as told to Isabella Taves. "I Live with a Genius." *McCall's* Feb. 1953: 38–41+.

Disney, Roy. "Unforgettable Walt Disney." *Reader's Digest* Feb. 1969: 212–18.

Disney Institute. *Be Our Guest: Perfecting the Art of Customer Service.* New York: Disney Editions, 2001.

"Disney Unveils Vision for Disney Springs." *About Walt Disney World* webpage. 14 Mar. 2013. Accessed 22 May 2013. http://wdwnews.com/releases/2013/03/14/disney-springs-unveiled/?CMP=SOC-DPFY13Q2AnnouncingDisneySpringsAtWaltDisneyWorldResort000312-03-13.

"Divinely Inspired: The Folk Art of Howard Finster." *Americana* Nov.–Dec. 1989: 26.

Doctorow, Cory. *Down and Out in the Magic Kingdom.* New York: Tom Doherty Associates, 2003.

Dorfman, Ariel. *The Empire's Old Clothes: What the Lone Ranger, Barbar, and Other Innocent Heroes Do to Our Minds.* Trans. Clark Hansen. New York: Pantheon, 1983.

Doris, David T. "'It's the Truth, It's Actual . . . ': Kodak Picture Spots at Walt Disney World." *Visual Resources: An International Journal of Documentation* 14 (1999): 321–38.

Doss, Erika. "Making Imagination Safe in the 1950s: Disneyland's Fantasy Art and Architecture." *Designing Disney's Theme Parks: The Architecture of Reassurance.* Ed. Karal Ann Marling. Paris: Flammarion/Canadian Centre for Architecture Montreal, 1997. 179–89.

Dunlop, Beth. *Building a Dream: The Art of Disney Architecture.* New York: Abrams, 1996.

Dunn, Maryjane, and Linda Kay Davidson. "Bibliography of the Pilgrimage: The State of the Art." *The Pilgrimage to Compostela in the Middle Ages: A Book of Essays.* Ed. Maryjane Dunn and Linda Kay Davidson. New York: Garland, 1996. xxiii–xlviii.

Durkheim, Émile. *The Elementary Forms of Religious Life.* Trans. J. W. Swain. London: Allen, 1915.

"Dynamite Ducks." *Architects' Journal* 20 Oct. 1994: 22–23.

Eco, Umberto. "Travels in Hyperreality" (1975). *Travels in Hyperreality: Essays.* Trans. William Weaver. 2nd ed. San Diego: Harcourt, 1986. 3–58.

Eisenman, Peter. "Architecture in a Mediated Environment." *Architectural Associations: The Idea of the City.* Ed. Robin Middleton. London: Architectural Association; Cambridge: MIT Press, 1996. 57–62.

Eisner, Michael. "Planetized Entertainment." *New Perspectives Quarterly* 12.4 (1995): 8–10.

Eisner, Michael, with Tony Schwartz. *Work in Progress: Risking Failure, Surviving Success.* New York: Hyperion, 1998.

Eliot, Marc. *Walt Disney: Hollywood's Dark Prince.* New York: Birch Lane-Carol, 1993.

Emerson, Chad Denver. *Project Future: The Inside Story behind the Creation of Disney World.* Pike Road, Ala.: Ayefour, 2010.

"Euro Disney Expects Losses to Continue, Even with Rescue Pact." *Wall Street Journal* 14 Mar. 1994, sec. B: 6.

"Euro Disney Reports Loss." *New York Times* 3 Feb. 1994, late ed., Business Day sec.: D7.

Everett, Marshall. *The Book of the Fair; The Greatest Exposition (the World Has Ever Seen—Photographed and Explained): A Panorama of the St. Louis Exposition.* Philadelphia: Ziegler, 1904.

Ewen, Stuart. *All Consuming Images: The Politics of Style in Contemporary Culture.* New York: Basic, 1988.

Featherstone, Mike. *Consumer Culture and Postmodernism.* London: Sage, 1991.

Feifer, Maxine. *Tourism in History: From Imperial Rome to the Present.* New York: Stein, 1985.

"50 Things You Didn't Know about Disney World." Orlando-Florida.net. Accessed 27 Sept. 2010. http://www.orlando-florida.net/press-releases/50-things-you-dont-know-about-disney-world.htm.

Finch, Christopher. *The Art of Walt Disney: From Mickey Mouse to the Magic Kingdoms.* New York: Abrams, 1973.

———. *Walt Disney's America*. New York: Abbeville, 1978.

Findlay, John M. *Magic Lands: Western Cityscapes and American Culture after 1940*. Berkeley: University of California Press, 1992.

Findling, John E., ed., and Kimberly D. Pelle, asst. ed. *Historical Dictionary of World's Fairs and Expositions, 1851–1988*. New York: Greenwood, 1990.

Fjellman, Stephen M. *Vinyl Leaves: Walt Disney World and America*. Boulder: Westview, 1992.

Flower, Joe. *Prince of the Magic Kingdom: Michael Eisner and the Re-Making of Disney*. New York: Wiley, 1991.

Foglesong, Richard E. *Married to the Mouse: Walt Disney World and Orlando*. New Haven: Yale University Press, 2001.

Foucault, Michel. "The Eye of Power." Interview with Jean-Pierre Barou and Michelle Perrot. *Power/Knowledge: Selected Interviews and Other Writings, 1972–77*. Ed. Colin Gordon. Trans. Colin Gordon, Leo Marshall, John Mepham, and Kate Soper. New York: Pantheon, 1980. 146–65.

Fowler, Sigrid H. "*Learning from Las Vegas* by Venturi, Brown and Izenour: Architecture and the Civic Body." *Journal of Popular Culture* 7.2 (1973): 425–33.

Francaviglia, Richard V. *Main Street Revisited: Time, Space, and Image Building in Small-Town America*. Iowa City: University of Iowa Press, 1996.

———. "Main Street U.S.A.: A Comparison/Contrast of Streetscapes in Disneyland and Walt Disney World." *Journal of Popular Culture* 15.1 (1981): 141–56.

Franz, Douglas. "Living in a Disney Town, with Big Brother at Bay." *New York Times* 4 Oct. 1998, Arts & Leisure sec.: 31.

Franz, Douglas, and Catherine Collins. *Celebration U.S.A.: Living in Disney's Brave New Town*. New York: Holt, 1999.

Freedberg, David. *The Power of Images: Studies in the History and Theory of Response*. Chicago: University of Chicago Press, 1989.

"Freemont Street Experience." *Architecture* Apr. 1996: 87–89.

"From the Wisdom of Walt Disney." *Wisdom* 32 (Dec. 1959): 76–80.

Frye, Roland Mushat. *Milton's Imagery and the Visual Arts: Iconographic Tradition in the Epic Poems*. Princeton: Princeton University Press, 1978.

Fung, Anthony, and Micky Lee. "Localizing a Global Amusement Park: Hong Kong Disneyland." *Continuum: Journal of Media & Cultural Studies* 23.2 (Apr. 2009): 197–208.

Fussell, Paul. "The Stationary Tourist." *Harper's* Apr. 1979: 31–38.

Gabler, Neal. *Walt Disney: The Triumph of American Imagination*. New York: Knopf, 2006.

Gabriel, Trip. "From Vice to Nice." *New York Times Magazine* 1 Dec. 1991: 68–71+.

Galantay, Ervin Y. *New Towns: Antiquity to the Present*. New York: Braziller, 1975.

Gauthier, Marie-Madeleine. *Highways of Faith: Relics and Reliquaries from Jerusalem to Compostela*. Trans. J. A. Underwood. 2nd ed. London: Alpine, 1987.

Gaver, Eleanor E. "Inside the Outsiders." *Art & Antiques* 7 (Summer 1990): 72–87+.

Geertz, Clifford. "Religion as a Cultural System." *Reader in Comparative Religion: An Anthropological Approach*. Ed. William A. Lessa and Evon Z. Vogt. 4th ed. New York: Harper, 1979. 78–89.

Gennawey, Sam. *Walt and the Promise of Progress City*. Pike Road, Ala.: Ayefour, 2011.

———. "Walt Disney's EPCOT and the Heart of Our Cities." *Four Decades of Magic: Celebrating the First Forty Years of Disney World*. Ed. Chad Denver Emerson. Pike Road, Ala.: Ayefour, 2011. 97–112.

Gerson, Paula, Annie Shaver-Crandell, and Alison Stones, with the assistance of Jean Krochalis. *The Pilgrim's Guide to Santiago de Compostela: A Critical Edition*. London: Miller, 1998.

Giamatti, A. Bartlett. *The Earthly Paradise and the Renaissance Epic*. Princeton: Princeton University Press, 1966.

Gibian, Peter. "The Art of Being Off-Center: Shopping Center Spaces and Spectacles of Consumer Culture." *Mass Culture and Everyday Life*. Ed. Peter Gibian. New York: Routledge, 1997. 238–91.

Gilbert, James. *Whose Fair? Experience, Memory, and the History of the Great St. Louis Exposition*. Chicago: University of Chicago Press, 2009.

Girardo, Norman, and Ricardo Viera. "Howard Finster." Interview with Howard Finster. *Art Journal* 53 (1994): 48–50.

Giroux, Henry A. *The Mouse That Roared: Disney and the End of Innocence*. Lanham, Md.: Rowman & Littlefield, 1999.

Goldberger, Paul. "Mickey Mouse Teaches the Architects." *New York Times Magazine* 22 Oct. 1972: 40–41+.

Goodnough, Abby. "Disney Is Selling a Town It Built to Reflect the Past." *New York Times* 16 Jan. 2004. Accessed 26 May 2011. http://www.nytimes.com/2004/01/16/us/disney -is-selling-a-town-it-built-to-reflect-the-past.html.

Gottdiener, Mark. "Disneyland: A Utopian Urban Space." *Urban Life* July 1982: 139–62.

———. *The Theming of America: Dreams, Visions, and Commercial Spaces*. Boulder: Westview-Harper, 1997.

The Greatest of Expositions Completely Illustrated: Official Views of the Louisiana Purchase Exposition. St. Louis: Myerson, Official Photographic Company of the Louisiana Purchase Exposition, 1904.

"The Greatest Triple Play in Show Business." *Reader's Digest* July 1955: 69–73.

Green, Amy Boothe, and Howard E. Green. *Remembering Walt: Favorite Memories of Walt Disney*. New York: Hyperion, 1999.

Greene, Katherine, and Richard Greene. *The Man behind the Magic: The Story of Walt Disney*. New York: Viking, 1991.

Greenwood, Davydd J. "Culture by the Pound: An Anthropological Perspective on Tourism as Cultural Commoditization." *Hosts and Guests: The Anthropology of Tourism*. Ed. Valene L. Smith. Philadelphia: University of Pennsylvania Press, 1989. 171–85.

Griffin, Al. *Step Right Up, Folks!* Chicago: Regnery, 1974.

Griffin, Sean. "Curiouser and Curiouser: Gay Days at the Disney Theme Parks." *Rethinking Disney: Private Control, Public Dimensions*. Ed. Mike Budd and Max H. Kirsch. Middletown, Conn.: Wesleyan University Press, 2005. 125–50.

———. *Tinker Belles and Evil Queens: The Walt Disney Company from the Inside Out*. New York: New York University Press, 2000.

———. "'You've Never Had a Friend Like Me': Target Marketing Disney to a Gay Community." *Gender, Race, and Class in Media: A Text-Reader.* Ed. Gail Dines and Jean M. Humez. 2nd ed. Thousand Oaks, Calif.: Sage, 2003. 206–10.

Gross, Daniel. "The Mickey Mouse MBA: What we can all learn from Disney World." *Slate* 10 Nov. 2007. http://www.slate.com/toolbar. aspx?action=print&id=2177693.

Grover, Ron. *The Disney Touch: How a Daring Management Team Revived an Entertainment Empire.* Homewood: Business One Irwin, 1991.

———. "Now Disneyland Won't Seem So Mickey Mouse." *Business Week* 29 Jan. 2001: 56–58.

Gruen, Victor. *The Heart of Our Cities: The Urban Crisis, Diagnosis and Cure.* New York: Simon & Schuster, 1964.

Gunther, Marc. "Disney's Call of the Wild." *Fortune* 13 Apr. 1998: 120–24.

Gurrieri, Francesco, and Judith Chatfield. *Boboli Gardens.* Florence: Editrice Edam, 1972.

Haas, Charlie. "Disneyland Is Good for You." *New West* 4 Dec. 1978: 13–19.

Haden-Guest, Anthony. *The Paradise Program: Travels through Muzak, Hilton, Coca-Cola, Texaco, Walt Disney and Other World Empires.* New York: Morrow, 1973.

Halevy, Julian. "Disneyland and Las Vegas." *Nation* 7 June 1958: 510–13.

Hall, Colin Michael. *Hallmark Tourist Events: Impacts, Management, and Planning.* London: Bellhaven, 1992.

Hannigan, John. *Fantasy City: Pleasure and Profit in the Postmodern Metropolis.* London: Routledge, 1998.

Harrington, Michael. "To the Disney Station: Corporate Socialism in the Magic Kingdom." *Harper's* Jan. 1979: 35–39+.

Harris, Neil. *Cultural Excursions: Marketing Appetites and Cultural Tastes in Modern America.* Chicago: University of Chicago Press, 1990.

———. "Expository Expositions: Preparing for the Theme Parks." *Designing Disney's Theme Parks: The Architecture of Reassurance.* Ed. Karal Ann Marling. Paris: Flammarion/Canadian Centre for Architecture Montreal, 1997. 19–27.

Harris, Neil, Wim de Wit, James Gilbert, and Robert W. Rydell. *Grand Illusions: Chicago's World's Fair of 1893.* Chicago: Chicago Historical Society, 1993.

Harrison, Helen A. Introduction. *Dawn of a New Day: The New York World's Fair 1939/40.* By Helen A. Harrison et al. New York: New York University Press/Queens Museum, 1980.

Harvey, David. *The Condition of Postmodernity: An Enquiry into the Origins of Cultural Change.* Oxford: Blackwell, 1989.

Harwood, Edward. "Rhetoric, Authenticity, and Reception: The Eighteenth-Century Landscape Garden, the Modern Theme Park, and Their Audiences." *Theme Park Landscapes: Antecedents and Variations.* Ed. Terence Young and Robert Riley. Washington, D.C.: Dumbarton Oaks Research Library and Collection, 2002. 49–68.

Hayden, Dolores. "An American Sense of Place (with an Afterword)." *Critical Issues in Public Art: Content, Context, and Controversy.* Ed. Harriet F. Senie and Sally Webster. 2nd ed. Washington, D.C.: Smithsonian Institution Press, 1998. 261–69.

Hazel, Dann, and Josh Fippen. *A Walt Disney World Outing: The Only Vacation Plan-*

ning Guide Exclusively for Gay and Lesbian Travelers. San Jose: Writers Club Press/ iUniverse, 2002.

Hearn, Jeff, and Sasha Roseneil. "Consuming Cultures: Power and Resistance." *Consuming Cultures: Power and Resistance*. Ed. Jeff Hearn and Sasha Roseneil. New York: St. Martin's, 1999. 1–13.

Helton, Sean. "The Other Side." Accessed 26 May 2011. http://www. impactpress.com/ articles/aprmay97/celebrat.htm.

Hench, John, with Peggy Van Pelt. *Designing Disney: Imagineering and the Art of the Show*. New York: Disney Editions, 2008.

"Here's Your First View of Disneyland." *Look* 2 Nov. 1954: 82–84+.

Hess, Alan. *Viva Las Vegas: After-Hours Architecture*. San Francisco: Chronicle, 1993.

Hiaasen, Carl. *Team Rodent: How Disney Devours the World*. New York: Library of Contemporary Thought–Ballantine, 1998.

Hinsley, Curtis M. "The World as Marketplace: Commodification of the Exotic at the World's Columbian Exposition, Chicago, 1893." *Exhibiting Cultures: The Poetics and Politics of Museum Display*. Ed. Ivan Karp and Steven D. Lavine. Washington, D.C.: Smithsonian Institution, 1991. 344–65.

Hoberman, J. "Stardust Memories." *Artforum* Jan. 1996: 9–10.

Hofmeister, Sallie. "Disney Vows to Seek Another Park Site." *New York Times* 30 Sept. 1994, National Report: A12.

Holmes, Scott, and Carol Holmes. "Whatever Happened to Beastly Kingdom?" *Four Decades of Magic: Celebrating the First Forty Years of Disney World*. Ed. Chad Denver Emerson. Pike Road, Ala.: Ayefour, 2011. 139–51.

Howard, Catherine Ryan. *Mousetrapped: A Year and a Bit in Orlando, Florida*. Charleston: CreateSpace, 2010.

Howard, Ebenezer. *Garden Cities of To-Morrow*. Ed. F. J. Osborn. 1902. Cambridge: MIT Press, 1970.

Hunt, John Dixon. *Garden and Grove: The Italian Renaissance Garden in the English Imagination, 1600–1750*. 2nd ed. Philadelphia: University of Pennsylvania Press, 1996.

Huxtable, Ada Louise. *The Unreal America: Architecture and Illusion*. New York: New Press, 1997.

Imagineers. *The Imagineering Way*. New York: Disney Editions, 2003.

Izard, Ralph S. "Walt Disney: Master of Laughter and Learning." *Peabody Journal of Education* July 1967: 36–41.

Izenour, Steven, and David A. Dashiell III. "Relearning from Las Vegas." *Architecture* Oct. 1990: 46–51.

Jackson, John Brinckerhoff. *Discovering the Vernacular Landscape*. New Haven: Yale University Press, 1984.

Jackson, Kathy Merlock. *Walt Disney: A Bio-Biography*. Westport, Conn.: Greenwood, 1993.

———, ed. *Walt Disney Conversations*. Jackson: University Press of Mississippi, 2006.

Jameson, Fredric. *Postmodernism, or, The Cultural Logic of Late Capitalism*. Durham: Duke University Press, 1991.

Janofsky, Michael. "Town 'Devastated' by Loss of Project." *New York Times* 30 Sept. 1994, National Report: A12.

Jencks, Charles. *The Language of Post-Modern Architecture*. 5th ed. New York: Rizzoli, 1987.

Jenkins, Virginia Scott. *The Lawn: A History of an American Obsession*. Washington, D.C.: Smithsonian Institution, 1994.

Jethani, Skye. "Rethinking Tomorrowland: Disney's Lesson for the Church: The Future Isn't What It Used to Be." *Leadership* 26.1 (Winter 2005): 36–40.

Johnson, David. "Las Vegas: Buccaneer Bay." *TCI (Theatre Crafts International)* May 1994: 34–37.

Johnson, David M. "Disney World as Structure and Symbol: Re-Creation of the American Experience." *Journal of Popular Culture* 15.1 (1981): 157–65.

Johnson, Rossiter, ed. *A History of the World's Columbian Exposition*. 4 vols. New York: Appleton, 1897–98.

Jones, Karen, and John Wills. *The Invention of the Park: Recreational Landscapes from the Garden of Eden to Disney's Magic Kingdom*. Cambridge: Polity Press, 2005.

Jones, Wesley, with Michael Esola. *Mousecatraz: The Disney College Program*. 2nd ed. Pompano Beach, Fla.: Mantra Press, 2010.

Joselit, David. "Architecture: Moguls on Main Street." *Art in America* Jan. 1999: 50–53.

Kaufman, Edward N. "The Architectural Museum from World's Fair to Restoration Village." *Assemblage* 9 (1989): 21–39.

Kendall, Alan. *Medieval Pilgrims*. New York: Putnam, 1970.

Keys to the Kingdom Tour, 14 Jan. 2011, Magic Kingdom, Disney World Resort, Florida.

King, Margaret J. "Disneyland and Walt Disney World: Traditional Values in Futuristic Form." *Journal of Popular Culture* 15.1 (1981): 116–40.

———. "Empires of Popular Culture: McDonald's and Disney." *Ronald Revisited: The World of Ronald McDonald*. Ed. Marshall Fishwick. Bowling Green: Bowling Green University Popular Press, 1983. 106–19.

King, Thomas R. "Disney Plans to Perk Up an Enervated Epcot." *Wall Street Journal* 14 Mar. 1994, sec. B: 1+.

Kinsey, Leonard. *The Dark Side of Disney*. Bamboo Forest Publishing, 2011.

Kirshenblatt-Gimblett, Barbara. *Destination Culture: Tourism, Museums, and Heritage*. Berkeley: University of California Press, 1998.

Kirwin, Liza. "Papers of the Reverend Howard Finster." *Archives of American Art Journal* 28.2 (1988): 32–33.

Klingmann, Anna. *Brandscapes: Architecture in the Experience Economy*. Cambridge: MIT Press, 2007.

Knight, Cher Krause. "Adam and Eve . . . and Goofy: Walt Disney World as the Garden of Eden." *Visual Resources: An International Journal of Documentation* 14 (1999): 339–53.

———. "Beyond the Neon Billboard: Sidewalk Spectacle and Public Art in Las Vegas." *Journal of American and Comparative Cultures* 25.1–2 (Spring/Summer 2002): 9–13.

———. "Mickey, Minnie, and Mecca: Destination Disney World, Pilgrimage in the Twentieth Century." *Reclaiming the Spiritual in Art: Contemporary Cross-Cultural*

Perspectives. Ed. Dawn Perlmutter and Debra Koppman. Albany: State University of New York Press, 1999. 33–43.

Knott, John R., Jr. *Milton's Pastoral Vision*. Chicago: University of Chicago Press, 1971.

Koenig, David. *More Mouse Tales: A Closer Peek Backstage at Disneyland*. 2nd ed. Irvine: Bonaventure Press, 2002.

———. *Mouse Tales: A Behind-the-Ears Look at Disneyland*. Irvine: Bonaventure Press, 1994.

———. *Mouse under Glass: Secrets of Disney Animation and Theme Parks*. Irvine: Bonaventure Press, 1997.

———. *Realityland: True-Life Adventures at Walt Disney World*. Irvine: Bonaventure Press, 2007.

Korkis, Jim. *The Vault of Walt: Unofficial, Unauthorized, Uncensored Disney Stories Never Told*. Pike Road, Ala.: Ayefour, 2012.

Kostof, Spiro. *The City Assembled: The Elements of Urban Form through History*. Boston: Bulfinch-Little, 1992.

———. *The City Shaped: Urban Patterns and Meanings through History*. Boston: Bulfinch-Little, 1991.

———. *A History of Architecture: Settings and Rituals*. New York: Oxford University Press, 1995.

Kowinski, William Severini. *The Malling of America: An Inside Look at the Great Consumer Paradise*. New York: Morrow, 1985.

Kunstler, James Howard. *The Geography of Nowhere: The Rise and Decline of America's Man-made Landscape*. New York: Simon & Schuster, 1993.

Kurland, Gerald. *Walt Disney: The Master of Animation*. Charlotteville: SamHar, 1971.

Kurtti, Jeff. *Since the World Began: Walt Disney World the First 25 Years*. New York: Roundtable-Hyperion, 1996.

Kyriazi, Gary. *The Great American Amusement Parks: A Pictorial History*. Secaucus, N.J.: Citadel Press, 1976.

Labich, Kenneth. "Gambling's Kings." *Fortune* 22 July 1996: 80–82+.

Labriola, Albert C., and Edward Sichi Jr., eds. *Milton's Legacy in the Arts*. University Park: Pennsylvania State University Press, 1988.

Lainsbury, Andrew. *Once Upon an American Dream: The Story of Euro Disneyland*. Lawrence: University Press of Kansas, 2000.

Langdon, Philip. *A Better Place to Live: Reshaping the American Suburb*. Amherst: University of Massachusetts Press, 1994.

"Las Vegas." *TCI (Theatre Crafts International)* May 1994: 24–25.

Layton, T. A. *The Way of Saint James; Or, the Pilgrim's Road to Santiago*. London: Allen, 1976.

Lazzaro, Claudia. *The Italian Renaissance Garden: From the Conventions of Planting, Design, and Ornament to the Grand Gardens of Sixteenth-Century Central Italy*. New Haven: Yale University Press, 1990.

Leavitt, Stacey Eager. "When You Wish Upon a Star." *USA Today Magazine* Sept. 2005: 32–37.

Leccese, Michael. "Against the Odds." *Landscape Architecture* Apr. 1996: 66–73+.

Leighton, Albert C. *Transport and Communication in Early Medieval Europe, AD 500–1100*. Newton Abbot: David, 1972.

Levin, Bob. *The Pirates and the Mouse: Disney's War against the Counterculture*. Seattle: Fantagraphic Books, 2003.

Lévi-Strauss, Claude. *Myth and Meaning*. 2nd ed. New York: Schocken, 1979.

Levs, Josh. "Disney World Vows Action after Report of Wealthy Hiring Disabled to Skip Lines." *CNN U.S.* 15 May 2013. Accessed 9 June 2013. http://www.cnn.com/2013/05/15/us/disney-skipping-lines.

Lewis, Archibald R. *Nomads and Crusaders, A.D. 1000–1368*. Bloomington: Indiana University Press, 1988.

Lieb, Michael. *Poetics of the Holy: A Reading of* Paradise Lost. Chapel Hill: University of North Carolina Press, 1981.

"Lifestyle." *Summerlin* official website. Accessed 24 May 2011. http://www.summerlin.com/lifestyle/.

Lipsitz, George. "Consumer Spending as State Project: Yesterday's Solutions and Today's Problems." *Getting and Spending: European and American Consumer Societies in the Twentieth Century*. Ed. Susan Strasser, Charles McGovern, and Matthias Judt. Cambridge: Cambridge University Press, 1998. 127–47.

Lorentz, Brent. "Why 'Escape from Tomorrow' Likely Won't Make It to Theaters." *Law360*. 16 May 2013. Accessed 9 June 2013. http://www.law360.com/articles/441571/why-escape-from-tomorrow-likely-won-t-make-it-to-theaters.

Lovell, Margaretta M. "Picturing 'A City for a Single Summer': Paintings of the World's Columbian Exposition." *Art Bulletin* 78 (1996): 40–55.

Lowenthal, David. *The Past Is a Foreign Country*. Cambridge: Cambridge University Press, 1985.

Lukas, Scott A. "How the Theme Park Gets Its Power: Lived Theming, Social Control, and the Themed Worker Self." *The Themed Space: Locating Culture, Nation, and Self*. Ed. Scott A. Lukas. Lanham, Md.: Lexington Books, 2007. 183–206.

———. "A Politics of Reverence and Irreverence: Social Discourse on Theming Controversies." *The Themed Space: Locating Culture, Nation, and Self*. Ed. Scott A. Lukas. Lanham, Md.: Lexington Books, 2007. 271–93.

———. *Theme Park*. London: Reaktion Books, 2008.

Lutz, Catherine A., and Jane L. Collins. *Reading National Geographic*. Chicago: University of Chicago Press, 1993.

Lyon, David. *Jesus in Disneyland: Religion in Postmodern Times*. Cambridge: Polity Press, 2000.

MacCannell, Dean. "Staged Authenticity: Arrangements of Social Space in Touristic Settings." *American Journal of Sociology* 79 (1973): 589–603.

———. *The Tourist: A New Theory of the Leisure Class*. New York: Schocken, 1976.

MacDonald, William L., and John A. Pinto. *Hadrian's Villa and Its Legacy*. New Haven: Yale University Press, 1995.

MacFadyen, J. Tevere. "The Future as a Walt Disney Production." *Next* July–Aug. 1980: 24–32.

Magnet, Myron. "No More Mickey Mouse at Disney." *Fortune* 10 Dec. 1984: 56–58+.

Malamud, Randy. "Walt Disney, Reanimated." *Chronicle Review* 26 Mar. 2010, sec. B. Accessed 12 Apr. 2010. http://chronicle.texterity.com/chronicle/20100326b/?sub_id= RancijgeBN8.

Malins, Edward. *English Landscape and Literature, 1660–1840.* London: Oxford University Press, 1966.

Mann, Dennis Alan. "Ritual in Architecture: The Celebration of Life." *Rituals and Ceremonies in Popular Culture.* Ed. Ray B. Browne. Bowling Green: Bowling Green University Popular Press, 1980. 61–80.

Mannheim, Steve. *Walt Disney and the Quest for Community.* Hampshire: Ashgate, 2002, rpt. 2004.

Marcus, Greil. "Forty Years of Overstatement: Criticism and the Disney Theme Parks." *Designing Disney's Theme Parks: The Architecture of Reassurance.* Ed. Karal Ann Marling. Paris: Flammarion/Canadian Centre for Architecture Montreal, 1997. 201–7.

Marin, Louis. "Disneyland: A Degenerate Utopia." *Glyph.* Johns Hopkins Textual Studies 1. Baltimore: Johns Hopkins University Press, 1977. 50–66.

———. *Utopics: Spatial Play.* Trans. Robert A. Vollrath. Atlantic Highlands, N.J.: Humanities, 1984.

Marling, Karal Ann. *As Seen on TV: The Visual Culture of Everyday Life in the 1950s.* Cambridge: Harvard University Press, 1994.

———. "Disneyland, 1955: Just Take the Santa Ana Freeway to the American Dream." *American Art* 5.1–2 (1991): 168–207.

———. "Imagineering the Disney Theme Parks." *Designing Disney's Theme Parks: The Architecture of Reassurance.* Ed. Karal Ann Marling. Paris: Flammarion/Canadian Centre for Architecture Montreal, 1997. 29–177.

Mason, Peter. "From Presentation to Representation: *Americana* in Europe." *Journal of the History of Collections* 6.1 (1994): 1–20.

Mattie, Erik. *World's Fairs.* Princeton: Princeton Architectural Press, 1998.

Mazur, Eric Michael, and Tara K. Koda. "The Happiest Place on Earth: America and the Commodification of Religion." *God in the Details: American Religion in Popular Culture.* Ed. Eric Michael Mazur and Kate McCarthy. New York: Routledge, 2001. 299–315.

McBride, Sarah. "Death at Disney World Prompts Investigations." *Wall Street Journal* (Eastern ed.) 19 Aug. 2009: B.5. ProQuest. Emerson College Library. Accessed 23 Nov. 2009. ProQuest document ID: 1836055171.

McColley, Diane Kelsey. *A Gust for Paradise: Milton's Eden and the Visual Arts.* Urbana: University of Illinois Press, 1993.

McLuhan, Marshall, and Quentin Fiore. *The Medium Is the Massage.* 1967. New York: Touchstone-Simon, 1989.

McLuhan, Marshall, and Bruce R. Powers. *The Global Village: Transformations in World Life and Media in the 21st Century.* New York: Oxford University Press, 1989.

McReynolds, William Irvin. "Disney Plays 'The Glad Game.'" *Journal of Popular Culture* 7.4 (1974): 787–96.

———. "Walt Disney in the American Grain." PhD diss., University of Minnesota, 1972.

Meet Me at the Fair: Memory, History, and the 1904 World's Fair. Promotional literature by Katherine T. Corbett, Carol Diaz-Granados, Howard Miller, and Robert Rydell in conjunction with exhibition. St. Louis: Missouri Historical Society, 1996–97.

Menen, Aubrey. "Dazzled in Disneyland." *Holiday* July 1963: 68–70+.

Merritt, Howard S. "Appendix I: Correspondence between Thomas Cole and Robert Gilmor, Jr." *Annual II: Studies on Thomas Cole, an American Romanticist*. Baltimore: Baltimore Museum of Art, 1967. 41–81.

Mesters, Carlos. *Eden: Golden Age or Goad to Action*. Trans. Patrick J. Leonard. 2nd ed. New York: Orbis, 1974.

Michalos, Alex C. "Combining Social, Economic and Environmental Indicators to Measure Sustainable Human Well-Being." *Social Indicators Research* 40.1–2 (1997): 221–58.

Mickey Mouse Monopoly: Disney, Childhood and Corporate Power. Media Education Foundation, 2001. (Chyng Feng Sun, producer/writer; Miguel Picker, director/editor).

"The Mirage Volcano: A Las Vegas Icon Reborn." *The Mirage* official website. Accessed 23 Dec. 2010. http://mirage.com/attractions/volcano.aspx.

Mitchell, Chris. *Cast Member Confidential*. New York: Citadel Press, 2010.

Mitchell, William J., Charles W. Moore, and William Turnbull Jr. *The Poetics of Gardens*. Cambridge: MIT Press, 1988.

Moehring, Eugene P. *Resort City in the Sunbelt: Las Vegas, 1930–2000*. 2nd ed. Reno: University of Nevada Press, 2000.

Moehring, Eugene P., and Michael S. Green. *Las Vegas: A Centennial History*. Reno: University of Nevada Press, 2005.

Mohl, Raymond A., and Gary R. Mormino. "The Big Change in the Sunshine State: A Social History of Modern Florida." *The New History of Florida*. Ed. Michael Gannon. Gainesville: University Press of Florida, 1996. 418–47.

Monk, Samuel H. *The Sublime: A Study of Critical Theories in XVIII-Century England*. New York: Modern Language Association, 1935.

Moore, Alexander. "Walt Disney World: Bounded Ritual Space and the Playful Pilgrimage Center." *Anthropological Quarterly* 53.4 (Oct. 1980): 207–18.

Moore, Charles W. "You Have to Pay for the Public Life." *Perspecta: Yale Architectural Journal* 9–10 (1965): 57–106.

More, Thomas. *Utopia*. 1516. Ed. George M. Logan and Robert M. Adams. Cambridge: Cambridge University Press, 1989.

Morgenstern, Joseph. "Walt Disney (1901–1966): Imagineer of Fun." *Newsweek* 26 Dec. 1966: 68–69.

Morinis, Alan. "Introduction: The Territory of the Anthropology of Pilgrimage." *Sacred Journeys: The Anthropology of Pilgrimage*. Ed. Alan Morinis. Westport, Conn.: Greenwood, 1992. 1–30.

Morison, Elting E. "What Went Wrong with Disney's World's Fair." *American Heritage* Dec. 1983: 70–79.

Morley, Simon. "Introduction: The Contemporary Sublime." *The Sublime: Documents of Contemporary Art*. Ed. Morley Simon. London: Whitechapel Gallery; Cambridge: MIT Press, 2010. 12–21.

Mukerji, Chandra. *Territorial Ambitions and the Gardens of Versailles*. Cambridge: Cambridge University Press, 1997.

Mumford, Lewis. *The City in History: Its Origins, Its Transformations, and Its Prospects*. New York: Harcourt, 1961.

Munro, Eleanor. *On Glory Roads: A Pilgrim's Book about Pilgrimage*. New York: Thames, 1987.

Muschamp, Herbert. "Disney: Genuinely Artificial, Really Surreal." *New York Times* 4 Oct. 1998, Arts & Leisure sec.: 41.

Nagourney, Adam, and Brooks Barnes. "In New Exhibit, Disney Lends Its Star Power to Reagan, and Vice Versa." *New York Times* 21 July 2011. Accessed 23 July 2012. http://www.nytimes.com/2012/07/22/us/disney-and-reagan-united-at-presidential-library.html?_r=1.

Nasaw, David. *Going Out: The Rise and Fall of Public Amusements*. New York: Basic Books, 1993.

Naylor, Lois Anne. "Las Vegas for Families." *Better Homes & Gardens* Nov. 1994: 21–22+.

Negley, Glenn, and J. Max Patrick. *The Quest for Utopia*. College Park, Md.: McGrath, 1971.

Neil, J. Meredith. "Las Vegas on My Mind." *Journal of Popular Culture* 7.2 (1973): 379–86.

Neuman, Robert. "Disneyland's Main Street, USA, and Its Sources in Hollywood, USA." *Journal of American Culture* 31.1 (Feb. 2008): 83–97.

Newcomb, Chris. "Crossing the Berm: The Disney Theme Park as Sacralized Space." PhD diss., Florida State University. Ann Arbor: UMI Press, 2003.

Newman, Morris. "The Strip Meets the Flaming Volcano." *Progressive Architecture* Feb. 1995: 82–86.

Nicholas, David. *The Evolution of the Medieval World: Society, Government and Thought in Europe, 312–1500*. London: Longmans, 1992.

Noble, Louis Legrand. *The Life and Works of Thomas Cole*. Ed. Elliot S. Vesell. Cambridge: Belknap-Harvard, 1964.

Nolan, Mary Lee, and Sidney Nolan. *Christian Pilgrimage in Modern Western Europe*. Chapel Hill: University of North Carolina Press, 1989.

Norberg-Schultz, Christian. "On the Way to a Figurative Architecture." *GA Document* 14 (1985): 6–11.

O'Day, Tim. "Looking Back at the Future (with an introduction by Ray Bradbury)." *Disney Magazine* Fall 2002: 34–43.

Official Guidebook, New York World's Fair 1939. New York: Exposition, 1939.

Official Souvenir Book, New York World's Fair 1964/1965. New York: Time-Life, 1964.

Orvell, Miles. *The Real Thing: Imitation and Authenticity in American Culture, 1880–1940*. Chapel Hill: University of North Carolina Press, 1989.

Pahl, Jon. *Shopping Malls and Other Sacred Spaces*. Grand Rapids, Mich.: Brazos Press, 2003.

Parry, Ellwood C., III. *The Art of Thomas Cole: Ambition and Imagination*. Newark: University of Delaware Press, 1988.

Peacock, Robert, and Annibel Jenkins. *Paradise Garden: A Trip through Howard Finster's Visionary World*. San Francisco: Chronicle, 1996.

Pedersen, R. A. *The Epcot Explorer's Encyclopedia*. Encyclopedia Press/CreateSpace, 2011.

Pepper, Jeffrey. "Epcot 1939." *Four Decades of Magic: Celebrating the First Forty Years of Disney World*. Ed. Chad Denver Emerson. Pike Road, Ala.: Ayefour, 2011. 303–24.

Perry, Christopher W. *The Church Mouse: Leadership Lessons from the Magic Kingdom.* Cleveland: Pilgrim Press, 2011.

Perry, Nick. *Hyperreality and Global Culture.* London: Routledge, 1998.

Peterson, Kristen. "Vegas, Say Goodbye to Guggenheim." *Las Vegas Sun* 10 Apr. 2008. Accessed 24 Aug. 2011. http://www.lasvegassun.com/news/2008/apr/10/vegas-say -goodbye-Guggenheim/.

Philips, Deborah. "Consuming the West: Main Street, USA." *Space and Culture* 5.1 (Feb. 2002): 29–41.

Phillips, David. *Exhibiting Authenticity.* Manchester: Manchester University Press, 1997.

Pierson, Michele. *Special Effects: Still in Search of Wonder.* New York: Columbia University Press, 2002.

Pike, David L. "The Walt Disney World Underground." *Space and Culture* 8.1 (2005): 47–65.

Pine, Joseph, II, and James H. Gilmore. *The Experience Economy: Work Is Theatre and Every Business a Stage.* Boston: Harvard Business School Press, 1999.

Pinsky, Mark I. *The Gospel According to Disney: Faith, Trust, and Pixie Dust.* Louisville: Westminster John Knox Press, 2004.

Platt, Adam. "Something Wild." *Elle* July 1999: 72–73.

Pointon, Marcia R. *Milton and English Art.* Manchester: Manchester University Press, 1970.

Pollan, Michael. "Town-Building Is No Mickey Mouse Operation." *New York Times Magazine* 14 Dec. 1997: 56–63+.

Pontius, Larry (based upon story idea from Marty Cummins). *Waking Walt.* New York: Writer's Showcase/iUniverse, 2002.

Prest, John. *The Garden of Eden: The Botanic Garden and the Re-Creation of Paradise.* New Haven: Yale University Press, 1981.

Preston, James J. "Empiricism and the Phenomenology of Religious Experience." *Mentalities* 2.2 (1984): 10–20.

———. "The Rediscovery of America: Pilgrimage in the Promised Land." *Geographia Religionum: Pilgrimage in the United States.* Ed. Surinder Mohan Bhardwaj and Gisbert Rinschede. Berlin: Reimer, 1990. 15–26.

———. "Spiritual Magnetism: An Organizing Principle for the Study of Pilgrimage." *Sacred Journeys: The Anthropology of Pilgrimage.* Ed. Alan Morinis. Westport, Conn.: Greenwood, 1992. 31–46.

Project on Disney. *Inside the Mouse: Work and Play at Disney World.* Durham: Duke University Press, 1995.

Pulley, Brett. "Disney's Deal: A Special Report; A Mix of Glamour and Hardball Won Disney a Piece of 42nd Street." *New York Times* (Metropolitan Desk, Late Ed.) 29 July 1995, sec. 1, col. 4: A1, A9. LexisNexis. Emerson College Library. Accessed 7 July 2011.

Rafferty, Kevin, with Bruce Gordon (for the Imagineers). *Walt Disney Imagineering: A Behind the Dreams Look at Making the Magic Real.* New York: Welcome-Hyperion, 1996.

Rakoff, David. *Half Empty.* New York: Doubleday, 2010.

"Rambler." *Guide to Florida*. 1875. Reproduced with introduction by Rembert W. Patrick. Gainesville: University Press of Florida, 1904.

Raz, Aviad E. "The Slanted Smile Factory: Emotion Management in Tokyo Disneyland." *The Cultural Study of Work*. Ed. Douglas Harper and Helene M. Lawson. Lanham, Md.: Rowman & Littlefield, 2003. 210–27.

Reader, Ian, and Tony Walter, eds. *Pilgrimage in Popular Culture*. New York: Macmillan, 1994.

Real, Michael R. "The Disney Universe—Morality Play." *Mass-Mediated Culture*. Englewood Cliffs, N.J.: Prentice, 1977. 44–89.

"Recreation: Disneyland East." *Newsweek* 29 Nov. 1965: 82.

Reddy, John. "The Living Legacy of Walt Disney." *Reader's Digest* June 1967: 165–70.

Reis, Raul. "Brazil: Love It and Hate It: Brazilians' Ambiguous Relationship with Disney." *Dazzled by Disney? The Global Disney Audiences Project*. Ed. Janet Wasko, Mark Phillips, and Eileen R. Meehan. London: Leicester University Press, 2001. 88–101.

"Religion." *Front Porch: The Celebration Community Web Site*. Accessed 26 May 2011. http://www.celebration.fl.us/religion.htm/.

Relph, E. *Place and Placelessness*. London: Pion, 1976.

Reps, John W. *The Making of Urban America: A History of City Planning in the United States*. Princeton: Princeton University Press, 1965.

Riddle, Lyn. "At Celebration, Some Reasons to Celebrate." *New York Times* 7 Mar. 1999. *New York Times* Archives. Accessed 26 May 2011. http://www.nytimes.com/1999/03/07/realestate.at-celebration-some-reasons-to-celebrate.html?pagewanted=print&src=pm.

Ridgway, Charles. *Spinning Disney's World: Memories of a Magic Kingdom Press Agent*. Branford, Conn.: Intrepid Traveler, 2007.

Ritchie, David. "Sea of Green: A Short History of the Lawn." Paper presented at the College Art Association Annual Conference, New York Hilton, New York, 13 Feb. 1997.

Ritz, Stacy. *Disney World and Beyond: The Ultimate Family Guidebook*. 3rd ed. Berkeley: Ulysses, 1995.

Ritzer, George. *Enchanting a Disenchanted World: Revolutionizing the Means of Consumption*. 2nd ed. Thousand Oaks, Calif.: Pine Forge, 2005.

———. *The McDonaldization of Society: An Investigation into the Changing Character of Contemporary Social Life*. Rev. ed. Thousand Oaks, Calif.: Pine Forge, 1996.

———. *The McDonaldization Thesis: Explorations and Extensions*. London: Sage, 1998.

Rockwell, David, with Bruce Mau. *Spectacle*. London: Phaidon Press Limited, 2006.

Rojek, Chris. "Disney Culture." *Leisure Studies* 12 (1993): 121–35.

Root, Deborah. *Cannibal Culture: Art, Appropriation, and the Commodification of Difference*. Boulder: Westview, 1998.

Rose, Frank. "Can Disney Tame 42nd Street?" *Fortune* 24 June 1996: 94–98+.

Rosenberg, Karen. "'A Life of Walt Disney.'" *New York Times* 9 July 2010. Accessed 29 July 2010. http://www.nytimes.com/2010/07/09/arts/design/09galleries-003.html?.

Ross, Andrew. *The Celebration Chronicles: Life, Liberty and the Pursuit of Property Values in Disney's New Town*. New York: Ballantine, 1999.

———. "The Mickey House Club." *Artforum* Feb. 1997: 25–26+.

Ross, Irwin. "Disney Gambles on Tomorrow." *Fortune* 4 Oct. 1982: 62–68.

Rothman, Hal K. *Devil's Bargains: Tourism in the Twentieth-Century American West.* Lawrence: University Press of Kansas, 1998.

———. *Neon Metropolis: How Las Vegas Started the Twenty-First Century.* New York: Routledge, 2003.

Rothman, Hal K., and Mike Davis. "Introduction: The Many Faces Of Las Vegas." *The Grit beneath the Glitter: Tales from the Real Las Vegas.* Ed. Hal K. Rothman and Mike Davis. Berkeley: University of California Press, 2002. 1–14.

Rowe, Anne E. *The Idea of Florida in the American Literary Imagination.* Baton Rouge: Louisiana State University Press, 1986.

Rowe, Colin, and Fred Koetter. *Collage City.* Cambridge: MIT Press, 1978.

Rowman, Monica, and Greg Evans. "Mouse in Manhattan: Beauty . . . Or Beast?" *Variety* 1–14 July 1996: 1, 50. Accessed 24 July 2011. LexisNexis. Emerson College Library.

Rudolph, Conrad. *Pilgrimage to the End of the World: The Road to Santiago de Compostela.* Chicago: University of Chicago Press, 2004.

Rugoff, Ralph. "Only in Vegas." *Harper's Bazaar* May 1994: 60–62+.

Rydell, Robert W. *All the World's a Fair: Visions of Empire at American International Expositions, 1876–1916.* Chicago: University of Chicago Press, 1984.

———. *The Books of the Fairs: Materials about World's Fairs, 1834–1916, in the Smithsonian Institution Libraries.* Chicago: American Library Association, 1992.

———. "Souvenirs of Imperialism: World's Fair Postcards." *Delivering Views: Distant Cultures in Early Postcards.* Ed. Christraud M. Geary and Virginia-Lee Webb. Washington, D.C.: Smithsonian Institution, 1998. 47–63.

———. *World of Fairs: The Century-of-Progress Expositions.* Chicago: University of Chicago Press, 1993.

Rydell, Robert W., and Nancy E. Gwinn, eds. *Fair Representations: World's Fairs and the Modern World.* Amsterdam: VU University Press, 1994.

Said, Edward W. *Culture and Imperialism.* New York: Knopf, 1993.

Sammond, Nicholas. *Babes in Tomorrowland: Walt Disney and the Making of the American Child, 1930–1960.* Durham: Duke University Press, 2005.

Sayers, Frances Clark. "Walt Disney Accused." *Horn Book Magazine* Dec. 1965: 602–11.

Schaap, Dick. "Culture Shock: Williamsburg and Disney World, Back to Back." *New York Times* 28 Sept. 1975, Travel and Resorts sec. 10: 1+.

Schama, Simon. *Landscape and Memory.* New York: Knopf, 1995.

Schickel, Richard. "Bringing Forth the Mouse." *American Heritage* Apr. 1968: 24–29+.

———. *The Disney Version: The Life, Times, Art and Commerce of Walt Disney.* Rev. ed. New York: Simon, 1985.

———. *The Disney Version: The Life, Times, Art and Commerce of Walt Disney.* 3rd ed. Lanham, Md.: Ivan R. Dee, 1997.

———. "Walt Disney: Myth and Reality." *American Heritage* Apr. 1968: 94–95.

Schroeder, Fred E. H. *Front Yard America: The Evolution and Meanings of a Vernacular Domestic Landscape.* Bowling Green: Bowling Green State University Popular Press, 1993.

Schultz, Elizabeth. "Las Vegas: A City That Never Sleeps." *Telephony* 16 Mar. 1987: 49+.

Schuman, Michael, and Jeffrey Ressner. "Disney's Great Leap into China." *Time* 18 July 2005: 52–54. Academic Search Premier. Emerson College Library. Accessed 5 Dec. 2009. Accession Number: 17575001.

Schweizer, Peter, and Rochelle Schweizer. *Disney, the Mouse Betrayed: Greed, Corruption and Children at Risk.* Washington, D.C.: Regnery, 1998.

Scully, Vincent. "Disney: Theme and Reality." Foreword in *Building a Dream: The Art of Disney Architecture.* By Beth Dunlop. New York: Abrams, 1996. 7–11.

Sears, John F. *Sacred Places: American Tourist Attractions in the Nineteenth Century.* New York: Oxford University Press, 1989.

Seelye, John. "The Mouse in the Machine." *New Republic* 22 Dec. 1973: 22–24.

Sehlinger, Bob. *The Unofficial Guide to Walt Disney World.* Multiple editions by different publishers, 1992–2011.

Serwer, Andrew E. "Welcome to the New Las Vegas." *Fortune* 24 Jan. 1994: 102–5.

Shearer, Lloyd. "How Disney Sells Happiness." *Parade* 26 Mar. 1972: 4–5.

Shepherd, J. C., and G. A. Jellicoe. *Italian Gardens of the Renaissance.* 2nd ed. New York: Architectural, 1966.

Shillingburg, Donald. "Entertainment Drives Retail." *Architectural Record* Aug. 1994: 82–89.

Short, John Rennie. *Global Dimensions: Space, Place and the Contemporary World.* London: Reaktion Books, 2001.

Shortsleeve, Kevin. "The Wonderful World of the Depression: Disney, Despotism, and the 1930s. Or, Why Disney Scares Us." *Lion and the Unicorn* 28.1 (Jan. 2004): 1–30.

Shuit, Douglas P. "Magic for Sale." *Workforce Management* 83.9 (Sept. 2004): 35–36, 38, 40.

Sicher, Efraim. "By Underground to Crystal Palace: The Dystopian Eden." *Comparative Literature Studies* 22 (1985): 377–93.

Sims, Calvin. "Family Values as a Las Vegas Smash." *New York Times* 3 Feb. 1994, late ed., Business Day sec.: D1+.

Sklar, Marty. "The Artist as Imagineer." *Designing Disney's Theme Parks: The Architecture of Reassurance.* Ed. Karal Ann Marling. Paris: Flammarion/Canadian Centre for Architecture Montreal, 1997. 13–17.

———. [Martin A. Sklar]. Introduction. *Walt Disney's EPCOT: Creating the New World of Tomorrow.* By Richard R. Beard. New York: Abrams, 1982. 11–29.

Sklar, Robert. *Movie-Made America: A Social History of American Movies.* New York: Random, 1975.

Smith, Dave. *Disney A to Z: The Official Encyclopedia.* New York: Hyperion, 1996.

———, ed. *Walt Disney: Famous Quotes.* Lake Buena Vista: Disney, 1994.

Smoodin, Eric. *Animating Culture: Hollywood Cartoons from the Sound Era.* New Brunswick: Rutgers University Press, 1993.

———, ed. *Disney Discourse: Producing the Magic Kingdom.* New York: Routledge, 1994.

Snow, Dennis. *Lessons from the Mouse: A Guide for Applying Disney World's Secrets of Success to Your Organization, Your Career, and Your Life.* Orlando: Snow & Associates, 2010.

Snow, Richard F. "Disney: Coast to Coast." *American Heritage* Feb.–Mar. 1987: 22+.

Sorkin, Michael. "Post-Sin City." *I.D.* Mar.–Apr. 1994: 44–49.

———. "See You in Disneyland." *Variations on a Theme Park: The New American City and the End of Public Space.* Ed. Michael Sorkin. New York: Noonday-Hill, 1992. 205–32.

Souther, J. Mark. "The Disneyfication of New Orleans: The French Quarter as Façade in a Divided City." *Journal of American History* 94.3 (Dec. 2007): 804–11.

Sperb, Jason. "'Take a Frown, Turn It Upside Down': Splash Mountain, Walt Disney World, and the Cultural De-rac[e]-ing of Disney's *Song of the South* (1946)." *Journal of Popular Culture* 38.5 (2005): 924–38.

Spirn, Anne Whiston. *The Language of Landscape.* New Haven: Yale University Press, 1998.

Starkie, Walter. *The Road to Santiago: Pilgrims of St. James.* 2nd ed. Berkeley: University of California Press, 1965.

Stein, Andi. *Why We Love Disney: The Power of the Disney Brand.* New York: Peter Lang, 2011.

Stein, Karen D. "Down the Strip." *Architectural Record* Oct. 1990: 68–75.

Stern, Robert A. M., assisted by Thomas Mellins and Raymond Gastil. *Pride of Place: Building the American Dream.* Boston: American Heritage-Houghton, 1986.

Stewart, James B. *Disney War.* New York: Simon & Schuster, 2005.

Stokstad, Marilyn. *Medieval Art.* New York: Icon-Harper, 1986.

———. *Santiago de Compostela: In the Age of the Great Pilgrimages.* Norman: University of Oklahoma Press, 1978.

Stone, James S. *The Cult of Santiago: Traditions, Myths, and Pilgrimages (A Sympathetic Study).* London: Longmans, 1927.

Stratton, David. *Ultimate Las Vegas and Beyond.* 2nd ed. Berkeley: Ulysses, 1995.

Streisand, Betsy. "Las Vegas Gamboling: The Neon City Has Reinvented Itself as a Vacation Mecca for Families." *U.S. News & World Report* 31 Jan. 1994: 61–63.

Stuever, Hank. "America Loves to Hate the Mouse: Behind the Fantasy Walt Disney Built Looms a Dark Reality. On His 100th Anniversary, It Can Now Be Revealed." *Washington Post* 5 Dec. 2001: C.1. Accessed 4 Aug. 2011. ProQuest Newspapers doc. i.d.: 93460834.

Stungo, Naomi. "Relearning from Vegas." *RIBA Journal* Jan. 1995: 24–25.

Sturken, Marita. *Tangled Memories: The Vietnam War, the AIDS Epidemic, and the Politics of Remembering.* Berkeley: University of California Press, 1997.

———. *Tourists of History: Memory, Kitsch, and Consumerism from Oklahoma City to Ground Zero.* Durham: Duke University Press, 2007.

Styron, William. "Slavery Is Not a Subject for Disney." *Sydney Morning Herald* 9 Aug. 1994.

Sullivan, Jeremiah. "You Blow My Mind, Hey Mickey!" *New York Times Magazine* 8 June 2011. Accessed 15 June 2011. http://www. nytimes.com/2011/06/12/magazine/a-rough -guide-to-disney-world.html?_r=1.

Sumption, Jonathan. *Pilgrimage: An Image of Mediaeval Religion.* 2nd ed. Totowa, N.J.: Rowman, 1975.

Susman, Warren I. *Culture as History: The Transformation of American Society in the Twentieth Century*. New York: Pantheon, 1984.

Susman, Warren, with the assistance of Edward Griffin. "Did Success Spoil the United States? Dual Representations in Postwar America." *Recasting America: Culture and Politics in the Age of the Cold War*. Ed. Lary May. Chicago: University of Chicago Press, 1989. 19–37.

Taylor, John. *Storming the Magic Kingdom: Wall Street, the Raiders, and the Battle for Disney*. New York: Knopf, 1987.

Taylor, Mark C. *Hiding*. Chicago: University of Chicago Press, 1997.

Telotte, J. P. *The Mouse Machine: Disney and Technology*. Urbana: University of Illinois Press, 2008.

Thomas, Bob. *Building a Company: Roy O. Disney and the creation of an entertainment empire*. New York: Hyperion, 1998.

———. *Walt Disney: An American Original*. 1st ed. New York: Simon, 1976.

———. *Walt Disney: An American Original*. 2nd ed. New York, Hyperion, 1994.

"Tinker Bell, Mary Poppins, Cold Cash." *Newsweek* 12 July 1965: 74–76.

Tomlinson, John. "Internationalism, Globalization and Cultural Imperialism." *Media and Cultural Regulation*. Ed. Kenneth Thompson. London: Sage/Open University, 1997. 118–53.

"Tripping on Disney." *Newsweek* 19 Jan. 1970: 88.

Trowbridge, Scott, and Christopher Stapleton. "Melting the Boundaries between Fantasy and Reality." *Computer* 42.7 (2009): 57–62.

Tselos, Dimitri. "The Chicago Fair and the Myth of the 'Lost Cause.'" *Journal of the Society of Architectural Historians* 26.4 (Dec. 1967): 259–68.

Tuan, Yi-Fu, with Steven D. Hoelscher. "Disneyland: Its Place in World Culture." *Designing Disney's Theme Parks: The Architecture of Reassurance*. Ed. Karal Ann Marling. Paris: Flammarion/Canadian Centre for Architecture Montreal, 1997. 191–99.

Tunnard, Christopher, and Boris Pushkarev. *Man-Made America: Chaos or Control? An Inquiry into Selected Problems of Design in the Urbanized Landscape*. New Haven: Yale University Press, 1963.

Turner, J. F. "Howard Finster: Man of Visions." *Clarion* 14 (1989): 38–43.

———. *Howard Finster, Man of Visions: The Life and Work of a Self-Taught Artist*. New York: Knopf, 1989.

Turner, Victor. "The Center Out There: Pilgrim's Goal." *History of Religions* Feb. 1973: 191–230.

———. "Liminal to Liminoid, in Play, Flow, and Ritual: An Essay in Comparative Symbology." *Rice University Studies* 60 (1974): 53–92.

———. "Pilgrimage and Communitas." *Studia Missionalia* 23 (1974): 305–27.

———. *Process, Performance and Pilgrimage*. Atlantic Highlands, N.J.: Humanities, 1979.

Turner, Victor, and Edith Turner. *Image and Pilgrimage in Christian Culture: Anthropological Perspectives*. New York: Columbia University Press, 1978.

Twilight Tuesdays: Along the Pike at the 1904 World's Fair. St. Louis: Missouri Historical Society, 1996–97.

Unofficial Walt Disney Imagineering Site. Accessed 1 Nov. 2010. http://imagineering.org .wordpress.com/.

Updike, John. "The Mystery of Mickey Mouse." *Art & Antiques* Nov. 1991: 60–65+.

Van Gennep, Arnold. *The Rites of Passage.* 1909. London: Routledge, 1960.

Van Maanen, John. "Displacing Disney: Some Notes on the Flow of Culture." *Qualitative Sociology* 15.1 (1992): 5–35.

———. "The Smile Factory: Work at Disneyland." *Reframing Organizational Culture.* Ed. Peter J. Frost, Larry F. Moore, Meryl Reis Louis, Craig C. Lundberg, and Joanne Martin. Newbury Park: Sage, 1991. 58–76.

Van Pelt, Peggy, ed. *The Imagineering Workout: Exercises to Shape Your Creative Muscles.* New York: Disney Editions, 2005.

Van Riper, A. Bowdoin, ed. *Learning from Mickey, Donald and Walt: Essays on Disney's Edutainment Films.* Jefferson, N.C.: McFarland, 2011.

Veness, Susan. *The Hidden Magic of Walt Disney World: Over 600 Secrets of the Magic Kingdom, Epcot, Disney's Hollywood Studios, and Animal Kingdom.* Avon, Mass.: Adams Media, 2009.

Venturi, Robert, Denise Scott Brown, and Steven Izenour. Foreword. *Viva Las Vegas: After-Hours Architecture.* By Alan Hess. San Francisco: Chronicle, 1993.

———. *Learning from Las Vegas: The Forgotten Symbolism of Architectural Form.* 1972. Cambridge: MIT Press, 1991.

Villmoare, Adelaide H., and Peter G. Stillman. "Pleasure and Politics in Disney's Utopia." *Canadian Review of American Studies* 32.1 (2002): 81–104.

Wagner, Roy. *The Invention of Culture.* Englewood Cliffs, N.J.: Prentice, 1975.

Walker, Jesse. "Disney Legalizes Same-Sex Unions." *Reason* 39.2 (June 2007): 61–67. Academic Search Premier. Emerson College Library. Accessed 5 Dec. 2009. Accession Number: 25147222.

Wallace, Michael. "Mickey Mouse History: Portraying the Past at Disney World." *History Museums in the United States: A Critical Assessment.* Ed. Warren Leon and Roy Rosenzweig. Urbana: University of Illinois Press, 1989. 158–80.

Wallach, Alan. "Thomas Cole: Landscape and the Course of American Empire." *Thomas Cole: Landscape into History.* Ed. William H. Truettner and Alan Wallach. New Haven: Yale University Press/Smithsonian Institution National Museum of American Art, 1994. 23–111.

Wallis, Brian. "Selling Nations: International Exhibitions and Cultural Diplomacy." *Museum Culture: Histories, Discourses, Spectacles.* Ed. Daniel J. Sherman and Irit Rogoff. Minneapolis: University of Minnesota Press, 1994. 265–81.

Walt Disney Family Museum website. Accessed 20 Sept. 2010. http://www.disney.go.com/ disneyatoz/familymuseum/.

"Walt Disney: Giant at the Fair." *Look* 11 Feb. 1964: 28–32.

"Walt Disney: Great Teacher." *Fortune* Aug. 1942: 90–95+.

Walt Disney World: The First Decade. Anaheim: Walt Disney Productions, 1982.

Ward, Annalee R. *Mouse Morality: The Rhetoric of Disney Animated Film.* Austin: University of Texas Press, 2002.

Wasko, Janet. "Challenging Disney Myths." *Journal of Communication Inquiry* 25.3 (July 2001): 237–57.

———. "Is It A Small World After All?" *Dazzled by Disney? The Global Disney Audiences Project.* Ed. Janet Wasko, Mark Phillips, and Eileen R. Meehan. London: Leicester University Press, 2001. 3–28.

———. *Understanding Disney: The Manufacture of Fantasy.* Cambridge: Polity Press, 2001.

Watts, Steven. *The Magic Kingdom: Walt Disney and the American Way of Life.* Boston: Houghton, 1997.

Weathersby, William, Jr. "Las Vegas: Luxor." *TCI (Theatre Crafts International)* May 1994: 27.

Weber, Jonathan. "The Ever-Expanding, Profit-Maximizing, Cultural-Imperialist, Wonderful World of Disney: The Serious Business of Selling All-American Fun." *Wired* 10.2 (Feb. 2002). Accessed 23 Nov. 2009. http://www.wired.com/wired/archive/10.02/Disney-pr.html.

White, Trumbull, and Wm. Ingleheart. *The World's Columbian Exposition, Chicago, 1893.* Boston: Standard Silverware-Ziegler, 1893.

"The Wide World of Walt Disney." *Newsweek* 31 Dec. 1962: 48–51.

Wiener, Jon. "Disney World Imagineers a President." *Nation* 22 Nov. 1993: 605+.

Williams, Alistair. "Tourism and Hospitality Marketing: Fantasy, Feeling, and Fun." *International Journal of Contemporary Hospitality Management* 18.6 (2006): 482–95.

Williams, Pat, with Jim Denney. *How to Be Like Walt.* Deerfield Beach, Fla.: Health Communications, 2004.

Wilson, Alexander. "The Betrayal of the Future: Walt Disney's EPCOT Center." *Socialist Review* Nov.–Dec. 1985: 41–54.

———. *The Culture of Nature: North American Landscape from Disney to the Exxon Valdez.* Cambridge: Blackwell, 1993.

———. "Technological Utopias." *South Atlantic Quarterly* 92 (1993): 157–73.

Wilson, A. N. *The Life of John Milton.* Oxford: Oxford University Press, 1983.

Wines, Michael. "A Disneyland of History Next to the Real Thing." *New York Times* 12 Nov. 1993: A14.

———. "Step Up, Folks! Check It Out! Nationhood!" *New York Times* 29 May 1994, Arts & Leisure sec. 2: 1+.

———. "Yes Virginia, the Past Can Be Plasticized." *New York Times* 28 Nov. 1993, late ed., sec. 4: E4.

Wolf, Jaime. "M-I-C-K-E-Y H-O-U-S-E." *Elle* July 1996: 28.

Wolfert, Ira. "Walt Disney's Magic Kingdom." *Reader's Digest* Apr. 1960: 144–47+.

Wolkomir, Richard. "Las Vegas Meets La-La Land." *Smithsonian* Oct. 1995: 50–59.

Wolters, Larry. "The Wonderful World of Walt Disney." *Today's Health* Apr. 1962: 26–31+.

"A Wonderful World: Growing Impact of the Disney Art." *Newsweek* 18 Apr. 1955: 60+.

"World's Fairs? Who Cares?" *American Demographics* Dec. 1989: 19.

Wright, Chris. "Natural and Social Order at Walt Disney World; The Functions and Contradictions of Civilising Nature." *Sociological Review* 54.2 (May 2006):303–17.

Wright, David E., and Robert E. Snow. "Consumption as Ritual in the High Technology Society." *Rituals and Ceremonies in Popular Culture*. Ed. Ray B. Browne. Bowling Green: Bowling Green University Popular Press, 1980. 326–37.

Wright, D. R. Edward. "Some Medici Gardens of the Florentine Renaissance: An Essay in Post-Aesthetic Interpretation." *The Italian Garden: Art, Design and Culture*. Ed. John Dixon Hunt. Cambridge: Cambridge University Press, 1996. 34–59.

Wu, Tim. "It's A Mad, Mad, Mad, Mad Disney World." *New Yorker: Culture Desk*. 22 Jan. 2013. Accessed 9 June 2013. http://www.newyorker.com/online/blogs/culture/2013/01/escape-from-tomorrow-disney-world-and-the-law-of-fair-use.html.

Yee, Kevin. *Mouse Trap: Memoir of A Disneyland Cast Member*. Orlando: Ultimate Orlando Press, 2008.

———. *Unofficial Walt Disney World 'Earbook 2010: One Fan's Review in Pictures*. Orlando: Ultimate Orlando Press, 2011.

———. *Walt Disney World Hidden History: Remnants of Former Attractions and Other Tributes*. Orlando: Ultimate Orlando Press, 2010.

Yoshimoto, Mitsuhiro. "Images of Empire: Tokyo Disneyland and Japanese Cultural Imperialism." *Disney Discourse: Producing the Magic Kingdom*. Ed. Eric Smoodin. New York: Routledge 1994. 181–99.

Young, Peter A. "Howard Carter in Luxorland." *Archaeology* May–June 1994: 72.

Young, Terence. "Grounding the Myth—Theme Park Landscapes in an Era of Commerce and Nationalism." *Theme Park Landscapes: Antecedents and Variations*. Ed. Terence Young and Robert Riley. Washington, D.C.: Dumbarton Oaks Research Library and Collection, 2002. 1–10.

Zaslow, Jeff. "Man behind the Mouse Befuddles the Children Dwelling on the Magic—Who's Walt Disney Anyway? 'He Lives in the Big Castle,' Or 'He Invented Florida.'" *Wall Street Journal* 29 Oct. 2001: A.1. ProQuest. Emerson College Library. Accessed 23 Nov. 2009. ProQuest document ID: 86731641.

Zehnder, Leonard E. *Florida's Disney World: Promises and Problems*. Tallahassee: Peninsular, 1975.

Zelinsky, Wilbur. "Imaginary Landscapes." *Landscape Architecture* June 1990: 46–49.

———. "Nationalist Pilgrimages in the United States." *Geographia Religionum: Pilgrimage in the United States*. Ed. Surinder Mohan Bhardwaj and Gisbert Rinschede. Berlin: Reimer, 1990. 253–67.

Ziebart, Eve. *The Unofficial Disney Companion: The Inside Story of Walt Disney World and the Man behind the Mouse*. New York: Macmillan, 1997.

Zukin, Sharon. *Landscapes of Power: From Detroit to Disney World*. Berkeley: University of California Press, 1991.

Index

Disney, Walt: apartment for, 42; "bee story" of, 13; character of, 42, 163; childhood of, 63; as Christian, 46; on completed films, 16; conservatism of, 157; death of, 12, 69, 187n5; as distributor, 13; drinking of, 181n93; on Great Moments with Mr. Lincoln, 126–27; Howard and, 57; legacy of, 163–64; Main Street, U.S.A., and, 40; on Marceline, 41; on Mickey Mouse, 12; motivations of, 24; on movement of people, 52; New York World's Fair and, 124, 127–28; official view of, 167; plans of, 9–10, 18, 58–59, 87, 112–13; Rouse and, 83; simulations and, 70; sources of inspiration for, 93; surveys of theme parks by, 58; tiger and, 68–69; on time, 93; trains, miniatures, and, 121–22, 125; values of, 63–66, 102, 114–15; visionary capitalism and, 11–12; vision of Paradise of, 44, 45–46, 47, 69

Disney Company: corporate culture of, 159; criticism of, 147–48; diversification of, 155–56; marketing by, 14–16; Mickey Mouse as symbol for, 12; postmodernism and, 21; publishing ventures of, 14; ranking of, 140; scholars and, 2; synergy and, 16; theme park business of, 153–54

Disney Cruise Line, 66

Disney Development Company, 84

Disney Dollars, 38

"Disneyfication," 140, 150

"Disney Gospel," 65

Disney Institute, 17–18

"Disneyization," 143

Disneyland: apartment on Main Street, 42; Disney World compared to, 5, 152; expectations for, 59; funding for and design of, 11; in Hong Kong, 145–46; Las Vegas compared to, 71; Monsanto "House of the Future" in, 122; opening of, 9–10, 15; in Paris, 144–45; Rouse

on, 83; site for, 57–58; in Tokyo, 143–44. *See also* Anaheim, California

Disneylandia, 65

Disneyland Paris, 144–45

Disneyland series, 15

Disney realism, 63

Disney's America, 97–98

Disney's California Adventure, 145

DisneySea, 145

Disney Springs, 19, 153

Disney Stores, 15–16, 150

Disney Studio, 181n103

Disney University, 17

Disney World: borders of, 47, 74; business performance of, 153–54; cost of, 18; criticism of, 4; description of, 19–20; W. Disney vision of, 62–63, 66, 69; environmental mandate of, 61; magic of, 169–70; modifications to, 153, 154–55, 158–59; naming of, 152; nationalistic associations of, 31–32; as pilgrimage center, 24–26, 29–34, 36–39; as placeless and timeless, 16; political autonomy of, 72; sale of land of, 150; studies of, 2–3, 4, 8; as theme park, 5, 154; urbanism and, 151. *See also* Epcot; Florida; Magic Kingdom theme park; Reedy Creek Improvement District; *specific attractions*

Disney World College Program, 173n40

Disney Worldwide Conservation Fund, 67

Dorfman, Ariel, 111

Dougall, Terry, 93

Downtown Disney, 19, 153

Dress code, 64, 173n38

Dreyfuss, Henry, 119, *120*

D23 fan community, 16

Duany, Andres M., 83–84

Durkheim, Émile, 25

Eco, Umberto, 22, 95

Education and entertainment, relationship between, 49–50, 65, 138

Lainsbury, Andrew, 146

Landscape: control of, 61–62; "Disneyfication" of, 140; as instilled with social significance, 46–47; manipulation of, 76; as place for enrichment and entertainment, 49–50. *See also* Gardens

Landscape tourism, 50–51, 66

Las Vegas: architecture of, 74–75; business collaboration in, 73–74; Caesars Forum Shops, 93–94; change as constant in, 80, 101; Circus Circus, 78; cultural venues in, 82; founding and development of, 70–71; history of, 73; identity crisis of, 71; luxe sensibility in, 81; Luxor Hotel and Casino, *79,* 79–80; MGM Grand, 80; The Mirage Hotel and Casino, 76–77, *77,* 78; Neon Museum, 78; planning issues in, 84; The Strip, 77–79; as themed environment, 72; Treasure Island, 80–81

Learning from Las Vegas (Venturi, Scott Brown, and Izenour), 74

Le Corbusier, *Plan Voisin* for La Cité Radieuse, 103, *104,* 114

Leopold of Anhalt-Dessau, 76

Liminal pilgrimages, 34

Linkletter, Art, 15, 189n50

London Zoo, 67

Louisiana Purchase Exposition (1904), 105, 108–10, 138

Lovell, Margaretta, 106, 117

Lowenthal, David, 97

Lukas, Scott, 106, 158

Luxor Hotel and Casino, *79,* 79–80

MacArthur, John D., 59

MacFadyen, J. Tevere, 129

Magical Express bus, 36

Magic Kingdom theme park: American culture and, 40; colonial imperialist message of, 136; as creationist myth, 31; early entrance to, 169; Fantasyland, 155; Jungle Cruise, 158–59, 165; Keys to the Kingdom Tour, 164–69; layout of, 52; movement through, 36–37; opening of, 18; plans for, 103; popularity of, 153–54; spaces as "scenes," 54; utilidors of, 62, 164, 167–68

Magic Skyway, 124, *125,* 125–26

Main Street, U.S.A., 36, 40–43, 94

Malamud, Randy, 2

Mall of America, 92

Malls, shopping, scale and design of, 91–93

MAPO design and fabrication, 126

Marceline, Missouri, 40–41, 42, 63

Marin, Louis, 69

Marketing, 14–16, 156–57

Marling, Karal Ann: on consumption, 94; as curator, 14; on *Disneyland* series, 15; on Epcot, 123; on Future World, 129; on Golden Gate International Exhibition, 121; on Harvey Houses, 93; on motifs as common culture, 31

Martin, Richard, *Paphian Bower,* 49

Marton, Marissa, 86

Mason, Peter, 139

Mazur, Eric Michael, 25

McDonald's, 166

McGee, J. W., 110

Mesters, Carlos, 45

Methodology, 5–6, 8

MGM Grand, 80

Michalos, Alex, 69

Mickey Mouse, 12, 31, 38–39

The Mickey Mouse Club series, 14–15

Mickey Mouse Monopoly (film), 147–48

Midway Plaisance of Chicago fair, 107–8

Miller, Diane Disney, 1

Milton, John, *Paradise Lost,* 46–47

Mineral King project, 66

Mintz, Charles, 13

The Mirage Hotel and Casino, 76–77, *77,* 78

Mitchell, Chris, 14

Moore, Alexander, 34, 36, 43

Moore, Charles, 151

Moore, Randy, 161–62

Moral behavior of Guests, 63–64
Moral code, 64–66, 114–15
More, Thomas, *Utopia*, 55
Morris, Tom, 146
Moses, Robert, 114, 117, 126–27
Mumford, Lewis, 56–57
MyDisneyExperience.com, 153
MyMagic+, 153

Nature parks and nature tourism, 49–51
Neon Museum, 78
Neuman, Robert, 41
Neuschwanstein, 95
Newman, Morris, 78
"New Towns," 83–84
"New Urbanism," 86
New York World's Fair (1939–40), 117–21, *118, 120*
New York World's Fair (1964–65), 124–28, *125*

Olmsted, Frederick Law, 106
Optimism, 65–66
Orlando, Florida, 73
Orvell, Miles, 75
Oswald the Lucky Rabbit cartoons, 13

Pahl, John, 39
Paphian Bower (Martin), 49
Paradisal traditions: Disney vision and, 44, 45–46, 47, 69; in Florida, 58–66; in literature and art, 46–49; in nature parks and formal gardens, 49–52, *53,* 54–55; overview of, 44–45; surveys of parks, 57–58; in utopian planning, 55–57; zoological models, 67–69
Paradise, definition of, 45
Paradise Lost (Milton), 46–47
Parigi, Giulio and Alfonso, 54
Pearson, Ridley, *The Kingdom Keepers* series, 155
Pepper, Jeffrey, 117–18
Perez, Shane, 161
Perisphere, 118, *118,* 119, 123

Philippine Reservation at St. Louis fair, 109–10
Pickett, Paul, 142
Pike, David, 168
Pike amusement district of St. Louis fair, 108–9
Pilgrimage: as act of faith, 43; crossing of thresholds and, 34, 36; culture and, 26–27; social functions of, 27–28; tourism and, 27, 33. *See also* Pilgrimage centers
Pilgrimage centers: corruption in, 39; Disney World, 24–26, 29–34, 36–39; geography and layout of, 33–34, 36–37; Main Street, U.S.A., 40–43; Santiago de Compostela, 29–34, *35,* 37–38; souvenirs of, 37–38, 40; traditional, 29–30; travel literature and, 32. *See also* Pilgrimage
The Pilgrim's Guide, 32
Pine, Joseph, 10
Pinsky, Mark, 65
Pirates of the Caribbean ride, 154
Planned communities, 55–57, *56,* 82–91
Plan Voisin for La Cité Radieuse (Le Corbusier), 103, *104,* 114
Plater-Zyberk, Elizabeth, 83–84
Pleasure gardens, 76, 77
Pleasure Island, 19, 153
"Plussing" practice, 74–75
Pollan, Michael, 88
Popular culture, shared culture compared to, 3
Postmodern architecture, 74–75
Postmodernism, 20–21
Potter, Joe, 113
Power sharing, 159
Progress City, 125
Public space: corporatization of, 72; Main Street, U.S.A., and, 94; privatization of, 150

Radio Corporation of America (RCA), 64
Raz, Aviad, 144

Tivoli Gardens, 58
Tokyo Disneyland, 143–44
Total Systems/Integrated Electronics Approach, 64
Tourism: Disney World and, 141–42; event, 110–11; goal of, 99; historical, 96–97; nature and landscape, 49–51, 66; nostalgic forms of, 28; pilgrimage and, 27, 33. *See also* Las Vegas
Tourists, 27
Travelers, 27
Travel literature and pilgrimage centers, 32
"Travels in Hyperreality" (Eco), 22
Treasure Island, 80–81
Tribolo, 52
Typhoon Lagoon, 19

Updike, John, 31
Urban explorers, 161
Urbanism, 83–84, 151
Urban Land Institute Award for Excellence, 61
Urban planning, 60, 62, 80, 113–14, 150. *See also* Ideal cities; Las Vegas; Planned communities
U.S. pavilion, 132–33
Utilidors, 62, 164, 167–68
Utopia, definition of, 45
Utopian planning, 55–57, 56, 58, 69. *See also* Ideal cities

Values and moral code, 64–66, 102, 114–15
Vaughn, Bruce, 155
Vdara, 81, 82
Venturi, Robert, 74, 75, 184n61
Victorian era of Main Street, U.S.A., 41–42

Villmoare, Adelaide, 159

Wagner, Catherine, 169
Walker, Card, 116, 149
Walker, Jesse, 156
Wallace, Michael, 41, 63, 97, 129, 133
Wallis, Brian, 135
Walt Disney Family Museum, 1–2
Walt Disney World. *See* Disney World
Water in formal gardens, 54–55
Watson, Ray, 113, 115
Watts, Steven, 4–5, 115, 124–25, 127–28, 157
Weber, Jonathan, 147
WED Enterprises, 13, 126
Wells, Frank, 84, 149
Whalen, Grover, 117
White City of Chicago fair, 107, 108
Wines, Michael, 98
World Columbian Exposition (1893), 105, 106–8, 137
World's Fairs: cultural opportunism and, 137; Epcot and, 7, 19, 103–5, 117–18, 137–38; as event tourism, 110–11; modernism and, 121; in New York, 105–10, 117–21, 118, 120, 124–28, 125; as temporary cities, 117; World Showcase compared to, 132, 134
World Showcase, 132, 134. *See also* Epcot
Worlitz garden, 76, 77
Wright, David, 40
Wynn, Steve, 80–81

Yee, Kevin, 14, 37, 39
Yosemite National Park, 50–51, 51
Young, Terence, 140

Zoological models of Eden, 67–69
Zukin, Sharon, 146

Cher Krause Knight is associate professor of art history at Emerson College in Boston. Her previous publications include *Public Art: Theory, Practice and Populism*. Dr. Knight is the co-founder of Public Art Dialogue, an international, interdisciplinary professional organization. She also co-founded and coedits the journal *Public Art Dialogue*.

The University Press of Florida is the scholarly publishing agency for the State University System of Florida, comprising Florida A&M University, Florida Atlantic University, Florida Gulf Coast University, Florida International University, Florida State University, New College of Florida, University of Central Florida, University of Florida, University of North Florida, University of South Florida, and University of West Florida.